Education and Gender

Also available in the Education as a Humanitarian Response series

Education as a Global Concern, Colin Brock

Education and Minorities, edited by Chris Atkin

Education and HIV/AIDS, edited by Nalini Asha Biggs

Education, Refugees and Asylum Seekers, edited by Lala Demirdjian

Education and Internally Displaced Persons, edited by Christine Smith Ellison and Alan Smith

Education, Aid and Aid Agencies, edited by Zuki Karpinska

Education and Disadvantaged Children and Young People, edited by Mitsuko Matsumoto

Education and Reconciliation, edited by Julia Paulson

Education and Natural Disasters, edited by David Smawfield

Education, Poverty, Malnutrition and Famine, edited by Lorraine Pe Symaco

Education in Indigenous, Nomadic and Travelling Communities, edited by Rosarii Griffin

Also available from Bloomsbury

Education around the World: A Comparative Introduction, Colin Brock and Nafsika Alexiadou

Comparative and International Education: An Introduction to Theory, Method and Practice (2nd edition), David Phillips and Michele Schweisfurth

Education and Gender

Education as a Humanitarian Response

Edited by

Debotri Dhar

BLOOMSBURY

NEW DELHI • LONDON • OXFORD • NEW YORK • SYDNEY

BLOOMSBURY INDIA
Bloomsbury Publishing India Pvt. Ltd
Second Floor, Building No. 4
DDA Complex LSC, Pocket C – 6 & 7
Vasant Kunj, New Delhi 110070
www.bloomsbury.com

BLOOMSBURY, Bloomsbury Academic India and the Diana logo are trademarks of Bloomsbury Publishing Plc

First published in India 2019
First published 2014

This edition published with permission from Bloomsbury Publishing Plc, 50 Bedford Square, London, WC1B3DP, UK

British Library Cataloguing-in-Publication Data
A catalogue record for this book is available from the British Library.

Library of Congress Cataloging-in-Publication Data
Education and gender / edited by DebotriDhar. pages cm. – (Education as a humanitarian response)
ISBN 978-1-4725-0834-8 (hardback) – ISBN 978-1-4725-0908-6 (paperback)
1. Sex differences in education–Cross-cultural studies. 2. Gender identity in education–Cross-cultural studies. 3. Women–Education–Cross-cultural studies.
4. Educational equalization–Cross-cultural studies. I. Dhar, Debotri, editor of compilation.
LC212.9.E37 2015 370.15'1–dc23
2014012553

ISBN: 978-93-87863-84-2

2 4 6 8 10 9 7 5 3 1

For sale in the Indian subcontinent only

Typeset by Integra Software Services Pvt. Ltd.
Digitally printed and bound in India by Replika Press Pvt. Ltd.

Contents

Notes on Contributors

Debotri Dhar holds a bachelor's degree (Honours) from the University of Delhi, India, a master's in Women's Studies from the University of Oxford, UK, and a Ph.D. in Women's and Gender Studies from Rutgers University, USA. Her research interests lie in feminist theory; gender in South Asia, with an emphasis on the politics, literatures and cultures of modern India; comparative politics and Global Studies; interdisciplinarity; and feminist/critical pedagogy. She has published articles and book chapters; presented papers at universities such as Yale, Princeton, Rutgers and Bonn; and delivered several public talks. Her academic awards and honours include an Excellence Fellowship, a South Asian Studies research award, an Institute for Research on Women Graduate Fellowship and a Distinction in Women's Studies. Currently, Debotri lectures at Rutgers University along with holding a Visiting Scholar position in Women's, Gender and Sexuality Studies at Boston University, where she is working on a monograph.

Patricia George works as Education Officer – Research in the Ministry of Education, Antigua and Barbuda. She also works as an overseas Research Fellow for the Centre for Commonwealth Education, University of Cambridge, UK. Previously, she taught Mathematics and Chemistry in secondary schools in Antigua and Barbuda. Patricia George obtained a Ph.D. in Education from the University of Leeds, UK, in 2007. She is particularly interested in issues concerning mathematics and science education, student identity, studies that provide cross-national comparisons and the general area of the sociology of education – in particular, gender and education, poverty and education and the interplay of these two. She recently conducted research and completed a report titled *Risk in Organisation of Eastern Caribbean States (OECS) Education Systems*, which looked at a number of factors (institutional, systemic and social) that impede and/or prevent students completing their education. The report informed in part the education strategy of 2021 for those countries.

Dorothy L. Hodgson is Professor of Anthropology at Rutgers University, USA. She has served as Chair of the Department of Anthropology, Director of the Rutgers' Institute for Research on Women, and as President of the Association for Feminist Anthropology. As a historical anthropologist, she has worked in Tanzania, East Africa, for almost thirty years on such topics as gender, ethnicity, cultural politics, colonialism, nationalism, modernity, the missionary encounter, transnational organizing and the indigenous rights movement. She is the author of *Being Maasai, Becoming Indigenous: Postcolonial Politics in a Neoliberal World* (2011), *The Church of Women: Gendered Encounters Between Maasai and Missionaries* (2005), and *Once Intrepid Warriors: Gender, Ethnicity and the Cultural Politics of Maasai Development* (2001); and editor of *Gender and Culture at the Limit of Rights* (2011), *Gendered Modernities: Ethnographic Perspectives* (2001) and *Rethinking Pastoralism in Africa: Gender, Culture and the Myth of the Patriarchal Pastoralist* (2000); and co-editor of '*Wicked' Women and the Reconfiguration of Gender in Africa* (2001).

Ann Mari May is Professor of Economics at the University of Nebraska, USA, and holds courtesy appointments in the departments of history, women's studies and agricultural economics. She has published widely in the area of feminist economics and much of her recent work focuses on women and higher education and the role of women in economics profession. Her work has been cited in the *Wall Street Journal, New York Times*, *USA Today* and several other news outlets. Along with the joys of doing interdisciplinary research, she teaches courses in nineteenth- and twentieth-century US economic history, history of women and work, gender, economics and social provisioning and a Ph.D. seminar on feminist economics. She has received numerous teaching awards and is a member of the Academy of Distinguished Teachers at the University of Nebraska. She currently serves as Executive Vice President and Treasurer of the International Association for Feminist Economics (IAFFE) – a position she has held since 2006.

Katie Orlemanski is a Ph.D. student in the Department of Anthropology at Rutgers University, USA. Her research focuses on gender and education in Tanzania, East Africa. Prior to graduate school, she worked as a programme officer for a girls' education project in western Kenya (2008–2012). She also has professional experience working in Ghana, Nigeria and South Sudan. Her graduate studies have been supported by a Graduate Research Fellowship from the National Science Foundation.

Yana van der Meulen Rodgers is Professor and Graduate Director in the Women's and Gender Studies department at Rutgers University, USA. Many of her studies have focused on East and South Asian economies, and she has travelled to and lived in Asia to conduct her research. She has published numerous articles in refereed economics journals and has recently completed a book entitled *Maternal Employment and Child Health: Global Issues and Policy Solutions* (2011). Yana became President-Elect for the International Association for Feminist Economics in June 2012, and she has served as an associate editor for *Feminist Economics* since 2005. She maintains a regular consulting relationship with the World Bank and the United Nations, and more recently with the Asian Development Bank.

Anahi Russo Garrido is the Allen-Berenson postdoctoral fellow in Women's and Gender Studies at Brandeis University, USA. She holds a Ph.D. in Women's and Gender Studies from Rutgers University, USA, and an MA in Cultural Anthropology from Concordia University, Canada. Her research currently focuses on gender and sexuality in Latin America, nationalism, space and place and queer theory. More particularly, her research investigates the transformation of intimacy in the lives of three generations of women participating in queer communities in Mexico City. She is the co-editor of *Building Feminist Movements and Organizations* and has published articles on queer Mexico City in *WSQ* and *NWSA Journal* among others.

Rumina Sethi is Professor at the Department of English and Cultural Studies, Panjab University, Chandigarh, India; she wrote her doctoral thesis at Trinity College, Cambridge, UK. She is the author of *Myths of the Nation: National Identity and Literary Representation* (1999) and *The Politics of Postcolonialism: Empire, Nation and Resistance* (2011). She has published extensively in *South Asian Review*, *Journal of Gender Studies*, *Modern Asian Studies*, *Textual Practice*, *New Formations*, *Journal of Contemporary Thought*, *World Literature Written in English* and *Postcolonial Text*. Professor Sethi has held academic fellowships at the University of Oxford and the Rockefeller Foundation at Bellagio, Italy, and is presently the editor of the journal *Dialog*.

Mike Younger was Director of International Initiatives in the Faculty of Education, University of Cambridge, UK (2011–2014), having served as Dean of Education and Head of the Faculty of Education (2006–2011). His main research and teaching interests are located in teacher education and professional development, gender studies and in school leadership and curriculum development. He co-directed, with Molly Warrington, a UK-government-sponsored project on raising boys' achievement within inclusive contexts – a project which led to a highly influential report, two major books and over twenty mainstream research publications. More recently, he worked collaboratively with colleagues in East Africa and the Caribbean, developing research and intervention projects exploring gender processes and patterns in upper primary and secondary schools and developing teacher education programmes in Tanzania, Namibia and the Caribbean. In 2012, he took responsibility as lead consultant for the faculty in establishing a new Graduate School of Education at Nazarbayev University, Kazakhstan, and in leading an initial teacher education project aimed at transforming teacher education in Kazakhstan.

Series Editor's Preface

Underlying this entire series on *Education as a Humanitarian Response* is the well-known adage in education that 'if we get it right for those most in need we will likely get it right for all if we take the same approach'. That sentiment was born in relation to those with special educational needs within a full mainstream system of schooling.

In relation to this series it is taken further to embrace the special educational needs not only of those experiencing disasters and their aftermath, whether natural or man-made, but also of other groups who may be significantly disadvantaged. Indeed, much can be learned of value to the provision of mainstream systems from the holistic approach that necessarily follows in response to situations of disaster and disadvantage. Sadly, very little of this potential value is actually perceived, and even less is embraced. Consequently, one of the aims of the series, both in the core volume, *Education as a Global Concern*, and the contributing volumes, is to bring the notion of education as a humanitarian response to the mainstream, and those seeking to serve it as teachers, other educators and politicians.

Among the factors that are very significant in educational terms and addressed in this series, none is more fundamental than that of gender. Though largely an issue of female disadvantage, that of males is an important phenomenon in some societies, whether to do with traditional economic roles or with male adolescent underachievement in more developed countries. Nonetheless, the overwhelming global picture is one of female disadvantage ranging from the application of patriarchal kinship systems and traditions in some countries to the 'glass ceiling' problem in others. Sometimes, both may occur in the same society, especially where modernization is occurring in some social sectors, including equal educational opportunity, while traditional restrictions remain in others. The well-known phrases of that doyen of gender and education scholarship, Professor Lalage Bown – 'women are development' and 'without women no development' – remain as true as ever.

Dr Debotri Dhar has made an exceptional contribution to the literature in this field through the case studies she has assembled in this volume, as well as through the extremely well researched and argued introductory and concluding chapters. I am most grateful to her for this outstanding contribution to the series *Education as a Humanitarian Response.*

Colin Brock
Honorary Professor of Education
University of Durham, UK

Education and Gender: An Introduction

Debotri Dhar

Chapter Outline

On 12 July 2013, Malala Yousafzai, a Pakistani teenager who was shot in the head by the Taliban for advocating that all girls should have the right to go to school, gave a moving speech at the UN Youth Assembly in New York City (*The Independent, 2013*). 'I am not against anyone. I am here to speak up for the right of education of every child,' she said. Speaking of the Talib who had shot her, she said she would not shoot him even if she had a gun in her hand and he were standing in front of her; this, Malala said,

> is the compassion I have learned from Mohammed, the prophet of mercy, Jesus Christ and Lord Buddha. This is the legacy of change I have inherited from Martin Luther King, Nelson Mandela and Mohammed Ali Jinnah. This is the philosophy of nonviolence that I have learned from Gandhi, Bacha Khan and Mother Teresa. And this is the forgiveness that I have learned from my father and from my mother. This is what my soul is telling me: be peaceful and love everyone.

Going on to speak of how the terrorists were misusing religion for their own personal benefit, Malala emphasized that peace was necessary for education. 'In many parts of the world, especially Pakistan and Afghanistan, terrorism, war and conflicts stop children from going to schools. We are really tired of these wars.' Pointing out how women and children were suffering in many different ways across the world due to problems such as child labour and early marriage, she said that 'poverty, ignorance, injustice, racism and the deprivation of basic rights are the main problems, faced by both men and women'. In her speech, Malala therefore called upon governments to end terrorism and violence; to ensure free, compulsory education for every child; and to support the expansion of education opportunities for girls in the developing world. She also called upon 'all communities to be tolerant, to reject prejudice based on caste, creed, sect, color, religion or agenda, and to ensure freedom and equality for women so they can flourish', because 'we cannot all succeed when half of us are held back'. Malala ended her speech with the powerful words: 'Let us pick up our books and our pens, they are the most powerful weapons. One child, one teacher, one book and one pen can change the world. Education is the only solution.'

The international spotlight on Malala Yousafzai, and her co-option by certain sections of the West in order to justify the latter's war against terror in one of the most troubled geopolitical areas of the world, has recently received a lot of criticism. Regardless of one's ideological stand on this issue – which cannot be separated from the issue of armed militants trying to kill an unarmed teenaged girl, in an extreme instance of the curtailment of freedom of expression – the fact remains that Malala's own speech does not admit to any such co-option. For that reason, the sixteen-year old Malala's formal address in the UN Youth Assembly serves as an apt introduction to this book on education and gender.

In her speech, an understanding of women's education as an instrument of global development shares equal space with an understanding of education as a fundamental human right for all men, women and children. Further, her speech does not treat gender as an isolated category, instead staying attentive to the ways in which gender intersects with class, race, ethnicity, religion and nationality to create shifting and complex structures of power. Most importantly, she strongly indicts totalitarianism by making a poignant connection between education, compassion and socio-political transformation; without meaningful education, it is impossible to cultivate empathy for the challenges faced by women and men around the world and to foster a commitment to democracy, diversity, dialogue and peaceful resolution of conflict.

Education, then, is the practice of freedom (Hooks, 1984), making us simultaneously human as well as humanitarian.

***

Gender and Education

Traditional as well as some contemporary literature on the relationship between women and education has tended to be instrumentalist in intent, viewing women's education as a means to larger ends (Bown, 1990; Ballara, 1992; Breierova and Duflo, 2004; UNICEF, 2005). Thus women's education has been seen to contribute to the welfare of the mother-child dyad and the family (through reduced maternal mortality, improved child health and better socialization patterns); to the economic and social development of family, community and country (through greater investment of income in the family and community, as well as through human resource development and increased productivity of the labour force for the country); and to a reduction in global inequality (through an improvement in the quality of half the world's population). For instance, the UNICEF's GAP report (2005) on gender disparities in education clearly states that 'Educating girls is a surefire way to raise economic productivity, lower infant and maternal mortality, improve nutritional status and health, reduce poverty and wipe out HIV/AIDS and other diseases [...] Educating girls benefits both boys and girls [...] Educating girls is a means to an end [...].'

Its merits notwithstanding, especially from a developmental perspective, this silver bullet, instrumentalist view of education has been widely criticized by the human rights approach, which advocates for women – and especially, 'third world' women – to be treated as individuals in their own right rather than as underutilized resources of nation-states (see for instance essays in Ray, 1994; Subrahmanian, 2002). While not denying the positive correlation between women's education on the one hand and community health, economic productivity and social development on the other, the rights-based approach appeals to the principles of natural justice, ethics and law in order to argue that education is a fundamental political and civil *right* for all individuals rather than merely a socio-economic *requirement*.

Among other frameworks for understanding the relationship between women and education, the human capability approach and the empowerment approach deserve special mention. The former, associated most closely with Amartya Sen and Martha Nussbaum, breaks with conventional development paradigms to demonstrate how education adds not just to human capital but also to human capability, enabling women to exercise their legal rights and strengthening their political and civic engagement in society (Sen, 1999; Nussbaum, 2003). The latter, as the name suggests, critiques the power differentials associated with gender stratification in society; education is thus seen as a way to effectively empower women (see for instance Heward, 1999;

Dhar, 2006). Needless to say, there are both gaps as well as overlaps between all the various approaches, even though their substantive focus may differ.

A similar substantive argument has ensued on the subject of quantity versus quality. For long, a disproportionate emphasis was placed on access rather than outcome (Stromquist, 1995; Heward, 1999), the key question faced by governments, non-governmental organizations (NGOs) and donor agencies being how to remove the obstacles that prevent girls from participating in education and devolving into quantitative concerns revolving around girls' enrolment and retention rates.

The importance of access to education for women around the world, of course, cannot be emphasized enough. A definitive study of seven developing countries in the nineties had identified a range of socio-cultural, political, legal, religious and economic factors which acted as deterrents to female participation in education (Brock and Cammish, 1997). In each case, the study had found that unfavourable circumstances affected girls more than boys, with a fundamental cultural bias in favour of males operating strongly through decisions about child care, nutrition, physical work, freedom of movement and marriage. Speaking of health, for instance, poverty and malnutrition affected both boys' and girls' access to education; boys, owing to their more favoured status, were however better nourished and received a more prompt treatment when they were ill (p. 22). In the case of the economic factor which was found to exert considerable pressure, female participation in schooling was deterred not only by the direct costs relating to materials such as textbooks and uniforms but also by the opportunity costs associated with the loss of assistance to parents in the home and on agricultural land, as well as to formal and informal sanctions operating against girls' education (p. 23).

More than a decade later, the findings of the above study still remain relevant in many parts of the globe. The Millennium Development Report compiled by the United Nations in 2005 confirmed that girls still lag behind boys in school enrolment levels (MDG Report, 2005). These disparities only increased at progressively higher levels of education; for example, in 2001–2002, of around sixty-five developing countries, only half had achieved gender parity in primary education, while only around 20 per cent had achieved parity in secondary and 8 per cent in higher education. A more recent report has found that in 47 out of 54 African countries surveyed, girls had a less than 50 per cent chance of completing primary school, with prospects of a widening gender gap at the secondary level (GCE, 2012, p. 6). Thus, while some authors have argued that a more nuanced understanding of educational attainment demonstrates how developing countries are becoming like developed countries, with gender gaps that increasingly favour rather than discriminate against girls (Grant and Behrman, 2010), studies using measures such as the primary completion rate of children and net enrolment ratios (Bruns et al., 2003; Hewett and Lloyd, 2005) do point to overlaps between older and new trends, albeit with significant differences *within* the 'developing' world; an example is Sub-Saharan Africa, where schooling attainment remains the lowest and gender gap the widest (Bloom, 2007).

However, access is only the tip of the proverbial iceberg. Decades ago, noted sociologist Emile Durkheim had argued that education is a social function; schools are ultimately responsible for passing on what society considers its crucial beliefs and value-systems (Durkheim, 1956). This understanding of education continues to remain valid in contemporary times; hence, even as economists and policymakers have touted the importance of increased access to education, sociologists as well as critical theorists have probed deeper in order to ascertain whether equal access and retention rates automatically translated into an 'equal' education. Here, an Open Systems model of education (for early discussions, see Ballantine, 1983; Burgess, 1986) that acknowledges how, rather than functioning in a vacuum, education as a dynamic subsystem is inextricably intertwined with other social subsystems is particularly useful. With specific reference to gender, the open systems model allows us to understand how sex roles, gendered behaviour and the traditional division of labour in a wider society can be reproduced within the realm of education.

A very visible indicator of such reproduction is gender stereotyping in curricula. Research on curricular bias has a long history – several scholars realized early on that the curriculum is what Stenhouse (1967) called a 'selection of culture' (p. 57) – but is generally considered to have assumed centre-stage with a collection of papers titled *Knowledge and Control*, edited by Michael Young (1971). Since then, there has been an increased understanding of how 'knowledge' is selected, organized and filtered through the education system via the curriculum such that what reaches the classrooms is often what Michael Apple calls 'official knowledge' (Apple, 1997). Curricular bias and stereotyping has attracted policy space even in the Millennium Development Goals, with most blueprints for equality in education emphasizing the need to eliminate gender bias in educational material (MDG Report, 2005).

However, even when formal curricular bias has been removed, gender stereotyping may continue through the 'hidden' or 'paracurriculum'. The concept of the hidden curriculum, developed by Benson Snyder (1971) and renamed by David Hargreaves as the paracurriculum (1978), refers to the unwritten and informal rules, regulations and routines that underwrite most formal organizational principles in school or, in other words, all that is learnt alongside the 'official' curriculum. The paracurriculum plays out in a variety of ways: through the value climate of the school, its validating or invalidating impact upon the student's prior socialization and self-concept, the transmission of sex role stereotypes by teachers via labelling, different disciplining tactics and assigning privileges and tasks by gender etc. As Ballantine (1983) had explained back in the eighties, 'Schools become important sources of information on sex-appropriate behaviour; children learn by observing and imitating adult roles, including the roles of teachers and administrators. They observe the ratio of males to females and the authority structure in the educational hierarchy. They learn their own sex-appropriate behaviour through positive and negative sanctions [...]' (p. 77). For instance, teachers may format discipline according to the gender of the student; girls may be scolded for playing 'rough and dirty' games, while boys might be mildly rebuked for 'crying like a girl'. In communication, boys may receive more individualized teacher attention, this in turn becoming a vicious circle because it reaffirms both girls' and boys' notion that the views of the former are not as important (Burgess, 1986, pp. 193–4; OECD, 1986, pp. 39–46). The OECD cross-national study of sex inequalities had found that teachers often rewarded girls' traditional behaviour such as attentiveness, cleanliness and timidity; whereas boys were encouraged to be self-reliant, girls were implicitly encouraged in passive dependency (pp. 39–40). Processes such as labelling and self-fulfilling prophesy theories further crystallize these notions; children become what, according to the teachers' expectations, they are presumed to be (Rist, 1977).

While these studies belong to earlier decades, recent research confirms many of their findings, including girls' continuing low self-esteem and overall invisibility and boys' domination of classroom space and teacher attention (Jones and Wheatley, 1990; Sanford, 2005; Liu, 2006), even though teachers in some contexts are now more alert to the dangers of boys dominating classroom interactions and spaces (Warrington and Younger, 2000). Many girls still tend to avoid subjects such as mathematics and science which are socially constructed as masculine (Walden, 1991). In particular, empirical studies show how cleverness, rationality and academic ability continue to be constructed as masculine (Renold, 2005), creating challenges for girls as they try to negotiate being clever as well as acceptably feminine in school (Renold,

2005; Renold and Allen, 2006; Francis, 2010; Skelton et al., 2011). Therefore, rather than act as an equalizer of gender inequalities, education may instead socialize children into hegemonic gender roles. This gendered socialization of different actors within the education system through curricular and paracurricular biases, acting in concert with prior socialization and gender dynamics of a wider society, can then lead to gendered choices, expectations and educational outcomes regardless of official indicators of education such as equal access and retention.

Gender, of course, does not function in isolation; instead, it intersects with a host of other markers of social identity such as class, race, age, geographical location, the rural-urban divide, nationality and so forth, in complex ways. These intersections then have a corresponding effect on the relationship between gender and education.

Social class, for instance, directly impacts educational performance, with household poverty having an obvious negative impact on children's education (Hammond et al., 2007; Hunt, 2008; Sabates et al., 2010). When poverty intersects with gender, interesting dynamics result; thus recent data demonstrates that in situations of household poverty, girls from poor households are less likely than boys to enter primary school while boys face greater risks of repeating grades and leaving school early (UIS, 2012). However, as discussed earlier, the relationship between social class and education transcends narrow considerations of economic capital, for economic capital is intimately bound up with cultural and social capital which shape what may otherwise be erroneously perceived as 'natural' scholastic abilities (Becker, 1964; Bourdieu, 1984, 1986, 1997). According to Bourdieu, cultural capital refers to cultural goods (such as books) and dispositions of the mind and body, while social capital refers to the aggregate of (actual or potential) resources accruing from a network of institutionalized and recognized relationships. The symbolic efficacy of cultural and social capital lies in the logic of its diffuse transmission, which may escape observation but is nevertheless responsible for the unequal scholastic achievement of children originating from different strata in society. Other early but still relevant studies on the class dimension of education and how the latter may reproduce the inequalities associated with the former instead of eliminating it include those by Aaron Cicourel and John Kituse (1977), Talcott Parsons (1983) and Samuel Bowles (1983).

Education opportunities, expectations and outcomes are also influenced by the rural-urban divide as well as inter-urban disparities, such as in cities with large slums (Hunt, 2008). Thus rural areas have consistently been linked with higher rates of early school leaving for children, especially in remote areas where children have to travel long distances to reach school (Hunt, 2008; Sabates et al., 2010). Age is another important factor. In many countries, the repetition rate is high in primary education, especially during the early grades; however, early school leaving is more likely to occur among older children, at an age when the opportunity cost of participation in school rises (UIS, 2012, p. 43).

Race, too, can have an impact on educational expectations, experiences and outcomes, for both students as well as their educators. Indeed, in race-stratified societies, bodies are consciously and unconsciously racialized in the classroom, just as outside of it, making the classroom terrain challenging to navigate and informing pedagogical choices in important ways. As a result of this understanding, feminist scholarship continues to emphasize race-class intersections alongside analyses of gender (Hooks, 1984; Darder, 1991; Montoya, 1995; Reyes, 1997; Srivastava, 1997; essays in Anderson and Hill Collins, 1998; essays in Macdonald and Sanchez-Casal, 2002).

Closer attention to geographical location as well as to history and culture further illuminate how education cannot be isolated from the larger context of the society of which it forms an integral part. For example, boys' disengagement from education and their apparent underachievement in countries such as the United Kingdom, Australia, New Zealand and Canada present an interesting contrast to the specific educational disadvantages faced by girls in countries of Africa and parts of Asia. The issue of boys' underachievement is, in fact, critical enough to have merited explicit attention in educational research both by academics (Kutnick, Layne, and Jules, 1997; Figueroa, 2000; Chevannes, 2002; De Lisle, Smith, and Jules, 2005) and in policy and advocacy circles (Jha and Kelleher, 2006; World Bank, 2009). These trends underscore how gender roles can negatively impact educational attainment of both men and women (Plummer et al., 2008), highlighting the need to move beyond essentialist understandings of boys and girls in order to focus on the social construction of masculinity and femininity in specific contexts.

This understanding of gender as a social construction has, in turn, motivated an analysis of the relationship between sexuality and education; thus queer theory has challenged the assumptions of heteronormativity that historically undergirded discussions of gender and education in order to fashion pedagogical practices that validate the realities of both heterosexual and homosexual students (Bryson and Castell, 1993; Zimmerman, 1994; Greene, 1996; Khayatt, 1999; Rabinowitz, 2002).

In other words, the link between gender and education confounds easy generalizations. Education is both a requirement and a right – yet a flattened understanding of education as a magic word, a great equalizer of difference and an exogenous, automatically empowering influence, can be problematic; at best it merely skims the surface, while at worst, it can overlook the complex dynamics that mark the field of education to reproduce patriarchy, social inequality, even bondage (Dhar, 2006). An interrogation of the relationship between gender and education must instead be nuanced, probing critically into how gender interacts with a range of social, geographical, political, historical, material and ideological indicators to impact educational expectations, opportunities and outcomes for women and men in multiple ways and across a variety of contexts. Such critical, multi-pronged interrogation is necessary if the humanitarian function of education in creating gender-equal, pluralistic societies is to be fully realized.

***

Organization of the Book

Through a focused and lively collection of cases drawn from the USA, the UK, India, Mexico, Sub-Saharan Africa and the Caribbean, this book examines the global relationship between gender and education. It explores a range of issues on gender and education including, but not limited to, female disadvantage and male underachievement; gender stereotyping in the curriculum and paracurriculum; the intersection of gender, race and class; the defining role of history, geography and culture; gender issues in education policy; heteronormativity; the persisting gender gap in STEM fields; non-governmental initiatives; and the pitfalls as well as possibilities of feminist pedagogy.

While questions pertaining to gender and education often tend to devolve into questions about boys and girls, these categories are sometimes necessary in order to identify current gaps and propose future strategies. That said, the book's definition of gender is, in most instances, broader and multi-layered; eschewing essentialist definitions of 'male' and 'female', it examines the cultural construction of gender and sexualities in specific geographical contexts and interrogates issues of both male and female disadvantage in education. Attention is paid to both formal as well as non-formal education and to the Global North as well as the Global South. A significant emphasis is on drawing from best practices worldwide in order to propose solutions rather than only identifying problems, the ultimate focus being on the humanitarian function of education in creating and promoting gender-just, equitable and pluralistic societies.

The book is interdisciplinary, drawing liberally from across disciplines in order to present a comprehensive picture and analyse issues from multiple vantage points. The research methods used in the individual chapters are also varied and include textual analysis, ethnography, participant observation, statistical analysis, discourse analysis and historical/archival research. As an academic book, each chapter strives for a high standard of scholarship. At the same time, a sincere attempt has been made to present a variety of voices, from the formal and conventional third-person analysis to the more informal first-person account, in order to keep readers engaged.

'Promoting Girls' Education in Kenya: Insights from an NGO Initiative' by Katie Orlemanski and Dorothy Hodgson analyses the 'Four Pillars PLUS' project, a non-governmental education initiative in western rural Kenya. Women in sub-Saharan Africa are often forced to forgo their education owing to factors such as poverty, absence of adequate government support, cultural barriers and lack of viable employment prospects. Growing out of this context, the Four Pillars PLUS project supported the primary education of hundreds of children, mostly girls, enabling their transition to secondary school. Drawing from four years of fieldwork, the chapter examines the project's design, implementation and overall effectiveness. Exploring a range of economic, social and cultural themes, including the benefits of prioritizing a community's own articulations of their needs and recognizing community members as critical agents of change, the chapter emphasizes the need to strategically address barriers to girls' education beyond accessibility.

The Caribbean presents an interesting contrast, with girls emerging as the success story due to their overall higher academic achievement as compared to boys. Yet research in other contexts has shown that a focus on boys' apparent academic underachievement often masks other problems and inequalities, such as girls' continuing low self-esteem, boys' domination of classroom space and teacher attention, continued inequitable power dynamics and beliefs that it is still better to be a boy. 'Gender, Schooling and Achievement in the Caribbean' by Mike Younger and Patricia George explores both aspects of the issue. The extent to which boys achieve less well than girls is explored in different Caribbean contexts, and different explanations are examined and debated; at the same time, the issue of 'achieving girls' is also contested, and gender inequalities that have been masked by a focus on achievement scores are exposed, with discussion revolving around how the gender regime impacts upon the quality of schooling and overall well-being for girls.

In other words, significant strides in many parts of the globe notwithstanding, hegemonic constructions of gender often continue to militate against genuine equality in the realm of education. Women's low representation in the STEM fields (Science, Technology, Engineering, and Math) is a case in point. 'Gender and Graduate Education in the United States: Women's Advancement in STEM Fields' by Ann Mari May and Yana van der Meulen Rodgers focuses on this critical issue. Utilizing data on doctoral programmes in US universities published by the National Research Council, the study examines the concentration of women graduate students and faculty in US doctorate programmes. Analysing the link between women's representation among the faculty and women's representation among the graduate student body across fields, in a context where women faculty members continue to be concentrated in less prestigious universities, in lower academic ranks and in non-tenure track instructional positions, the authors argue for greater gender diversity among graduate student and faculty populations, and for policy and institutional reforms that support diversity in academia and the labour market.

Policy and institutional reforms are, of course, a complex matter, especially when we consider the role of the historical past in shaping the present. India is an interesting example. The development of women's education in India has been integrally linked with the perception of gendered roles within Indian society itself. From the ancient period when women were denied access to formal education, to the colonial period when the *zenana* or home-oriented system of women's education continued, the emphasis was on the right kind of women's education; women were to be trained as competent wives and mothers in a way that did not necessarily challenge the sexual division of labour in society. 'Nineteenth-Century Social Reform, Gender Politics and the Contemporary Indian Education System' by Rumina Sethi uses a historical lens to examine women's education in India. Analysing how the issue of women's education was first framed within nineteenth-century debates on socio-political reform, and working its way through women's subversive literature in nineteenth-century Bengal to a confrontation with distinguished educational commissions and committees of independent India that set the guidelines for school and university curricula, the chapter traces the links between the nineteenth-century nationalist agenda and contemporary policy concerns related to women's education.

'The Gender and Education Agenda in the United Kingdom, 1988–2013: The Ever-turning Wheel' by Mike Younger takes up yet another dimension of educational policy and praxis, interrogating the assumptions underlying the reorientation of the gender equity debate in the UK, as concerns about equal opportunities in education for girls are replaced with a preoccupation with equal opportunities policies for boys. As the emphasis shifts to 'underachieving boys' and what policymakers, teachers and parents should do about them, teacher recruitment policies have focused on recruiting more men as primary school teachers; educational consultants have promoted 'boy-friendly' teaching strategies; school leaders have promoted whole school recuperative masculinity approaches. But the gender gap remains, resilient, resistant, unchanging in many respects. Reflecting on the ineffectiveness of these short-term approaches linked to recuperative masculinity, this chapter argues for a more inclusive, multi-faceted educational approach that challenges essentialist notions of 'boy' and 'girl'.

In analysing the relationship between gender and education, the importance of formal schooling as well as of non-governmental efforts directed towards helping students transition into the formal education system cannot be emphasized enough. At the same time, civil society efforts to educate a general populace about the social construction of gender also deserve attention, especially since such education helps further dismantle essentialist notions of gender, bringing us to a timely discussion on the heteronormativity that permeates mainstream gender and education discourse. 'Unlearning Gender and Sexuality: The pedagogical work of LGBTTT organizations in Mexico City' by Anahi Russo Garrido examines the ways in which lesbian and queer women's organizations challenge heteronormativity through their pedagogical activities. Examining the work of two organizations, Grupo Lésbico Universitario (GLU) and Musas de Metal, through ethnographic research (more specifically, a combination of participant observation and interviews, supplemented by newspaper reviews), the chapter investigates how the organizations' formal workshops as well as informal networks destabilize dominant norms on gender and sexuality to redefine sexual citizenship in Mexico City.

A nuanced understanding of education as a deeply marked yet potentially transformative field of endeavor then leads up to an inevitable question: what concrete steps can educators take to create gender-equal, inclusive learning environments that promote equal opportunity, diversity and a fuller development of individuals' and communities' scholastic abilities? 'Teaching for the Future: Feminist Pedagogy and Humanitarian Education' by Debotri Dhar suggests that feminist – and critical – pedagogy may hold at least some answers. Using examples based on a range of Women's and Gender Studies courses at a US public university, the chapter presents a comprehensive discussion of feminist pedagogy; offers examples of implementing feminist pedagogy in the classroom, from syllabus design to classroom instruction; and explores some of the pitfalls as well as the possibilities of these pedagogical strategies.

Questions for reflection

a) What are some of the approaches to understanding the relationship between women and education? What is the key difference between a developmental approach and a human rights approach?
b) Does access to education continue to be a problem for girls and women? What are some of the limitations of framing women's education in terms of access rather than outcome?
c) What did sociologist Emile Durkheim mean when he said education is a social function? What is the Open Systems Model of education?
d) What effect do the intersections between gender and other markers of social identity such as class, race, age, geographical location and the rural-urban divide have on the relationship between gender and education?

Further Reading

Halsey, A. H., Lauder, Hugh, Brown, Phillip and Wells, Amy Stuart (eds.). (1997) *Education, Culture, Economy, Society*. Oxford: Oxford University Press.

This edited volume is a comprehensive introduction to major theoretical approaches within the sociology of education. It examines major changes taking place within this field – and within cultural theory more broadly – in the late twentieth century and offers directions for future research.

Subrahmanian, Ramya. (2002), 'Engendering education: Prospects for a rights-based approach to female education deprivation in India', in Maxine Molyneux and Shahra Razavi (eds.) *Gender Justice, Development, and Rights*. Oxford: Oxford University Press, 204–32.

This article critiques the instrumentalist view of education; while it takes up technical questions regarding barriers to the right to education, its ultimate focus is the formulation of a human rights approach to education.

Bibliography

Anderson, Margaret and Collins, Patricia Hill (eds.). (1998), *Race, Class and Gender: An Anthology*. Belmont: Wadsworth.

Apple, Michael. (1997), 'What postmodernists forget: Cultural capital and official knowledge', in A. H. Halsey, Hugh Lauder, Phillip Brown and Amy Stuart Wells (eds.) *Education: Culture, Economy, Society*. Oxford: Oxford University Press, 595–604.

Ballantine, Jeanne. (1983), *The Sociology of Education: A Systematic Analysis*. New Jersey: Prentice-Hall.

Ballara, Marcela. (1992), *Women and Literacy*. London: Zed.

Becker, Gary. (1964), *A Theoretical and Empirical Analysis with Special Reference to Education*. New York: National Bureau of Economic Research.

Bloom, David. (2007), 'Measuring global educational progress', in Joel Cohen, David Bloom, and Martin Malin (eds.) *Education for All: A Global Agenda*. Cambridge: American Academy of Arts and Sciences, 33–120.

Bourdieu, Pierre. (1984), *Distinction: A Social Critique of the Judgment of Taste*, trans. Richard Nice. Boston: Harvard University Press.

——. (1986), 'The forms of capital', in J. Richardson (ed.) *Handbook of Theory and Research for the Sociology of Education*. New York: Greenwood, 241–58.

——. (1997), 'The forms of capital', in A. H. Halsey, Hugh Lauder, Phillip Brown and Amy Stuart Wells (eds.) *Education, Culture, Economy, Society*. Oxford: Oxford University Press.

Bowles, Samuel. (1983), 'Unequal education and the reproduction of the social division of labour', in Ben Cosin and Margaret Hales (eds.) *Education, Policy and Society: Theoretical Perspectives*. London: Routledge & Kegan Paul, 27–50.

Bown, Lalage. (1990), *Preparing the Future: Women, Literacy and Development*. Somerset: Action Aid.

Breierova, L. and Duflo, E. (2004), 'The impact of education on fertility and child mortality: Do fathers really matter less than mothers?' National Bureau of Economic Research Working Paper No. 10513.

Brock, Colin and Cammish, Nadine. (1997), *Factors Affecting Female Participation in Education in Seven Developing Countries*. London: Department for International Development.

Bruns, Barbara, Mingat, Alain and Rahotomala, Ramahatra. (2003), *Achieving Universal Primary Education by 2015: A Chance for Every Child*. Washington, DC: World Bank.

Bryson, Mary and de Castell, Suzanne. (1993), 'Queer pedagogy: Practice makes im/perfect', *Canadian Journal of Education*, 18, 3, 285–305.

Burgess, Robert. (1986), *Sociology, Education and Schools: An Introduction to the Sociology of Education*. London: Batsford.

Chevannes, B. (2002), 'What you sow is what you reap: Violence and construction of male identity in Jamaica', *Current Issues in Comparative Education*, 2, 51–61.

Cicourel, Aaron and Kituse, John. (1977), 'The school as a mechanism of social differentiation', in Jerome Karabel and A. H. Halsey (eds.) *Power and Ideology in Education*. New York: Oxford University Press, 282–92.

Darder, Antonia. (1991), *Culture and Power in the Classroom*. New York: Bervin and Garvey.

De Lisle, J., Smith, P. and Jules, V. (2005), 'Which males or females are most at risk and on what? An analysis of gender differentials within the primary school system of Trinidad and Tobago', *Educational Studies*, 31, 393–418.

Dhar, Debotri. (2006), *Another Bondage: Rethinking Women, Education and Empowerment.* Unpublished M.St Thesis. Oxford University.

Durkheim, Emile. (1956), *Educationand Sociology*. Glencoe: Free Press.

Figueroa, M. (2000), 'Making sense of male experience: The case of academic underachievement in the English-speaking Caribbean', *IDS Bulletin*, 31, 68–74.

Francis, B. (2010), 'Re/theorizing gender: Female masculinity and male femininity in the classroom?' *Gender and Education*, 22, 477–90.

Global Campaign for Education (GCE). (2012), '*Gender discrimination in education: The violation of rights of women and girls*', Report submitted to the Committee on the Elimination of Discrimination against Women (CEDAW), Johannesburg.

Grant, Monica and Behrman, Jere. (2010), 'Gender gaps in educational attainment in less developed countries', *Population and Development Review*, 1, 7, 71–89.

Greene, Fredrick. (1996), 'Introducing queer theory into the undergraduate classroom', *English Education*, 18, 325–39.

Hammond, Cathy, Linton, Dan, Smink, Jay and Drew, Sam. (2007), 'Dropout Risk Factors and Exemplary Programs: A Technical Report'. National Dropout Prevention Center. Available at http://www.dropoutprevention.org/sites/default/files/uploads/major_reports/DropoutRisk FactorsandExemplaryProgramsFINAL5-16-07.pdf.

Hargreaves, David. (1978), 'Power and the paracurriculum', in C. Richards (ed.) *Power and the Curriculum: Issues in Curriculum Studies*. Driffeld: Nafferton.

Heward, Christine. (1999), 'Introduction: The new discourses of gender, education and development', in Christine Heward and Shiela Bunwaree (eds.) *Gender, Education and Development: Beyond Access to Empowerment*. London: Zed, 4–9.

Hewett, Paul and Lloyd, Cynthia. (2005), 'Progress toward education for all: Trends and current challenges in sub-saharan Africa', in Cynthia Lloyd, Jere Behrman, Nelly Stromquist and Barney Cohen (eds.) *The Changing Transition to Adulthood in Developing Countries: Selected Studies.* Washington, DC: National Academies Press, 84–117.

Hooks, Bell. (1984), *Teaching to Transgress*. New York: Routledge.

Hunt, Francis. (2008), *Dropping Out from School: A Cross-Country Review of Literature*. CREATE Pathways to Access, Monograph No 16. University of Sussex: CREATE.

Jha, J. and Kelleher, F. (2006), *Boys' Underachievement in Education: An Exploration in Selected Commonwealth Countries*. London: Commonwealth Secretariat.

Jones, M. G. and Wheatley, J. (1990), 'Gender differences in teacher-student interactions in science classrooms', *Journal of Research in Science Teaching*, 27, 861–74.

Khayatt, Didi. (1999), 'Sex and pedagogies: Performing sexualities in the classroom', *GLQ: A Journal of Lesbian and Gay Studies*, 5, 1, 107–39.

Kutnick, P., Layne, A. and Jules, V. (1997), *Gender and School Achievement in the Caribbean*. London: Department for International Development.

Liu, F. (2006), 'School culture and gender', in C. Skelton, B. Francis and L. Smulyan (eds.) *The SAGE Handbook of Gender and Education*. Thousand Oaks: Sage, 425–38.

Macdonald, Amie and Sanchez-Casal Susan (eds.). (2002), *Twenty-First-Century Feminist Classrooms: Pedagogies of Identity and Difference*. New York: Palgrave Macmillan.

Montoya, M. (1995), 'Un/Masking the self while Un/Braiding latina stories', in R. Delgado (ed.) *Critical Race Theory: The Cutting Edge*. Philadelphia: Temple University Press, 529–39.

Nussbaum, M. (2003), 'Women's education: A global challenge', *Signs: Journal of Women in Culture and Society*, 29, 2, 325–55.

Organisation for Economic Co-operation and Development. (1986), *Girls and Women in Education*. Paris: OECD.

Parsons, Talcott. (1983), 'The school class as a social system: Some of its functions in American society', in Ben Cosin and Margaret Hales (eds.) *Education, Policy and Society: Theoretical Perspectives*. London: Routledge and Kegan Paul, 85–105.

Plummer, D., McLean, A. and Simpson, J. (2008), 'Has learning become taboo and is risk-taking compulsory for Caribbean boys? Researching the relationship between masculinities, education and risk', *Caribbean Review of Gender Studies*, 2, 1–14.

Rabinowitz, Nancy. (2002), 'Queer theory and feminist pedagogy', in Amie Macdonald and Susan Sanchez-Casal (eds.) *Twenty-First-Century Feminist Classrooms: Pedagogies of Identity and Difference*. New York: Palgrave Macmillan.

Ray, Douglas (ed.) (1994), *Education for Human Rights: An International Perspective*. Paris: UNESCO.

Renold, E. (2005), *Girls, Boys and Junior Sexualities: Exploring Childrens' Gender and Sexual Relations in the Primary School*. London: Routledge Falmer.

——— and Allen, A. (2006), 'Bright and beautiful: High achieving girls, ambivalent femininities, and the feminisation of success in the primary school', *Discourse: Studies in the Cultural Politics of Education*, 27, 457–73.

Reyes, Maria. (1997), 'Chicanas in academe: An endangered species', in Suzanne de Castell and Mary Bryson (eds.) *Radical Interventions: Identity, Politics and Differences in Educational Praxis*. Albany: State University of New York Press, 15–37.

Rist, Ray. (1977), 'On understanding the processes of schooling: The contributions of labeling theory', in Jerome Karabel and A. H. Halsey (eds.) *Power and Ideology in Education*. New York: Oxford University Press, 292–305.

Sabates, Ricardo, Akyeampong, Kwame, Westbrook, Jo and Hunt, Frances. (2010), 'School Dropout: Patterns, Causes, Changes and Policies'. Background paper for *Education for All Global Monitoring Report 2011: The Hidden Crisis: Armed Conflict and Education*. Sussex: CIESES.

Sanford, K. (2005), 'Gendered Literacy Experiences: The Effects of Expectation and Opportunity for Boys' and Girls' Learning', *Journal of Adolescent & Adult Literacy*, 49, 302–15.

Sen, Amartya. (1999), *Development as Freedom*. New York, NY: Knopf Publishing.

Srivastava, Aruna. (1997), 'Anti-racism inside and outside the classroom', in Leslie Roman and Linda Eyre (eds.) *Dangerous Territories: Struggles for Difference and Equality in Education*. New York: Routledge, 113–26.

Skelton, C., Francis, B. and Read, B. (2011), 'Gender, popularity and notions of in/authenticity amongst 12–13 year old school girls', *British Journal of Sociology of Education*, 21, 169–83.

Snyder, Benson. (1971), *The Hidden Curriculum*. New York: Knopf.

Stenhouse, Lawrence. (1967), *Culture and Education*. London: Thomas Nelson.

Stromquist, Nelly. (1995) 'Romancing the state: Gender and power in education', *Comparative Education Review*, 39, (4), 423–54.

Subrahmanian, Ramya. (2002), 'Engendering education: Prospects for a rights-based approach to female education deprivation in India', in Maxine Molyneux and Shahra Razavi (eds.) *Gender Justice, Development, and Rights*. Oxford: Oxford University Press, 204–32.

'The Full Text: Malala Yousafzai delivers defiant riposte to Taliban Militants with Speech to the UN General Assembly', *The Independent*, 12 July 2013.

The Millennium Development Goals Report. (2005), New York: United Nations.

United Nations Children's Fund. (2005), *Gender Achievements and Prospects in Education: The Gap Report*. New York: UNICEF.

UNESCO Institute for Statistics. (2012), *Opportunities Lost: The Impact of Grade Repetition and Early School Leaving*. Montreal: UIS.

Walden, J. (1991), 'Gender issues in classroom organisation and management', in C. McLaughlin, C. Lodge and C. Watkins (eds.) *Gender and Pastoral Care*. Oxford: Blackwell.

Warrington, M. and Younger, M. (2000), 'The other side of the gender gap', *Gender and Education*, 12, 493–508.

World Bank. (2009), *Proceedings of Regional Caribbean Conference, 'Keeping Boys Out of Risk*. New York: World Bank/Commonwealth Secretariat.

Young, Michael. (1971), *Knowledge and Control: New Directions for the Sociology of Education*. London: Collier-Macmillan.

Zimmerman, Bonnie. (1994), 'Lesbian studies in an inclusive curriculum', *Transformations*, 5, 18–27.

Promoting Girls' Education in Kenya: Insights from an NGO Initiative

1

Katie Orlemanski and Dorothy L. Hodgson

Chapter Outline

On 11 October 2012, US Secretary of State Hillary Clinton delivered a speech to mark the United Nations' first annual 'International Day of the Girl Child'.[1] Seven thousand miles away, as evening fell over the rural farming community of North Gem in western Kenya, twelve-year old Anna[2] hummed to herself as she gathered firewood for her elderly uncle. She and her younger sisters had been living with their uncle since the death of their parents a few years before. Although he earned a small income from carving and selling wooden spoons, they had very little money. Anna had started skipping school on market days to sell vegetables from the family's kitchen garden in order to earn a few extra shillings. Despite her new responsibilities, Anna still performed well at school. But when the school principal called Anna into her office, it wasn't to congratulate her. 'Anna, I know you have been working hard', Madam Beatrice began, 'but I can't allow you and your sisters to continue coming to school without paying fees. I am sorry. Try to talk to your uncle to raise the money.' Although Anna knew that her uncle would try to negotiate with the principal, she recognized that they could not pay the school fees. On the walk home, she remembered the news of her aunt's baby in nearby Kisumu. Perhaps she could move to the city to work for her relatives and send money home for her sisters' fees?

Just as Anna considered dropping out of school, an international NGO, Family Health International 360 (FHI 360), began an education project in her area called 'Four Pillars PLUS: Improving Girls' Education in Kenya'.[3] The 'Four Pillars PLUS' project was conceived as an education initiative in western Kenya that initially supported the primary education of over 800 children (mostly girls) and enabled 200 of these children to transition to secondary school. The project recruited Anna and her sisters into the programme, guaranteeing the payment of all of their school fees for primary and secondary school. Today, Anna attends a provincial secondary school where she is ranked fourth in her class. During the holidays, she returns to her community to mentor other young girls.

Few African girls are as fortunate as Anna; a recent report found that in 47 out of 54 African countries surveyed, girls had a less than 50 per cent chance of completing primary school with prospects of a widening gender gap at the secondary level (GCE, 2012, p. 6). Like Anna, young women in sub-Saharan Africa (as elsewhere in the Global South) are often forced to forgo their education because of poverty (Achola, 1984); reduced government support as a result of neo-liberal and structural adjustment policies (Stromquist, 1998; Swadener et al., 2008); and gendered expectations about marriage (Bledsoe, 1990), domestic work (McSweeney and Freedman, 1980) and the different futures and responsibilities of boys and girls (Saunders, 2002). Moreover, even those girls who are able to complete primary school and attend secondary school often face challenges during and after their schooling, including harassment, rape and pregnancy (Chege, 2006); poor education (Aikman et al., 2005); pressure to leave school and marry (Bledsoe, 1990); accusations that they are no longer appropriate 'daughters' or prospective 'wives' (Njeuma, 1993); and a lack of viable employment prospects (Magubane, 2001). Finally, the 'value' of formal education itself is often debated by parents, scholars and policymakers (Bloch et al., 1998b; Stambach, 2003; Archambault, 2011).[4] Positive outcomes include learning skills such as literacy and numeracy; exposure to new ideas and ways of being; and the ability to navigate the intricacies of courts, banks, hospitals, the Internet and more (King and Hill, 1993). But there can also be costs, including alienation from their families, communities and cultural and social worlds (Anderson-Levitt et al., 1998); reluctance to pursue agriculture, pastoralism and other non-wage based livelihood strategies (Day, 1998; Englund, 2006); the risks of unplanned pregnancies, HIV-AIDs, tarnished reputations and dropping out (Archambault, 2011); and the tremendous financial sacrifices and other stresses on their families to find ways to pay for their school fees and replace their household labour (Kiluva-Ndunda, 2000; Stambauch, 2000).[5]

Given that most people support the right of girls to pursue their education (despite the endless debates about the form, content and value of education for girls), how can an education project address some of the challenges described earlier? If we broaden our understanding of a girl's 'right' to education, to her right to a safe, secure, quality education that will enhance her life and ensure the support of her family and community, what might this kind of education programme look like? In this chapter, we analyse the Four Pillars PLUS project's design, implementation and effectiveness in order to explore both the possibilities and perils of girls' education. Drawing on four years of work with the project by Katie Orlemanski (2008–2012), we suggest that there are at least four critical lessons to be learned from the project: (1) that adolescence is the key moment for intervention in girls' educational cycles; (2) the need to strategically address barriers to girls' education beyond accessibility; (3) the importance of obtaining 'buy-in' from local leaders and institutions in order for the project to gain legitimacy; and (4) the benefits of recognizing and incorporating community members as the critical agents of change. Together, these four principles promote compromise between the goals of the project and the community; address context and history; and prioritize a community's own articulations of their needs – all of which can effectively convert international goodwill into positive changes in the lives of young women.

The challenges of girls' education in Kenya

In Kenya, stark inequalities of wealth produce disparities in the provision of and access to quality education. Macroeconomic indicators that classify Kenya as 'wealthy' such as GDP mask a highly stratified wealth distribution; the elite 1 per cent of the population earns thousands of times the median wage earned by the bottom 90 per cent (DPMF, 2013). The vast majority of the country's population, both rural and urban, lives in conditions of poverty, a poverty produced in part by the legacies of exclusionary development practices during the colonial and post-colonial period and the retreat of the neo-liberal state from supporting social welfare initiatives (see, for example, Berman and Lonsdale, 1992a, 1992b; Smith, 2008; Swadener et al., 2008).

Poverty is therefore the biggest obstacle that children in rural western Kenya confront as they try to complete their education. The community of North Gem is located within Siaya County in Nyanza Province, an area that was historically known for producing highly educated doctors and elites who later became some of Kenya's political leaders. Education is still highly valued for both girls and boys but the structural conditions of poverty and disease put pressure on families to find alternative ways to support their kinship network. The area continues to face low infrastructure investment and few livelihood opportunities beyond subsistence farming. The general poverty of western Kenya has been exacerbated by the spike in AIDS-related deaths (especially prior to access to anti-retroviral treatment). The epidemic has left an extraordinary number of children, like Anna and her sisters, in need of care by their already impoverished extended families.[6]

In 2003, the Kenyan government reintroduced the Free Primary Education (FPE) programme, which greatly subsidizes the costs of enrolling children in classes one through eight. But caretakers must still pay an average of $30 to $50 a year per student for non-subsidized exam fees, school maintenance levies, uniforms, textbooks and other necessities. For secondary schooling, the costs are even higher. Payment to send a student to a local secondary school can exceed $200, a prohibitive cost for many families whose livelihoods depend on subsistence farming or other small-scale trades. Moreover, the general poverty of the area affects the quality of education provided by these rural schools. Although more students now enroll with the support of the FPE initiative and more classrooms have been built, the Ministry of Education (MoE) cannot afford to hire enough teachers to handle the influx of students. Class size in North Gem often exceeds fifty students. A lack of textbooks and instructional materials, minimal supervision and low salaries contribute to demoralized teachers, some of whom record higher truancy rates than their students. Given these conditions, most wealthy families choose to send their children to elite, private primary and secondary schools that can afford to recruit better qualified teachers; have smaller teacher-student ratios; and provide textbooks, computers, advising and other support for curricular and co-curricular activities – resulting in better exam grades; higher retention and completion rates; and more successful placement in colleges, universities and jobs in the formal sector.

Gender becomes a key consideration as poorer families decide how best to allocate their meagre monetary resources in order to secure the livelihoods and care of all their dependents, weighing the costs, benefits and consequences of different options like education. Gendered differences in the provision of crucial domestic labour, post-marital residence, responsibilities for supporting elderly parents, prospects for formal employment and other avenues for economic security (such as marriage) – all influence a family's difficult decision (cf. Archambault, 2011). In North Gem, young women generally spend more time on household chores than their male counterparts. Their labour is viewed as essential for the social reproduction of the family as they care for siblings and sick family members, process food, prepare meals, clean the house and compound, care for animals and collect firewood and water. Upon marriage, daughters are expected to move in with their husband's family and rely on them for support, while sons are expected to continue to support their natal families through their labour (and that of their wives and children), remittances and gifts. Of course, many married women return regularly to their father's home to visit, care-take and even contribute financially while not all sons can be relied upon for their support. For these and other reasons, poor families in North Gem often decide to use their limited resources to support the education of their sons instead of their daughters.

In Kenya, while the enrolment rates of girls in primary and secondary school have increased, many of them drop out (GCE, 2012, p. 6). Young women continue to face complex challenges to staying in school and excelling while there. They may have a long and unsafe walk to school. Curriculum and teaching methods often reinforce gender stereotypes. Girls report instances of sexual harassment from male peers and sometimes teachers (Ruto, 2009). They often have less time to study because of the gendered division of household labour. Addressing these factors requires a holistic approach to girls' education that supports not only increased accessibility to schools but also improved learning environments and outcomes for young women.

The Four Pillars PLUS project

In 2008, FHI 360 implemented the 'Four Pillars PLUS: Improving Girls' Education in Kenya' (formerly Academy for Educational Development (AED) 'Four Pillars') project to improve the educational outcomes of girls and other vulnerable children in Kenya under an initial three-year grant from the GE Foundation (2008–2011). The GE Foundation already supported a health initiative in a hospital serving the North Gem community, and, based on data linking girls' education and improved community health, the foundation provided an initial $1.2 million grant to implement Four Pillars PLUS in ten primary schools in the area. The project's goals included assisting and supporting female students (and some male students) who were at risk for dropping out of primary school or underperforming while enrolled.[7] Encouraged by the project's successes in increasing girls' enrolment, retention and performance rates in these schools over three years, the foundation financed a second four-year phase of the project (2011–2015) to expand support to students pursuing secondary schooling and vocational training. In addition to providing educational scholarships, the project aimed to support young women (and some young men) in transitioning successfully into the workforce through professional mentoring, internship programmes and advising for tertiary education options. Based on the quantitative and qualitative success of Four Pillars PLUS, the foundation provided another grant to FHI 360 to replicate the project in Nigeria.

Dr. May Rihani, a leading global advocate for women's rights and a former senior Vice President of AED (now FHI 360), conceived the original 'four pillars' approach as a holistic model to support girls' education. Rihani directed the implementation of the Four Pillars PLUS project along with a team of dedicated staff based in Washington DC and headed by Dr. Andrea Bertone. In Kenya, the project hired an experienced project director, Percilla Obunga, five field staff, and a chief finance officer. The field team comprised three Kenyan women, three Kenyan men and one American woman (Katie Orlemanski).

In partnership with the (MoE) and the Ministry of Gender and Children's Affairs, field staff aligned the 'four pillars' framework with the National Kenyan Policy for Orphans and Vulnerable Children. The outcome was a programme based on the following 'four pillars' adapted for girls' success in rural Kenyan schools:

1) **Scholarships** in the form of school fees for primary, secondary and vocational education; and schoolbooks, uniforms and school supplies awarded on a need and merit basis;
2) **Girls' Mentoring** to discuss important topics such as reproductive health, hygiene and future planning while developing qualities such as high self-esteem, knowledge of rights and critical decision-making skills;
3) **Teacher Development** to improve the overall quality of classroom learning and ensure gender-sensitive teaching methods;

4) **Community Development** in the implementation and sustainability of the project. Four Pillars PLUS worked to strengthen the capacity of community members to be the project's advocates, supporters and decision-makers, with both the ability and willingness to continue the vision for girls' education into the future. In addition, the project worked together with other NGOs, government ministries, and community- and faith-based organizations to link the community with other service providers. These pillars were designed to provide a holistic approach to the education of girls that would overcome some of the challenges outlined above.

Scholarships

Given the increasing impoverishment of many households in rural western Kenya and the difficult decisions faced by households in allocating their meagre resources, scholarships were an essential component of the Four Pillars PLUS project. The scholarships helped needy families overcome the financial barriers that prevented them from sending all of their children to school. They also enabled caretakers to pay for other necessities like food and healthcare for the entire household. Based on an assessment of student needs, the project designed a scholarship package that included the payment of government exam fees and the provision of a school uniform, school shoes, a school bag, an annual supply of sanitary towels and underwear (for female students) and learning materials. Each annual scholarship was valued at about $50 in primary schools (awarded based on need); $250 in secondary day schools (awarded based on need and merit); $650 in secondary boarding schools (awarded to top students only); and $250 in post-primary vocational training centres (awarded based on need). For every scholarship, caretakers agreed to pay a portion of the costs of school fees or supplies, which many of them did as 'in-kind' contributions of labour or maize.

While the provision of scholarships is a seemingly straightforward intervention, determining which students are 'in need' can be one of the most challenging steps for a scholarship programme. Recruiting students too hastily, without community input, can produce major problems in the future. Four Pillars PLUS collaborated with community members to design an extensive recruitment programme aimed at minimizing the risk of such common mistakes as: double-sponsoring a child who was recruited under two different names; sponsoring 'ghost' children in which names in the project database could not be matched to a physical student; recruiting beneficiaries because of nepotism or favouritism; recruiting students already sponsored by another programme (an increasingly common problem as scholarship models became popularized); and sponsoring relatively non-needy students while overlooking vulnerable cases.

Four Pillars PLUS spent substantial time and resources on the process of interviewing and confirming needy beneficiaries, which entailed understanding complex family networks; conducting household assessments; collecting birth and death certificates; and seeking community approval of the final list of beneficiaries for scholarships.[8] Initially the programme recruited only female students in classes six through eight, but support was eventually expanded to students pursuing secondary school and vocational training. When community members voiced concerns about vulnerable boys at risk of dropping out of school, Four Pillars PLUS agreed to allocate at least 30 per cent of scholarships to male students.

Until 2010, most of the scholarships were awarded to students in classes six through eight (approximately 300 girls and 100 boys in 2009 and 450 girls and 150 boys in 2010). In 2010, the project piloted a small scholarship initiative for students entering secondary school. By 2011, the project began shifting more resources to post-primary education scholarships. Through discussion with female students and other community members, project staff learned that primary school fees were only one reason that students dropped out. Another reason was that the unsubsidized fees for secondary school were too expensive for families to support even one child, leading to a sense of futility among students, especially young women and their families about the promises of an improved future through education. Young people and their families therefore sought other means of securing their futures outside of formal schooling. As a result of this concern, Four Pillars PLUS shifted from a focus on primary school scholarships to secondary and vocational training. The project increased secondary school scholarships from only 33 in 2010 to almost 150 in 2011, necessitating a reduction in the less expensive primary school scholarships to 360. By 2012, the majority of scholarship funds supported secondary and vocational training (200 students) instead of primary school education (200 students). By this time, as discussed later, the project had started a Savings and Internal Lending Community (SILC) with caretakers, who could use the funds to cover the relatively lower costs of primary school fees while the project offered scholarships for the prohibitive fees of secondary education and vocational training. The shift in the allocation of scholarships, coupled with continued mentoring and teaching initiatives in primary schools, resulted in improved enrolment, completion and transition rates for girls in North Gem.

Girls' mentoring

The second pillar, girls' mentoring, provided a safe space for girls to share with one another and learn from their peers in order to develop skills and knowledge about life choices, leadership and the dilemmas of adolescence. Twice a month, Four Pillars PLUS supported after-school girls mentoring sessions led by an adult role model. The mentoring programme welcomed all adolescent female students from the ten schools and reached about 1,000 girls twice a month through seventy-five trained mentors. The mentors were respected women elected by their community and were trained and paid by the project. In their meetings with the girls, they addressed issues of concern raised by the girls themselves in discussions and through anonymous questions posted in a collection box such as:

> *Is medical advice free at the health centre?*
> *Why are there fewer women in science than men?*
> *Can a young person visit a VCT to find out their HIV-status without their parents?*
> *What can I feed my younger brother who has reddish hair and a bloated belly?*

Mentors used comics, posters and instructional guides developed by FHI 360 to facilitate discussions on these questions and topics like reproductive health, HIV/AIDS, goal making, peer pressure and child rights. The project also provided healthy snacks including a milk packet, boiled eggs and a loaf of bread during the mentoring sessions to supplement young women's nutritional intake. As one mentor noted in 2008, 'The most valuable part of my mentoring experience is that through story-telling and role-plays, the girls are empowered to make good decisions' (Four Pillars, 2009, p. iv).

The girls' mentoring pillar also sought to develop leadership qualities in young women through peer-to-peer (P2P) mentoring and an annual girls' leadership conference. The P2P component linked younger girls in primary school with older peer role models in secondary school. It provided the student mentor an opportunity to give back to her community and develop leadership skills as she shared her experiences and advice. P2P exposed younger girls to positive role models for their futures. As Anna explained, 'I became the girls' education ambassador in my village due to the mentoring program. I currently lead a group of 50 girls in my school. This has helped in developing my leadership skills. I have become more knowledgeable in various issues including healthy decision making, hygiene, and HIV/AIDS thanks to my mentors' (Four Pillars, 2009, p. iv).

Teacher development

The third pillar of the project, teacher development, encompassed a broad scope of activities that addressed concerns put forward by the school and community to improve teaching and learning. Teacher development focused on barriers to girls' education like gender-biased curriculum, demoralized teachers, corporal punishment and sexual harassment by targeting not only teachers but also government officials, school management committees, church sponsors, parents, student leaders and others through sensitization campaigns and discussion forums. Some of these activities were straightforward – helping with exam fees, providing teaching supplies and materials, methodology workshops and sponsoring 'exposure' activities such as visits for the top students to a national university. The methodology workshops explored topics ranging from conducting learner-centred teaching in overcrowded classrooms to delivering gender-sensitive curriculum. The project supported increased supervisory visits by MoE officers in order to hold teachers accountable and to encourage their many heroic efforts. The project also motivated school staff through teaching awards and the provision of instructional materials like textbooks, posters and mathematical instruments.

Other activities arose from the specific problems encountered in North Gem. For example, in 2009, Four Pillars PLUS facilitated a 'jigger eradication campaign' when the mud-floored classrooms, lack of desks and lack of shoes led to severe jigger-related infections among students.[9] They sponsored Ministry of Health (MoH) officials to train local teachers to remove the parasites and treat the sores as well as to visit and treat the infested households of some students. Following the training, teachers conducted a 'jigger eradication day' in every school for affected students; the MoE sprayed infected classrooms with pesticide; and Four Pillars PLUS donated shoes to students without them.

Similarly, Four Pillars PLUS collaborated with School Management Committees (SMC) to support the formation of 4K Clubs. These clubs focused on action-oriented learning for students about agriculture, forestry and livestock. Ministry of Agriculture (MoA) officials visited the schools to help students start their own 4K projects. Four Pillars PLUS donated start-up supplies like seeds, fertilizer and fencing materials so that the 4K clubs could grow fruits, vegetables, seedlings or raise small livestock to sell. Some of the vegetables were used to support the school's lunch programme for needy children. Students managed the profits themselves, using them to buy uniforms, purchase school notebooks and pay exam fees for needy students. Moreover, the 4K Clubs were also learning projects for the community. For example, in the 4K gardens, MoA officials introduced a new sweet potato variety, a disease-resistant banana plant and a method for spacing vegetables during particularly dry seasons. The 4K Clubs encouraged students to practise the new techniques in their farms at home and welcomed community members to visit the learning gardens. By 2012, some of the 4K Clubs recorded annual profits up to $250 (Four Pillars, 2012, p. 10).

Community development

The purpose of the final pillar, community development, was to prioritize local knowledge and recognize community members as the project's key leaders and decision-makers. To do so, the project followed a two-pronged approach. First, project staff held open forums for community members to share their ideas and concerns about the design and implementation of the project. Second, the project recognized that communities had unmet needs beyond girls' education and provided support to address some of those needs.

Community members, students and teachers consistently cited poverty as a major community challenge that affected not only education but also nutrition, healthcare and dignified livelihoods. In response, Four Pillars PLUS facilitated the formation of SILC. SILC groups brought together individual community members to leverage their collective savings into small loans, thereby enabling participants to expand their small businesses or farms through rotating credit. Every month, members contributed about $1 each (or an amount agreed upon by group members) and then voted as a group on ways to invest the collective money. One SILC group, for example, used their savings to start a small business together. They bought plastic chairs and a tent to rent out for local events and funerals. Profits were distributed to group members every month. Another group loaned money on a rotating basis to individuals, some of whom used the funds to transport their farm products to larger markets in nearby cities. The farmers profited from the access to new markets and repaid the SILC loan with interest. A percentage of the funds accumulated by SILC groups went into a 'school-fee savings fund' that members could access at the beginning of each school term to pay their required contribution. Beyond small loans for monthly business needs, SILC provided essential support for members in times of emergency through funds for burial or medical assistance that did not have to be repaid. Three years after initiation of SILC in the North

Gem community, some groups recorded up to $950 in savings that could be distributed on a monthly basis to individuals as a loan or be reinvested in a group business (Four Pillars, 2012, p. 10).

Finally, Four Pillars PLUS often collaborated with the government and other service providers to expand community access to required services and expertise. For example, in conjunction with the Ministry of Health (MoH), Four Pillars PLUS facilitated free monthly visits by mobile Voluntary Counseling and Testing (VCT) units. Many community members attended the clinics individually or with their partner to find out their HIV status, receive counseling on ARV treatment and obtain condoms. The project also collaborated with other groups including the Federation of Women Lawyers in Kenya (FIDA) to conduct community trainings on how to respond to rape and assault; community-based youth groups who worked to reach out-of-school youth; and a re-usable sanitary towel initiative to sustain access to the products for female students.

Outcomes

Four Pillars PLUS measured the project outcomes for girls' education in North Gem through three key indicators: enrolment, retention and transition rates. While exclusive attention to one indicator may mask other inequalities, the three indicators taken together can evaluate progress in eliminating gender discrimination in education. For example, many studies only analyse primary school enrolment figures, which are often measured only on the first day of school. While useful, enrolment rates provide no insight into whether the girls stay in school (retention) or succeed in securing a place in secondary school or a vocational training programme (transition). Four Pillars PLUS kept detailed records of all three indicators and met regularly with students, teachers and parents to discuss the qualitative outcomes of the project. The project measured enrolment rates by counting the number of male and female students who attended class during the first week of school; retention rates by comparing the enrolment numbers in each class to the number of students who took the final exam at the end of each school year; and transition rates by tracking whether students who completed the prior class enrolled in the next class the following term. These indicators were often difficult to measure because some students repeated classes; 'dropped out' and then returned to school in the same year; or had high truancy rates.

Despite the difficulty of measuring outcomes, Four Pillars PLUS recorded well-defined improvements in all three rates for young women in North Gem. In the first year of the project, the number of girls who dropped out of two primary schools (mainly from upper primary classes) was thirty-three and twenty-nine. By 2009, the number of female dropout cases in these schools fell dramatically to four and three respectively (Four Pillars, 2009, p. 10). Aggregate enrolment of girls in the ten schools also increased in the first year, jumping from 1,647 in 2008 to 2,476 in 2009 (Four Pillars, 2009, p. 9). Longitudinal data shows the positive trends continuing into 2012. Finally, the number of young women in the ten project schools who enrolled in class 8 to complete their Kenya Certificate of Primary Education (KCPE) (a mandatory national exam that students must pass to finish primary school and proceed to secondary education) also increased during the project period from 155 in 2007 (the year before the project started) to 207 in 2012 (Four Pillars, 2013). Moreover, almost all of the female students who enrolled in KCPE remained in school the entire year and completed their final exam. In 2011, of the 182 female students who took the KCPE exam, 143 of them obtained scores high enough to secure positions in secondary schools or vocational training and successfully transitioned.

Lessons learned

So what were the lessons learned from the Four Pillars PLUS programme that might be useful in designing similar interventions?

First, the project recognized that adolescence is a crucial period for interventions that seek to address the immediate risk of girls dropping out of school. During adolescence, changes occur in young people's bodies, minds and feelings – as well as in community and family responsibilities. In some cases, the transition from childhood to adulthood signals the start of a young woman's role as a potential wife and mother and the end of her time as a student. Moreover, exam fees and the costs of additional preparatory 'tutoring' increase as students enter the upper primary classes that prepare them for the KCPE exam. The provision of scholarships to young women at this moment encourages families to keep them in school. Mentoring programmes support the students to support themselves as they make complex negotiations and decisions about their education, families and futures.

While adolescence remains a critical point of intervention, what emerged from the Four Pillars PLUS project suggests that addressing the root causes of high female drop-out rates requires interventions that extend to the years before and after the upper primary grades. The families of adolescent girls' who left school cited the lack of realistic possibilities to continue their education and then translate it into viable livelihoods. According to Caroline Archambault (2011, p. 638, citing Nyerere, 2009) 'Formal-sector salaried jobs in Kenya seem to demand increasingly higher levels of education, and the Kenyan school system is highly competitive, with positions in secondary school available for only just over half (55 per cent) of primary graduates.' Thus without the aspirational possibility of continuing education, young women sometimes chose to leave school to pursue their futures through marriage or informal jobs such as 'house helps' in cities. In response to this trend, Four Pillars PLUS reallocated its resources towards providing scholarships to secondary school for young women who achieved high enough marks on KCPE. The project also offered scholarships to vocational and technical training institutions for students who were not accepted into secondary school or were not interested in continuing their formal education. Vocational training provided a viable alternative to formal education and a more direct path to income generation.

But interventions at the adolescent stage alone cannot overcome the gender-biased schooling girls may face throughout their education cycle. In order for young women to perform at par with their male counterparts, a comprehensive reform of gender-sensitive learning must take place from Early Childhood Development (ECD) through secondary school. Four Pillars PLUS provided over 4,000 textbooks and other instructional materials for classes from ECD through secondary school in North Gem, and the project facilitated workshops on gender-sensitive learning methods for teachers at all levels.

Second, Four Pillars PLUS succeeded because it addressed a range of barriers to girls' education. Girls required both access to schools and high-quality learning once they enrolled. Scholarships subsidized the substantial financial costs of education, enabling more families to send their girls (and boys) to school. But forms of gender discrimination in the schools like gender-biased curricula or sexual harassment by teachers and male students required a holistic approach and intensive collaboration with the government education ministry. While the Kenyan MoE supported such commendable policies as gender-sensitive classroom teaching; strict punishment for sexual harassment; a ban on corporal punishment; and continuing education for pregnant students, translating these national policies into the local context of rural schools was a challenge. Four Pillars PLUS facilitated workshops for MoE officials to discuss these and other policies with school staff and develop methods for implementing them in the North Gem schools.

During community days sponsored by Four Pillars PLUS, female students used poems, dramas and songs to recount some of the gendered problems that detracted from their success in school, including being required to cook staff meals during classes, suffering from a lack of sanitary towels and having to meet the time demands of domestic chores. The project facilitated workshops for mentors on children's rights in and out of the classroom, including how to respond to sexual harassment in schools. Four Pillars PLUS also paid for tutors to work with underperforming female students.[10]

A third lesson is the importance of obtaining buy-in from local leaders and institutions for the project to gain legitimacy and adapt its framework to a local context. Involving, from the very beginning, a broad and diverse cross-section of actors including students, parents, school officials, government officials, local administration (Chiefs), church members and local business owners, through open discussion forums, provided a critical foundation for the success of Four Pillars PLUS. At the start of the project, staff held meetings with community members to discuss the project goals, hear from community members about their needs and decide together whether a beneficial relationship could be established. A dynamic forum conducted in the local language meant that compromises between project and community objectives were negotiated in a spirit of accountability and collaboration. For example, community members in eight of the ten forums expressed a need for a school-feeding programme. Although project staff recognized the value of such a programme, it was beyond the scope of their budget. As a compromise, the project agreed to indirectly support such a school-feeding programme by funding a MoA extension officer to conduct food-security training in the ten communities, which led to the start-up of the 4K Club school gardens. Today, eight school farms run by the 4K Clubs provide vegetables and maize for the school-feeding programme.

Fourth, the project demonstrated the benefits of recognizing and incorporating community members as the critical agents of change. In order to privilege local understandings and categories, Four Pillars PLUS conducted discussion forums for all community members interested in shaping the project. In the forums, participants debated the importance of girls' education and established their own definitions of key terms like gender, education, NGO, scholarship and mentor. These forums provided an avenue for Four Pillars PLUS to root project objectives in the language and needs of the community as a whole. For example, in order to determine which students should benefit from the programme, the project initially used international statistics to prioritize the most vulnerable children as adolescent girls who had lost both parents. But this approach was critiqued by participants in the discussion forums, many of whom asked 'What about the boy-child?' Although community members agreed that girls faced unique challenges in school, they also recognized that many boys had difficulties as well. As they explained, while NGO staff may prioritize a 'total orphan girl' as needing assistance over a 'boy with both parents', the orphaned girl may live with well-off relatives who provide for her school fees while the boy lives with parents who are 'sickly' and unable to work on the farm, much less pay school fees. Community members pressed the project staff to embrace a more complicated concept of 'vulnerability' and to understand and accommodate the complex social situation of each child beyond a simple categorization on paper. As a result of these discussions, Four Pillars PLUS agreed to allocate 30 per cent of its scholarships to male students, use individual assessments to determine 'vulnerability', and review, modify and approve the proposed list of scholarship students through public deliberation with community members.[11] Cases involving falsifying documents or answers were also discussed publically at the forum, often with a great deal of humour and shy admittance by the caretaker.

Similarly, the project openly discussed its eventual exit from the North Gem community and worked to strengthen the capacity and willingness of local institutions and groups to continue the vision for girls' education into the future.[12] Four Pillars PLUS linked each of the 'four pillars' for girls' education with a sustainability and ownership measure. Scholarships would be partially sustained through school garden 4K Clubs and the school-fee kitty in SILC groups. The project helped the seventy-five mentors to register themselves as an independent Community-based Organization (CBO) to provide guidance and counseling to girls and their families. For teacher development, the project trained the ten school management committees on their proper oversight function. The committees eventually formed the North Gem Child Support Network, which was committed to ensuring that schools remain girl-friendly environments after Four Pillars PLUS exits. The network linked with other service providers to ensure equal education for all and is currently in the process of applying to government grants to fund its mission. All of these sustainability initiatives support community development. Underlying each of the strategies, and ultimately the successful continuation of girls' education support in North Gem, is a pronounced commitment of Four Pillars PLUS to reinterpret its plans and goals in conversation with North Gem's community resources, priorities and ideas.

In conclusion, the international focus on the 'girl child' has generated significant educational, social and economic benefits for some young women like Anna and their families. The Four Pillars PLUS project successfully helped almost a thousand students attend primary, secondary and vocational school. Many more students benefitted from the project's mentoring programme, provision of classroom resources, support for the school feeding programme, improvements in the learning environment, teacher development programmes and other initiatives. The project provided broad support to community members by increasing their access to social service providers, developing income-generating opportunities like SILC and, perhaps most importantly, soliciting and responding to community ideas, needs and critiques. But as our analysis suggests, it takes more than scholarships for school fees to address the complex factors that influence the decisions and abilities of poor, rural families to educate girls and the capacity and likelihood for the girls to succeed in school. In Kenya, as elsewhere in the Global South (and even much of the Global North), rural families are struggling to survive in a world of increasing economic and political stratification, marginalization and insecurity. These inequities are reflected and reproduced in the schools, which lack sufficient trained teachers, classroom materials, resources and oversight, and in the lives of young girls, who confront unique challenges both within and outside of the classroom. While educational initiatives, governmental or non-governmental, can only do so much to overcome historical, geographical and gendered disparities of power, resources and opportunities, the lessons learned from Four Pillars PLUS may be helpful in designing similar projects and addressing some of the conventional pitfalls of girls' educational initiatives.

***

Acknowledgements: Both authors would like to thank the directors and staff of the Four Pillars PLUS project for permission to use project reports. Katie would like to thank the North Gem community and the young women who demonstrated their daily determination to go to school; the Malanga Mentors CBO; Four Pillars PLUS colleagues, especially Percilla Obunga, an insightful and patient project director with a fine sense of humour to boot; and Dr. Andrea Bertone, an invaluable leader of the project and personal mentor. We are both grateful to Dr. Debotri Dhar for providing us an opportunity to assess the Four Pillars PLUS project and clarify our positions on the value and challenges of girls' education.

Notes

1 The spotlighting of the 'girl child' (Croll, 2006; Switzer, 2010; Archambault, 2011) as an international icon for development coincides with the increased dominance of rights-based approaches to development (Cornwall and Nyamu-Musembi, 2004; Hodgson, 2011) and the popularization of female empowerment approaches to improvement schemes (Kabeer, 1994).

2 Anna and all other names are pseudonyms, unless otherwise noted.

3 Family Health International 360 is a non-profit human development organization dedicated to improving lives in lasting ways by advancing integrated, locally driven solutions and serves more than sixty countries and all US states and territories (http://www.fhi360.org). FHI acquired the Academy for Educational Development (AED), a non-profit organization dedicated to global education, health and economic development, to form FHI 360 in 2011, thereby combining their expertise. Primary funding for the Four Pillars PLUS project comes from the GE Foundation, the philanthropic arm of General Electric (GE).

4 Since the colonial period in Africa, formal education in a 'Western' mode of classrooms, teachers and textbooks has been seen as a key strategy to alleviate poverty by 'improving' the attitudes, skills, ideas and thus futures of young boys and, eventually, girls (Beck, 1966; White, 1996).

5 This very brief review of the challenges of and debates about the education of girls is based on the authors' work and experiences in impoverished, rural areas in Kenya (Orlemanski) and Tanzania (Hodgson) and is confirmed in the scholarly literature and NGO research and reports. For sub-Saharan Africa, see Bloch et al. (1998a). Valuable recent case studies from East Africa include Stambach (2000), Vavrus (2007), Switzer (2010) and Archambault (2011).

6 According to one government official, 40 per cent of primary school children in Nyanza Province have lost one or more parents due in large part to the AIDS epidemic (Oloo, 2008).

7 The Four Pillars PLUS project also conducted outreach programmes to families of children with disabilities, both girls and boys, a group grossly under-represented in formal schooling in Kenya. The project facilitated government assessments to determine each child's specific learning needs and provided scholarships for these students to attend specialized schools or acquire specialized learning equipment for the regular classroom.

8 Official documents like birth and death certificates and identity cards may be difficult to obtain for some students in Kenya. A letter from the local Chief explaining the case could be substituted in such cases.

9 A jigger is a parasite that embeds itself under the fingernails and toenails of a host and eats away at the skin causing painful sores and at times the loss of toes or fingers.

10 Tutoring outside of school by teachers is known as 'tuition' in Kenya. The MoE has attempted several times to ban tuition because it serves as a profit-making venture for some teachers who demand hefty payments from parents to deliver curriculum to students after school rather than during class. Additional tutoring is still needed, however, for students with learning challenges, inadequate prior training and those who want to compete with students from private schools for coveted spots in public secondary schools.

11 In order to capture the nuances of vulnerability, Four Pillars PLUS designed an assessment tool to collect complex census data on each child and their household through a face-to-face interview with the student and the caretaker. The data ranged from basic biological statistics like gender and age to more complex questions about a child's access to physical, social and financial capital. Four Pillars PLUS staff reviewed every complete file in a round-table discussion to establish a list of programme beneficiaries based upon their 'vulnerability' ranking and the funds available. The final list was approved by community members in a public forum.

12 Due to limited funding, Four Pillars PLUS initially operated under a three-year timeframe which would have allowed sponsored students in classes 6–8 to have completed primary school by the project's expected exit. Because of the project's documented success during its initial phase, however, Four Pillars PLUS received renewed funding for four additional years.

Questions for reflection

a) What are some of the possible benefits and risks of education for girls? Should girls always receive preference in educational programmes and assistance?
b) How are gender, poverty and education related? What kinds of educational approaches are more successful than others in addressing gender inequities and poverty?
c) What role did the community play in shaping the Four Pillars PLUS project? How do the goals of community members compare to those of NGO projects? What are the responsibilities of the project to the community and the community to the project?
d) Initially, the project thought that sponsoring girls in their final three years of primary school would help them enter secondary school. Why did this prove to be difficult? What changes did the project make?

Further Reading

Archambault, Caroline. (2011), 'Ethnographic empathy and the social context of rights: "Rescuing" maasai girls from early marriage', *American Anthropologist*, 113, 4, 632–43.

This article explores the complex factors that inform parental decisions about whether or not to send girls to school in a Maasai community in rural Kenya. Based on her long-term ethnographic data, Archambault argues that as structural conditions make it increasingly difficult for boys and girls in a semi-pastoralist community to convert their education into secure livelihoods, parents turn to local, social networks for their families' protection – including marriage for their daughters.

Vavrus, Frances Katherine. (2003), *Desire and Decline: Schooling Amid Crisis in Tanzania.* New York: P. Lang.

This ethnography of schooling in Moshi, Tanzania examines why the failed promises of education – like access to formal employment, social mobility and overall better economic development – do not deter Tanzanians in their pursuit of education. Vavrus's detailed interviews with students and their families provide a complex, gendered picture of the increasing desire for schooling in the face of declining economic conditions. Her interlocutors make great sacrifices for school fees not because they link education to a better economic future but because they desire to become part of a broader imagined community of educated persons with its associated prestige and identity.

Bibliography

Achola, P. P. W. (1984), 'Women and equality in Zambia: Trends in educational opportunities and outcomes', *Zambia Educational Review*, 5, 2, 105–23.

Aikman, S., Unterhalter, E. and Challender, C. (2005), 'The education MDGs: Achieving gender equality through curriculum and pedagogy change', in C. Sweetman (ed.) *Gender and the Millennium Development Goals*. Oxford: Oxfam GB, 44–55.

Anderson-Levitt, K., Bloch, M. and Soumaré, A. M. (1998), 'Inside classrooms in Guinea: Girls' experiences', in M. Bloch, J. Beoku-Betts and B. Tabachnick (eds.) *Women and Education in Sub-Saharan Africa: Power, Opportunities, and Constraints*. Boulder, CO: L. Rienner Publishers, 99–130.

Archambault, C. (2011), 'Ethnographic empathy and the social context of rights: "Rescuing" Maasai girls from early marriage', *American Anthropologist*, 113, 4, 632–43.

Beck, A. (1966), 'Colonial policy and education in British East Africa, 1900–1950', *Journal of British Studies*, 5, 2, 115–38.

Berman, B. and Lonsdale, J. (1992a), *Unhappy Valley: Conflict in Kenya and Africa. Book One: State and Class*. Athens: Ohio University Press.

—— and Lonsdale, J. (1992b), *Unhappy Valley: Conflict in Kenya and Africa. Book Two: Violence and Ethnicity*. Athens: Ohio University Press.

Bledsoe, C. (1990), 'School fees and the marriage process for mende girls in Sierra Leone', in P. R. Sanday and R. G. Goodenough (eds.) *Beyond the Second Sex: New Directions in the Anthropology of Gender*. Philadelphia: University of Pennsylvania Press.

Bloch, M. Beoku-Betts, J. A. and Tabachnick, B. R. (eds.). (1998a), *Women and Education in Sub-Saharan Africa: Power, Opportunities, and Constraints*. Boulder, CO: L. Rienner Publishers.

—— and Vavrus, F. (1998b), 'Gender and educational research, policy, and practice in sub-Saharan Africa: Theoretical and empirical problems and prospects', In M. N. Bloch, J. A. Beoku-Betts and B. R. Tabachnick (eds.) *Women and Education in Sub-Saharan Africa: Power, Opportunities, and Constraints*. Boulder, CO: L. Rienner Publishers, 1–24.

Chege, F. (2006), 'Teachers' gendered identities, pedagogy, and HIV/AIDS education in African settings within the ESAR', *Journal of Education*, 38, 26–44.

Cornwall, A. and Nyamu-Musembi, C. (2004), 'Putting the "rights-based approach" to development into perspective', *Third World Quarterly*, 25, 8, 1415–37.

Croll, E. (2006), 'From the girl child to girl's rights', *Third World Quarterly*, 27, 7, 1285–97.

Day, L. R. (1998), 'Rites and reason: Precolonial education and its relevance to the current production and transmission of knowledge', in M. N. Bloch, J. A. Beoku-Betts and B. R. Tabachnick (eds.) *Women and Education in Sub-Saharan Africa: Power, Opportunities, and Constraints*. Boulder, CO: L. Rienner Publishers, 49–72.

Development Poverty Management Forum (DPMF) (2013), 'A brief profile of inequality in Kenya', http://www.dpmf.org/dpmf/index.php?option=com_content&view=article&id=97:a-brief-general-profile-on-inequality-in-kenya&catid=43:social-policy-development-and-governance-in-kenya&Itemid=94 (accessed March 2013).

Englund, H. (2006), *Prisoners of Freedom: Human Rights and the African Poor*. Berkeley: University of California Press.

Four Pillars. (2009), 'Annual report 2008–2009 of Four Pillars: Improving Girls' Education Project in Kenya', a report produced for the Academy for Educational Development (AED), Washington DC.

——. (2012), 'Overview of project, March 2012', a presentation prepared for Family Health International (FHI 360), Kenya.

——. (2013), 'Summary of Four Pillars PLUS scholarship support, enrolment, completion, and transition rates, 2009–2013', a report prepared for Family Health International (FHI 360), Kenya.

Global Campaign for Education (GCE). (2012), 'Gender discrimination in education: the violation of rights of women and girls', a report submitted to the Committee on the Elimination of Discrimination against Women (CEDAW), Johannesburg.

Hodgson, D. L. (ed.) (2011), *Gender and Culture at the Limit of Rights*. Philadelphia: University of Pennsylvania Press.

Kabeer, N. (1994), *Reversed Realities: Gender Hierarchies in Development Thought*. London: Verso.

Kiluva-Ndunda, M. M. (2000), *Women's Agency and Educational Policy: The Experiences of the Women of Kilome, Kenya*. New York: State University of New York Press.

King, E. M. and Hill, M. A. (1993), '*Women's Education in Developing Countries: Barriers, Benefits, and Policies', a Report Published for the World Bank*. Baltimore: Johns Hopkins University Press.

Magubane, Z. (2001), 'Globalization and the South African woman: A historical overview', in AAWORD (ed.) *Visions of Gender Theories and Social Development in Africa: Harnessing Knowledge for Social Justice and Equality*. Dakar, Senegal: AAWORD Book Series.

McSweeney, B. G. and Freedman, M. (1980), 'Lack of time as obstacle to women's education: The case of Upper Volta (Part 2)', *Comparative Education Review*, 24, 2, S124–S139.

Njeuma, D. L. (1993), 'An overview of women's education in Africa', in J. K. Conway and S. C. Bourque (eds.) *The Politics of Women's Education: Perspectives from Asia, Africa, and Latin America*. Ann Arbor: University of Michigan Press, 123–31.

Nyerere, J. (2009), *Technical and Vocational Education and Training (TVET) Sector Mapping in Kenya, a Report*. Amersfoort: Edukans Foundation.

Oloo, E. (2008), 'Poverty to blame for rise in drop outs', *Daily Nation*, 21 November: Provincial News 37.

Ruto, S. J. (2009), 'Sexual abuse of school age children: Evidence from Kenya', *Journal of International Cooperation in Education*, 12, 1, 177–92.

Saunders, K. (2002), 'Introduction: Towards a deconstructive post-development criticism', in K. Saunders (ed.) *Feminist Post-Development Thought: Rethinking Modernity, Post-Colonialism, and Representation*. New York: Palgrave, 1–38.

Smith, J. H. (2008), *Bewitching Development: Witchcraft and the Reinvention of Development in Neoliberal Kenya*. Chicago: University of Chicago Press.

Stambach, A. (2000), *Lessons from Mount Kilimanjaro: Schooling, Community, and Gender in East Africa*. New York: Routledge.

——.(2003), 'World-cultural and anthropological interpretations of "choice programming" in Tanzania', in K. M. Anderson-Levitt (ed.) *Local Meanings, Global Schooling: Anthropology and World Culture Theory*. New York: Palgrave Macmillan, 141–60.

Stromquist, N. (1998), 'Agents in women's education: Some trends in the African context', in M. N. Bloch, J. A. Beoku-Betts and B. R. Tabachnick (eds.) *Women and Education in Sub-Saharan Africa: Power, Opportunities, and Constraints*. Boulder, Colorado: L. Rienner Publishers, 25–48.

Swadener, E., Wachira, P., Kabiru, M. and Njenga, A. (2008), 'Linking policy discourse to everyday life in Kenya: Impacts of neoliberal policies on early education and childrearing', in M. Garcia, A. R. Pence and J. L. Evans (eds.) *Africa's Future, Africa's Challenge: Early Childhood Care and Development in Sub-Saharan Africa*. New York: World Bank Publications, 407–26.

Switzer, H. (2010), 'Disruptive discourse: Kenyan Maasai schoolgirls make themselves', *Girlhood Studies*, 3, 1, 137–55.

Vavrus, F. (2007), *Desire and Decline: Schooling and Crisis in Tanzania*. New York: Peter Lang Publishing.

White, B. W. (1996), 'Talk about school: Education and the colonial project in French and British Africa (1860–1960)', *Comparative Education*, 32, 1, 9–26.

Gender, Schooling and Achievement in the Caribbean

2

Mike Younger and Patricia George

Chapter Outline

Introduction

Any discussion of educational achievement in the countries of the Caribbean has to acknowledge the diversity of the geographical and historical contexts – thirty territories, covering a north-west–south-east distance of close to 3,000 kilometres, exploited to different degrees by Dutch, French, English and Spanish colonizers – which impacts upon the particular and gives a specificity and uniqueness to any one nation. Within the educational sphere, however, there is uniformity in the concerns about the gender profile of academic engagement, with a focus on two overarching concerns confronting the educational systems: quantity concerns, in terms of expanding educational access, and quality concerns related to improving student achievement (George, 2013).

In both of these concerns, gender is distinctly prominent, since across the region as a whole, there appears to have been a significant improvement in educational access and achievement by girls, whereas retention, completion and achievement of boys appear to be regressing (Plummer et al., 2008).

Indeed, within the Commonwealth, the gendered pattern of engagement and achievement in education is much closer, in the Caribbean, to that experienced in the 'old' Commonwealth countries of the United Kingdom, Australia, New Zealand and Canada than it is to the 'newer' Commonwealth countries in Africa and parts of Asia. Thus it is that boys' disengagement from education, and their apparent underachievement, has emerged as the key issue which has been prioritized by policymakers and academics; 'failing' boys, 'poor boys', 'problem boys' and the need to 'rescue boys' became the dominant discourse – to address the perceived crisis of male underachievement.

Closer examination of recent data available through the EFA Global Monitoring Report (UNESCO, 2011), however, presents an ambivalent picture about gender equity in the Caribbean as a whole. At one level, there seems little significant inequality: for both pre-primary schooling and for primary education, the gross enrolment ratios stands close to parity (1.01 and 1.03 respectively in the 2008 school year, indicating slightly more girls present in the system), and indeed, at secondary level, the data show slightly more boys proceeding to secondary schools than girls (97 per cent compared to 94 per cent). In terms of formal schooling, the school life expectancy (the expected number of years of formal schooling from primary to tertiary education) is only slightly lower for boys (11.1 years) than for girls (11.4 years).

Disaggregation of these data within the Caribbean, however, reveals some inequalities across the region, with the net enrolment ratio at secondary level varying considerably, from Grenada, where the gender parity index (GPI) is in favour of boys (0.91), to Dominica (GPI: 1.21) and the Dominican Republic (GPI: 1.22), where significantly more girls access secondary education (Table 2.1). Moreover, across the Caribbean, the pupils' survival rate to grade 5 (generally the completion of formal primary education in the region) is significantly in favour of girls (GPI 1.07); more boys than girls are classified as out-of-school adolescents (51.6 per cent of the population); and 60 per cent of the enrolment in tertiary education in 2008 is female (93,000 women compared with 61,000 men). Indeed, this preponderance of women in tertiary education has been noted for some time: as early as 2000, Figueroa (2000) pointed out that 70 per cent of the graduates from the Mona campus of the University of the West Indies were female while in 1948, 70 per cent had been male, and this remained evident at the end of the decade, with women's 'share' of tertiary education across the Caribbean in 2009 varying from 56 per cent in Trinidad/ Tobago to 84.6 per cent in St Lucia (Reddock, 2009).

In terms of academic achievement, the data are even starker. Sixty four per cent of the entry for the Caribbean Secondary Examinations Certificate in

Table 2.1: Net enrolment ratio in secondary education (%): School year ending in 2008.

Selected countries	Total (%)	Male (%)	Female (%)	Gender parity index (F/M)
Bahamas	85	83	87	1.05
Belize	63	61	66	1.09
Cuba	83	82	83	1.01
Dominica	68	62	74	1.21
Dominican Republic	58	52	63	1.22
Granada	89	93	85	0.91
Jamaica	77	75	79	1.05
Montserrat	96	95	96	1.01
Saint Lucia	80	77	82	1.06
Saint Vincent the Grenadines	90	85	95	1.12
Trinidad & Tobago	74	71	76	1.07

Source: EFA Global Monitoring Report, 2011 (UNESCO, 2011).

2010 was female, and significant gender differentials in achievement were evident (Table 2.2). Forty four per cent of girls (compared with 33 per cent of boys) achieved grades 1 or 2 in English (defined as showing a comprehensive or good grasp of the key concepts, knowledge, skills and competencies

Table 2.2: Percentage of students achieving grades 1 and 2, by gender, Caribbean Secondary Examinations Certificate, 2010

	Number of candidates	%/number achieving grade 1	%/number achieving grade 2	%/number achieving grades 1/ 2
English				
Boys	36,885	13.5/ 4979	19.5/7193	33.0/12172
Girls	55,464	21.2/11578	23.0/ 12757	44.2/24335
Maths				
Boys	34,275	8.6/2948	12.3/4216	20.9/7164
Girls	54,098	7.6/4111	11.5/6221	19.1/10332
Social Studies				
Boys	16,848	4.9/826	29.9/5037	34.8/5863
Girls	28,865	8.4/2427	35.6/10276	44.0/12703
Science				
Boys	31,461	13.0/4090	27.0/8494	40.0/12584
Girls	52,643	14.0/7370	26.0/13687	40.0/21057
All subjects				
Boys	206,441	11.6/23947	24.6/50784	36.2/74,731
Girls	330,987	14.5/47993	26.2/86719	40.7/134,712

Source: Caribbean Examinations Council Annual Report (2010).

required by the syllabus), with similar gender gaps in Social Studies (10 per cent in favour of girls). Although gender parity *apparently* existed in science and boys *apparently* outperformed girls in mathematics (20.9 per cent of boys achieving grades 1/2 as against 19.1 per cent of girls), the *absolute* data show that even in these stereotypical male domains, more girls than boys were awarded grades 1 and 2 in these subjects, with 21,057 girls awarded grades 1 or 2 in science (compared to 12,584 boys) and 10,332 girls awarded the higher levels grades in Maths (compared to 7,164 boys). Indeed, the relative data conceal the extent of the gender disparity; Table 2.2 suggests that the gender gap is quite narrow (only 4.5 per cent) when all subjects are considered, in that 40.7 per cent of girls achieved grades 1/2 in all subjects across the Caribbean compared to 36.2 per cent of boys. The fact, though, that only 38 per cent of actual examination entries were from boys (206,441 compared to 330,987 from girls) means that whereas 134,712 grade 1–2 passes were awarded to girls, only 74,731 were awarded to boys; thus, of those awarded grade 1–2 passes, only 36 per cent were boys, and almost 60,000 grade 1 and 2 awards were made to girls than to boys.

These data are not unusual; similar outcomes emerge from De Lisle, Smith and Jules's (2010) report on Trinidad and Tobago's participation in the 2006 Progress in International Reading Literacy Survey, showing that – in international terms – Trinidad and Tobago ranked third in the magnitude of the gender gap, with a difference of thirty-one points in favour of females, higher than the international mean difference of seventeen points. In the Eastern Caribbean, 2009 data for the Common Entrance Examination (CEE) at the end of primary schooling in Antigua and Barbuda offer a similar scenario, with a gender disparity of 13 percentage points: 79 per cent of girls achieved the pass level compared with 66 per cent of boys; this disparity is sustained at secondary level, with 69 per cent of girls achieving the pass level in CSEC English compared with 63 per cent of boys.

Boys' 'underachievement' as *the* problem?

It is within this context, then, that boys' apparent 'underachievement' in the Caribbean has been constructed in the political and academic landscape, at least since the early 90s, as *the* problem to be solved, and it has ever since retained its status as an issue legitimately requiring political attention throughout the Anglophone Caribbean. So, there has been an explicit focus on research which has problematized boys (Kutnick, Layne, and Jules, 1997; Figueroa, 2000; Chevannes, 2002; De Lisle, Smith, and Jules, 2005) and the advocacy of policies and initiatives to address the 'underachieving boys' agenda (Jha and Kelleher, 2006; World Bank, 2009; Commonwealth Secretariat, 2011). Here, as elsewhere in the 'old' Commonwealth (Martino and Berrill, 2003), ideological agendas grounded in essentialist mindsets have come to dominate and dictate policy, driving forward a focus on boys' education (Figueroa, 2010). A great deal of energy has thus been invested, within education ministries and at inter-governmental organizational level, aimed at 'solving' the problem (World Bank, 2009; Commonwealth Secretariat, 2011). Thus, for example, 'affirmative-action-for-boys strategies' have been developed so that single-sex schooling has been promoted in Trinidad and Tobago, to encourage boys to remain focused on academic work, and in parts of Barbados, policy consideration has been given to protecting places in most-favoured selective schools for boys, even though some girls may outperform them in entrance examinations. In the regional context, the Commonwealth Secretariat announced in April 2011 that it was commissioning a three-year longitudinal study to identify factors contributing to the educational underachievement of boys in the Caribbean, and through case studies in Jamaica, St Lucia and Trinidad and Tobago, to identify a number of intervention strategies and activities to assist countries in addressing the issue (Commonwealth Secretariat, 2011). Although this initiative brought forward a strong negative reaction, because of the danger of 'downplaying real issues of gender disparity that perpetuate discrimination against girls throughout the school system and after it' (Rampersad, 2011, p. 1) and because of the dangers already apparent in some controversial strategies already implemented in the region, it is symptomatic of the strategies and approaches which dominate the regional agenda.

It is crucial, however, to recognize that these disparities are not simply a reflection of gender. Work in the UK (Francis, 2000, Skelton, 2001, Younger et al., 2005), in Australia (Lingard, 2003; Mills, 2003), in Scandinavia (Jóhannesson et al., 2009) and in the United States (Weaver-Hightower, 2003) has long established that such disparities in educational engagement and academic achievement are the outcome of a complex and multi-faceted intersection of different factors, and that ethnicity, class and location are equally as crucial as gender in explanatory frameworks. In the Caribbean, the work of Bailey (2004, 2009), Plummer et al. (2008) and George (2009, 2013) are seminal in this respect. Bailey's analysis (2004) of educational achievement in Jamaica concluded that students' performance in single-sex schools was better than in co-educational schools; that students in schools in high or middle socio-economic status locations performed better than those from lower socio-economic status locations; that better academic performances were observed in private, church-run schools than in state-run schools; and that students in schools in urban areas performed better than those in rural areas. On the basis of such evidence, she argued that within-group differences are evidently at least as important as between-group differences, with socio-economic status, ethnicity, religion, family structure and cultural norms assuming key significance in any search for theoretical and explanatory frameworks of differential achievement patterns. Similarly, a close examination of achievement data for Antigua and Barbuda has revealed (George, 2013) that more boys in private schools (84 per cent) regularly passed the CEE than girls in government schools (70 per cent); the lowest achieving group in private schools (boys in zone four of the island, where 76 per cent passed) did better than the best achieving group in government schools (girls in zone three, where 74 per cent passed), and there were significant variations in government schools across the four zones of the island, with boys' pass rates varying from 36 per cent to 58 per cent and girls' pass rates from 56 per cent to 74 per cent. This led George (2009, 2013) to suggest that poor girls achieve better than their male counterparts but less well than more privileged boys and to conclude that socio-economic status, poverty and social class is more closely related to achievement than is gender.

Boys' apparent 'underachievement': A deconstruction of the 'problem'?

How far, then, is boys' apparent underachievement *the* problem facing educational policymakers in the Caribbean? The moral panics about boys' underachievement in different parts of the world over the last three decades have too often been obsessed with the interpretation and definition of the issue, and on the struggle to satisfy the need or intervene appropriately, rather than discussing the validity (or not) of the issue – that is, whether it is a problem legitimately requiring attention. Literature from both the Caribbean and the wider Commonwealth illustrates clearly indicates that the 'problem' of boys' underachievement is one which has been addressed in ways that remain 'skewed in favour of dominant groups' (Parry, 1997; Roulston and Mills, 2000; Bailey, 2004; Arnot and Miles, 2005; Warrington and Younger, 2006). It is also one in which the modes of subjectification have varied including 'failing boys', 'poor boys', 'boys as the new disadvantaged' and, more recently, 'problem boys'. It is crucial, then, to explore contestations over the reality and complexity of educational underachievement and to consider whether this relates to broader political-economic marginalization (or privileging) of boys. How far are these perceptions accurate and a part of empirical reality? *Is* it a simplistic picture of male marginalization, or do (middle-class) men remain the privileged gender in many aspects of social life? Given that boys in socio-economically privileged schools are achieving better than girls in socio-economically deprived schools, what are the ethical concerns which this raises about the equity of any interventions which seek to target boys?

Miller has argued strongly – in 'Marginalization of the black male' (1986) and 'Men at risk' (1991) – that such educational underachievement for boys relates to the gendered economy and translates into 'male marginalisation', with boys and men occupying peripheral economic and social positions which disadvantage them. Miller depicts a depressing scenario of the position of men in Caribbean society, describing them as underachieving at school, constituting the bulk of the unemployed and unskilled; predominant in gangs; and involved in self-destructive behaviour such as drug and alcohol abuse. This is related, in Miller's view, to the ways in which black men, through colonial times, were confined within society to unskilled labour in agriculture and industry, with the controlling forces within the society sponsoring black women in order to minimize the possibility of militant, black, educated men emerging who might challenge the existing power structure. To Miller, deliberate policies were fostered to turn teaching from a male-dominated to a female-dominated profession, with the consequence that this feminization of the teaching profession has reduced boys' aspirations in school and has led parents to believe that the rates of return for educating girls are higher than those for boys; the outcome, Miller argues, has been widespread underachievement of boys. This thesis that boys' underachievement is related to the feminization of schooling, and the accompanying 'poor boys' discourse which stems from this, retains popularity and is frequently articulated as a reason why schools need to develop more 'relevant' curricula for boys and implement 'boy-friendly' pedagogies (Evans, 1999; De Lisle et al., 2005). The recuperative masculinity agenda, with its strong advocacy of initiatives such as 'Male Empowerment Now' models, father and son activity days, and single-sex classes in mixed schools (Biddulph, 1998; Majors, 2001; Crump-Russell, 2009), is a similar response to this thesis.

The last decade has seen this explanatory framework strongly disputed, however, by those who argue not only that it is unduly essentialist, placing too much validity on dominant versions of hegemonic masculinity and assuming far more homogeneity among boys and girls than can be recognized at anything other than the most superficial of levels (Francis, 2000; Lingard, 2003; Mills, 2003; Warrington and Younger, 2006) but also that such a thesis is unproven by empirical research and practice (Younger et al., 2005). The notion of 'privileged women', which might be seen as the flip side of Miller's 'marginalised men', has also been disputed by the evidence from a CARICOM report (2008), which suggested that labour markets remain strongly segregated, often to the disadvantage of women, and that occupational segregation is often accompanied by lower pay and worse working conditions. The report revealed that although the entry of women into the labour market has been increasing, their participation rates are still lower than that of men, to the extent that 59 per cent of the economically active workforce is male, and female unemployment rates are higher in virtually all countries as women are 'crowded' into fewer occupations (especially tourism) which are seasonally variable and have more limited access to education and training. As significantly, female youth unemployment rates (15–24 age group) are often more than twice the rate of male unemployment; at the extreme, 49 per cent of young women were unemployed in Belize (compared with 23 per cent young men) and 43 per cent in Jamaica (compared with 26 per cent of young men). Similarly, Chevannes (2002) argues that in Jamaica there is a misperception that unemployment is higher among young men than among women, a misperception which persists because of the visibility of unemployed men on the streets compared to the invisibility of unemployed women in domestic settings. Again, this raises ethical questions about a 'boys at risk' thesis when girls may be equally marginalized, albeit in less visible ways. In a similar vein, research by Figueroa and Mortley (2009) suggests that women rarely occupy positions of political leadership despite their educational success because their schooling equips them with collaborative, negotiational and non-confrontational skills which are not allied to those needed for political leadership.

Miller's thesis has also been challenged from a different perspective: Figueroa (2000, 2004) disputes the 'male marginalisation' thesis, arguing that the men within the Caribbean have been privileged rather than marginalized, having more access to resources, opportunity and social space and commanding greater power. Figueroa argues, however, that it is socialization practices within the home which prepare girls for schooling but fail to do this effectively for boys. This is a by-product of constraint rather than freedom: since boys are given the freedom to roam the streets while girls are kept at home 'for their own protection', their school work is more closely monitored and they are required to undertake mundane domestic duties. Ironically, this greater freedom which boys enjoy and which stems from their positions of power leads them to be disadvantaged at school since their socialization does not prepare them for the disciplined environment of the classroom. A similar facet of this argument emerges in George's study (2011) of risk in OECS education systems: she reports the view that Caribbean cultural beliefs of child rearing sees parents holding on to girls and letting go of boys, with girls tending to get more attention and care such that even within the same family there was some tendency to send girls to the 'better' schools.

There is another aspect of Figueroa's thesis, however, linked to current economic realities. This line of argument maintains that boys underachieve not only because of historic male privileging but also – in the current Caribbean economic context – because boys need fewer qualifications to get the same jobs as girls and boys are more likely to find work in the informal sector. This theme has been developed by Bailey, who, writing in relation to the Jamaican context, argues that explanations for boys' underachievement must take cognizance of 'the socio-economic value of certification to the different sexes and the inverse relationship between educational outcomes and social outcomes that favour males rather than females' (2004, p. 53). Bailey accepts that girls do outperform boys overall and are also less likely to drop out of school but argues that this does not translate into economic gain because of the subject choices presented to and made by girls as well as discrimination in the wider society. Indeed, she suggests that boys, schooling in the Caribbean is better described as being characterized by underparticipation rather than underachievement, since those boys who continue through the education system perform well in the financially lucrative areas of medicine, law, science and technology. Likewise, in relation to sex-role stereotyping in the curriculum, Lindsay (2002) argues that Caribbean schooling is premised on ideas of creating domesticated, dependent women and public, independent men.

Lindsay (2002) and Bailey (2004) both contest the view that boys' educational underachievement is a 'problem' requiring intervention and political attention. In their perspective, boys are positioned neither as 'poor' nor as 'troubled' but as 'powerful' and 'privileged'. Indeed, boys who opt out of the educational system or consciously disengage from academic work are constructed as economically rational actors who may 'choose' not to participate in the education system due to their lack of need for schooling. Given this continuing male social and economic dominance, it might be argued that a more appropriate 'gender agenda' within the Caribbean – rather than focusing on the 'problem' of boys' underachievement – is to continue to critique the attention it is receiving and to give higher profile on the educational agenda to contesting issues such as the schooling of girls for domesticity (Lindsay, 2002) and the lack of development of leadership skills for girls (Figueroa and Mortley, 2009).

There is little doubt that images of masculinity and stereotypical perspectives of what it is 'to be boy' do impact negatively on some boys' identification with schooling and the goal of striving for academic success (Cobbett, 2013). Thus, Plummer et al. (2008) see boys as being placed 'in a straight jacket' by constructions of masculinity that make education taboo and lead them towards activities that put them at physical risk rather than seeing boys as rationally rejecting education due to their lucrative employment options in the informal sector. They conclude that 'gender roles create a trap that disadvantages both men and women' (Plummer et al., 2008, p. 12). Other writers have made similar points, demonstrating a consensus that certain aspects of masculine identity are incongruent with academic success (Clarke, 2005; Plummer et al., 2008). In particular, the construction of schooling as feminine and 'gay' in the context of deeply homophobic cultures has been demonstrated as pressurizing boys to avoid educational success. Parry's (1997) research in Jamaica, for example, shows the pressure boys are under to act sufficiently macho, which includes avoiding school work, in order to avoid being labelled as gay; her research also demonstrates the consequences of this label, such as being beaten up and ridiculed by classmates.

This drive to avoid academic work is particularly apparent in the Caribbean in relation to gendered achievement in Language Arts (English). Quantitative evidence discussed earlier highlighted that this is the area where the gender gap in achievement is most marked, but explanations offered have not always been adequate. DeLisle et al. (2005), for example, account for the findings of their quantitative research by proposing that boys do less well in languages because large class sizes in most schools prohibit the use of collaborative approaches and encourage didactic teaching. This, they argue, is particularly inimical to language learning, and particularly so for boys since didactic approaches are not boys' preferred methods. But this line of argument is problematic due to the essentialist underpinnings of claims that boys prefer specific styles of teaching, made seemingly without evidence in this case, but also due to the consequent implication that boys need high-quality teaching, but girls, due to their compliant natures, will learn regardless. In contrast, Parry (1996) shows how English, the language of education, is constructed as feminine and consequently boys who speak it are labelled as 'sissy', 'girlish' and 'gay'. This specific aspect of boys' underachievement is not explained with reference either to material advantage or to essentialist calls for 'boy-friendly' pedagogies. This is a clear example of how restrictive gender codes work to disadvantage boys in specific ways, even while those boys may exercise dominance as a social group. The idea of 'boy-friendly' curricular and pedagogies is turned on its head, since rather than needing to be 'more masculine', schools can best help boys by promoting cultures characterized by greater freedom to perform gender in different ways.

There is a range of other Caribbean research which highlights the complex ways in which boys are both advantaged and disadvantaged by their gender. Chevannes (2002) disputes that males are being marginalized, if the main factor being considered is power. However, his research, along with that of Plummer et al. (2008) and Plummer and Geofroy (2010), highlights how increasingly restrictive norms of masculinity lead boys to engage in behaviours – such as violence, crime and risky sexual behaviour – which put both themselves and others at risk. Thus George's work on risk in the Eastern Caribbean states (2011) identifies boys between the ages of thirteen and fifteen years, those involved with drugs (both users and sellers, seen as particularly affecting boys) and gang membership (again seen as particularly affecting boys, giving boys a sense of belonging where parental neglect persisted) as the dominant concerns. Plummer describes the increasingly rigid policing of masculinity by peer group cultures involving obligations and taboos as well as sanctions for those who transgress. He highlights how 'hard, risky, rebellious, sexually dominant masculinities' have turned behaviours such as crime and violence into the 'pinnacle of modern manhood'. This is explained in terms of the increasing role of peer groups in young people's socialization as well as the need for boys to establish masculine identity outside of schooling due to schooling having become 'common ground'. Boys, therefore, 'retreat to physicality' in order to establish their masculinity. How the performances of masculinity that Plummer describes play out in the school context, and the implications of this for girls and boys, seem to be an important area for exploration.

Chevannes (2002) paints a similar picture of hegemonic masculinity but provides an additional focus on how, from a young age, boys learn the importance of acquiring money to earn the respect of family, friends and community and that control over economic resources is a building block of masculine identity. This, in many ways, puts boys and men in a position of power and corroborates with the data showing lower unemployment rates for men than women. However, this also tallies with data that show that schoolboys are more likely to have part-time jobs than schoolgirls, leading to less time for school work, and that the most common reason for boys dropping out of school is to earn money (Evans, 1999). Hence, the 'provider identity' can be a source of disadvantage as well as power. Therefore, while male unemployment is not higher than female's, the outworking of it is likely to be different.

Writing on masculinities in the Caribbean has shown that while boys exhibit domination as a social group, restrictive gender codes lead to specific types of disadvantage, which have implications not only for men themselves but also for women. The way masculinity has been conceptualized has sometimes not been helpful, however, revealing aspects of essentialism which have weakened the arguments. Thus, the assertion that 'fundamental biological differences mean that physicality has been preserved as a way of asserting masculine difference' (Plummer et al., 2008, p. 1) and the statement that girls' 'naturally earlier development' leads them to be more favoured (Chevannes, 2002, p. 53) are somewhat restrictive in that they preclude analysis of diversity and reify constructions of hegemonic masculinity. As the empirical data described earlier showed, particular groups of boys, as well as individual boys outside those groups, do achieve. Theorizing masculinity therefore needs to go beyond describing how hegemonic conceptions may disadvantage boys to understanding the psychic and social processes that allow particular boys to adopt subject positions which facilitate and enable achievement while other boys, as well as some girls, cannot. Otherwise, the myth that schools have been feminized to the advantage of all girls and the disadvantage of all boys will be perpetuated.

Girls: Successful, invisible and harassed?

It is evident, then, that emerging research challenges notions of male marginalization and disengagement, of the feminization of school environments and the construction of gender regimes which inherently favour girls (Epstein et al., 1998; Francis, 2000; Younger et al., 2005; Plummer et al., 2008; Bailey, 2009; Lingard et al., 2009; Mills et al., 2009; Skelton, 2010; Cobbett and Younger, 2012). It is becoming clear that there is a need for more inclusive gender relational approaches (Younger et al., 2005; Layne et al., 2008) and an acknowledgement that a focus primarily on boys' academic achievement often masks other problems and inequalities.

Although differential patterns of achievement by gender have been identified and analysed (Evans, 1999; Bailey, 2004; De Lisle et al., 2005; Kutnick, 2011), there has been relatively little empirical research which has explored the reality of schooling for girls in different parts of the Caribbean. While the rising achievement of girls in both the UK and the Caribbean has led to discourses of 'successful girls' who are 'having it all', it is unclear how far girls themselves identify with the aspirations of schools, enjoy schooling and see themselves as achieving and privileged. Indeed, recent research in the UK has challenged the perspective that achievement is not socially problematic for girls, demonstrating that girls continue to face challenges negotiating acceptable femininities and cleverness (Renold, 2005; Renold and Allen, 2006; Francis, 2010; Skelton et al., 2011). Although the finding that some boys avoid 'diligent' behaviour in order to avoid being labelled effeminate indicates that diligence would not be difficult for girls (who would want to be read as 'feminine'), the parallel concepts of 'cleverness' and 'rationality' are often constructed as masculine (Walkerdine, 1990; Renold, 2005). Furthermore, connections have long been made between cleverness and asexuality/unfemininity showing that there are contradictions between being educationally successful and a 'successful attractive girl' (Walkerdine, 1990; Renold, 2005; Archer et al., 2007) such that successful girls run risks of peer group resistance, ostracism and exclusion (Fordham, 1993; Wright, 2005; Morris, 2007).

The discussion which follows cannot claim to be valid across the whole Caribbean, let alone the Anglophone Caribbean, because it is specific in its context and scope. It draws upon intensive case-study research in schools in the eastern Caribbean, in Antigua and Barbuda, and examines how far there are tensions, contradictions and challenges which girls experience daily in schooling, both inside and outside the classroom. It seeks to open up and explore the realities of schooling for girls, in terms of issues of gender, sexuality and power, and looks at opportunities and inequalities which may be masked by a narrow focus only on achievement data; as such, it draws heavily upon our own work (Cobbett and Younger, 2012; Cobbett, 2013; Cobbett and Warrington, forthcoming).

Research on classroom dynamics and interactions in four secondary schools in Antigua and Barbuda (Younger and Cobbett, 2012) revealed that a key aspect of the gender regime of the schools was that boys received both more positive and more negative attention, which in itself was indicative of the complexity of gendered power dynamics as teachers worked to maintain an environment for learning in their classrooms. The view that boys received more negative, discipline-orientated attention than girls from teachers was widely acknowledged by students and teachers, with boys complaining frequently about the unfair treatment they received from teachers (Jules and Kutnick, 1997; Kutnick et al., 1997; Myhill and Jones, 2006) and broad agreement from girls and boys that boys got punished more regularly and more harshly for the same types of misdemeanour (Jules and Kutnick, 1997). These everyday physical interactions between boys and teachers were a component of the way in which masculinity was produced in the school context, with boys often enacting bodily resistance to teachers' physical roughness with them, thereby consolidating the construction of tough male bodies. Conversely, girls' 'smartness' and negotiation skills were widely recognized (Younger et al., 1999; Francis, 2000; Frank et al., 2003; Ringrose, 2007): indeed, it was commonly accepted by girls that 'you can suck up to teachers and they give you want you want', and 'if anything happens they (the teachers) would look to the boys more than anything', so that 'we can get away with things, some things that the boys don't get away with' (Warrington et al., 2000; Myhill, 2002).

Significantly, it was not just in the disciplinary regimes of schools, however, that boys received more attention than girls. In classroom observations, boys scored higher on all the types of interaction observed, being called upon more regularly by teachers to answers questions, offering more frequent unsolicited contributions to classroom discussions and demanding more of teachers' time in support of their learning. Often, this led to the invisibility of some girls, who were generally very quiet in class, very well behaved and did not demonstrate much interest in boys; indeed, it was evident that their lack of self-confidence and assertiveness led to a silent disengagement in lessons that rarely caused disturbances, generally went unnoticed in the classroom frenzy and frequently led to underachievement and academic failure. These girls were often observed quietly drawing pictures in their books while other students were working, with their bodily positions hunched over their books in a very different way to the disengaged boys who would tend to sprawl out over their desks. These girls were the 'invisible low achievers', adopting behaviour patterns which did not attract attention, almost hiding their work from teachers' scrutiny and going unnoticed and untroubled by teachers. These patterns of classroom interactions and dynamics suggest in some respects that the gendered practices of the schools are institutionalizing some girls to have low expectations, reiterated by the frequent assertion from girls as well as boys that 'girls should be seen and not heard' to such an extent that female quietness was clearly a normative expectation; in such a context, it is unsurprising that girls did not complain, or even notice, that boys received more positive support for their learning.

It was in the performance of gender outside the classroom, however, where girls faced the most extreme dilemmas. As in research from other parts of the world (Francis et al., 2009; Skelton et al., 2011), the prevailing gender regimes of the schools demanded that boys and girls behaved in particular ways in relation to gender if they were to win popularity, with an emphasis on particular behaviours, material possessions and looks. Normative behaviour for popular boys needed to be 'nuff'[1] embodying 'attitude', 'tough', showing a keen interest in the opposite sex and a willingness to 'scud'[2] class. To be popular, girls needed to be rude, mannerless, running after boys and not doing schoolwork. Inequitable power dynamics were implicit in this quest for popularity, with a common focus on boys as 'having girls' and 'protectors of girls' (Cobbett, 2013) while girls were depicted as making themselves attractive to boys through sexy and cute appearances. The need to meet these normative expectations was often a cause of stress, a focus for competition and at times a source of distress when failure and exclusion resulted (Reay, 2001). While some students resisted these stereotypes – some boys through cooperative and gentle behaviour and their beliefs set which contested rigid gender roles, some girls through keeping their hair short, cultivating a boyish look and stubbornly engaging with academic goals and targets – this equally caused stress and exposure to bullying if it involved too extreme a rejection of normative masculinity and femininity. The dilemmas here for some girls are self-evident; popularity did not rest easily with a striving for academic achievement, and to be quiet and working hard, in the words of one girl to be 'smart, nerdy, … have manners, they have more favour by the teachers', was usually associated with unpopularity, and with girls who don't really *study* boys (Cobbett, 2013). Thus as recent research from the UK has also started to show, academic achievement can be socially problematic for girls as well as boys (Renold, 2005; Renold and Allen, 2006; Francis, 2010).

The investments made by some girls in feminine attractiveness was a further problematic aspect of the gender regimes of these schools. Girls frequently saw themselves as being troubled by boys and, while this was seen as affirmation of their attractiveness and desirability, it also led to confusion and complex responses as girls walked a precarious tightrope, trying to maintain desirable heterofeminine identities while not becoming victims of sexual harassment. On occasions, girls were clearly the target of unwanted sexual advances by boys, were upset and uncomfortable by their experiences and by the inadequate responses of teachers to this behaviour, and yet they wanted to sustain their own image and conform to normative positions. While some girls clearly gained genuine pleasure and power from their experiences with boys and the attention they received from them, this power dynamic – with boys acting in a predatory fashion as possessors of entitlements to girls' bodies – is far from unproblematic, especially where the boys' advances are unwelcome by the girls.

Defining the boundaries was difficult for many girls, the more so because neither boys nor teachers seemed to acknowledge the inappropriateness of such behaviour. Contradictions were manifold in how girls tried to resolve this conflict in self and was apparent in the behaviour of many of the girls who – while genuinely upset and annoyed by the behaviour of the boys – simultaneously found it desirable and consolidating their own high status. While it is easy to offer ill-informed judgements of such behaviour, it is important to recognize that girls have the right to express their sexuality while having their personal boundaries respected and to recognize the dichotomy which regularly confronts many girls as they seek to negotiate desirable image and subject positions (Martino and Pallotta-Chiarolli, 2005; Youdell, 2005). More disturbingly, such sexual harassment was not seen as problematic or behaviour from which boys ought to desist, neither by boys themselves nor by their teachers, and appeared to be part of the normalized gender regime that boys participated in, in order to preserve and sustain their own macho image rather than to resist or discourage in others. Indeed, to resist would be interpreted as weakness, or non-macho behaviour, and boys persistently seemed unable to distinguish between sexual harassment and consensual sexual touching, confirming that harassment is what they would define as 'normal' and an inevitable part of growing up.

It seems that social issues in general, and inequalities affecting girls in particular, were masked in the schools, in the sense that teachers had limited awareness of them. Problems affecting girls seemed to be rendered invisible by the immediate concern that managing unruly students (particularly boys) in the classroom presented. There was a sense in which teachers did not have the time, space or energy to be concerned about (or even notice) problems that students who were not 'acting out' may have been encountering. While the physical nature of some boys' disputes, and the involvement of some boys in gang membership, meant that these often had high visibility in schools, the manifestation of girls' social problems (becoming withdrawn, involvement in transactional sexual relationships with other men) meant that these were not far less visible. In a context where there is already a preoccupation with boys' underachievement, these differences are likely to further exacerbate the neglect of girls. Equally, the structure of the secondary schools in which students are taught by different teachers for every subject and spend limited time with their form tutor also made pastoral care difficult, and it appears likely that the harassment which a significant number of girls face, and to which they object, is masked by teachers' concerns to sustain an ordered teaching environment and by an undue focus on achievement scores. Thus in Antigua, as in the UK, 'the dominance of the "standards" discourse and the concomitant focus on attainment has led to issues and concerns about pupils' experiences of school being sidelined or obscured' (Jackson et al., 2010, p. 6).

A number of issues emerge, then, in this discussion of girls' experiences of their schooling. Some girls within particular school communities were experiencing the kind of peer pressure to disengage from school that is commonly associated predominantly with boys. While there were differences in girls' and boys' classroom behaviour, it was clear that popular girls, as well as popular boys, disengaged from learning activities and felt social pressure in doing so, 'scudding' class on occasions to conform to peer group expectations which were not necessarily gender determined. Although a small number of high-achieving girls appeared to have avoided unpopularity or being Othered as geeks, such identity work is extremely arduous, and the nature of the productions of gender that were necessary to combine (relative) popularity with high achievement involved what McRobbie (2009) refers to as the 'subtle retrenchment of gender inequalities'. In essence, this meant that many girls had to balance their achievement by performing heterofemininity to ensure they did not compromise their sexual attractiveness – a finding which is in common with UK-based research (Renold and Allen, 2006; McRobbie, 2009; Francis, 2010; Skelton et al., 2011). Equally, as in the UK (Jackson, 2006), some girls were adopting increasingly disruptive 'ladette' behaviours in school, of a similar nature to groups of boys, to win acceptance and preserve image. In this context, then, girls may be relatively successful, in the narrow terms of academic achievement when compared to boys, but the costs of sustaining an acceptable image which marries achievement with popularity, which resists invisibility without courting attention as a 'keen' student, and which on occasions reluctantly accepts the possibility of harassment, are high. These costs are real for many girls, revealing not hidden but latent tensions which are masked by an unremitting focus on achievement scores and certainly challenges the prevailing notion that girls 'have it all'.

Concluding thoughts

Much of the debate about gender issues in Caribbean schools, in common with discussions in Europe, North America and Australasia, is contextualized within a 'raising achievement' framework, with academic achievement often conceptualized within an overtly narrow and competitive framework (Mahony, 1998; Martino, 1999). Achievement data do show that the underachievement of some groups of boys is an empirical reality in parts of the Caribbean, worthy of some further attention on the gender and education agenda. But boys' underachievement does not always relate to male disadvantage but frequently exists in a context of male socio-economic dominance; as such, it does not automatically need to be a cause for concern or affirmative action since many boys (and men) are not 'poor' but 'powerful'. In such a context, it is hard to endorse the assertion that 'boys' underachievement' is *the* dominant educational issue to be addressed and 'solved'.

Exploration of the gender regimes of secondary schools reveals other fundamental issues which need to be exposed and addressed. Girls' continuing low self-esteem, boys' domination of classroom space and teacher attention and the continuing inequitable power dynamics and beliefs that help to sustain the view that it is still better to be a boy – all need to be more high profile in the gender discourse about the inequalities of secondary schooling. So it becomes crucial to draw more explicit attention to the masking and silencing of girls' experiences and to provide significant insight into the girls' experiences of their own schooling, since overall these experiences continue to be marginalized in dominant neo-liberal approaches to boys' education (Hey, 1997; Kenway et al., 1998; Martino and Pallotta-Chiarolli, 2005). Contexts where many girls feel genuinely threatened and unsafe, where there are unacceptable levels of harassment and fear, where girls are at-risk because of predatory behaviour from boys and where there are conflicts of identity about being a girl (or a boy) and developing one's individuality need challenging and rectifying if schooling is to be a rewarding and stimulating experience for more students.

This discussion suggests that the working out of gender within Caribbean secondary schools is complex and multi-faceted and revealing of so many different performances of masculinity and femininity which are lost within the essentialism of the 'boys' underachievement' discourse. This discourse downplays the real tensions that high-achieving girls and high-achieving boys are facing in terms of fitting in, resisting ridicule from classmates and constructing gendered identities which acknowledge their own selves. It misses consideration of low-achieving girls, who are likely to comprise a particularly disadvantaged group post-school since there are more employment options for men lacking qualifications than women, leading to significantly higher youth unemployment rates for females than males across the Caribbean. It misses the other girls and boys who strive to realize and yet have to hide their own, different sexualities. In such a context, a single-minded focus on academic achievement (of boys or girls) is a severely limited agenda for conceptualizing educational 'success'. A sole focus on achievement scores masks other inequalities and challenges faced by girls in school, making it essential that these aspects concerning girls' education gain priority on the Caribbean agenda.

Research on gender and schooling, whether in the Caribbean, countries of the old Commonwealth or those in Asia and Africa, has shown that it is important to understand constructions of masculinity as these have implications for girls as well as boys, and that there is a need to look at gender relations within and between girls and boys, rather than simply focus on boys or girls. In the contexts of the Caribbean and elsewhere, feminist educational researchers have arguably been hesitant to explore the ways in which some men may experience specific types of gender-based disadvantages. This is unsurprising, given the seemingly unproblematic ways that boys' underachievement has dominated education agendas to the detriment of girls' needs. However, it can be argued that some focus on boys' underachievement should not provoke anxiety among feminists since awareness that restrictive gender codes are detrimental to men as well as women can provide an important impetus for social change, challenging the notion that power is a zero-sum game.

Such a view argues that it is problematic to assume that the issues of boys and girls are entirely separate; girls do exercise agency and as such have a significant role in the production of gender regimes, carving out spaces, behaviour patterns and relationships for themselves within schools. If we are to understand the complexity of gendered regimes in schools, we need to be open to examining the way both girls and boys act to produce, resist and contest them, and this involves moving beyond simple good girl/bad boy binaries into a complex gender relational analysis. The needs are clear, then, to shift the thinking of academics and policymakers and to create a new discourse, moving from an exclusive focus on boys' underachievement to a broader analysis of gender and education within a relational framework. Only then will we be able to go beyond looking at how notions of hegemonic masculinity disadvantage boys to understanding the processes by which particular boys and girls are enabled to adopt subject positions which are conducive to learning and why some boys and girls are prohibited from engaging with such positions. Greater depth of conceptual engagement with issues of masculinity and femininity, as well as greater attention to pupils' and teachers' views, voices and experiences, will give us more insights and enable more specific understandings of the diversity of experiences that boys and girls have at school.

Notes

1 Nuff: enough, as in 'good enough to win and impress friends'.

2 To scud class: to play truant.

Questions for reflection

a) Why has there been an explicit education policy focus on 'underachieving boys' in the Caribbean?

b) How are the disparities in educational engagement and academic achievement between boys and girls an outcome of a complex intersection of different factors such as ethnicity, social class and location rather than only gender?

c) What are some of the limitations of an educational approach that focuses solely on male academic underachievement? What are some of the challenges that 'achieving' girls continue to face? In other words, does an approach that focuses primarily on boys' academic achievement mask other gender inequalities?

Further Reading

Cobbett, M. and Younger, M. (2012), 'Boys' educational "underachievement" in the Caribbean: Interpreting the "problem"', *Gender and Education*, 24, 611–25.

This article examines various aspect of boys' educational underachievement in the Caribbean in detail, including prevalent notions of male marginalization and disengagement and the feminization of school environments. It explores the realities of schooling for girls, especially in terms of issues of gender, sexuality and power to uncover inequalities which may be masked by a narrow focus only on achievement data.

Bibliography

Archer, L., Halsall, A. and Hollingworth, S. (2007), 'Class, gender, (hetero) sexuality and schooling: Paradoxes within working-class girls' engagement with education and post-16 aspirations', *British Journal of Sociology of Education*, 28, 165–80.

Arnot, M. and Miles, P. (2005), 'A reconstruction of the gender agenda: The contradictory gender dimensions in New Labour's educational policy', *Oxford Review of Education*, 31, 173–89.

Bailey, B. (2004), 'Gender and education in Jamaican: Who is achieving and by whose standard?', *Prospects*, XXXIV, 53–70.

——. (2009), Needed! A paradigm shift in addressing boys' underachievement in education. Paper presented at the Regional Caribbean Conference on Keeping Boys Out of Risk, 5–9 May, Montego Bay.

Biddulph, S. (1998), *Raising Boys: Why Boys Are Different – and How to Help them Become Happy and Well-balanced Men*. Sydney: Finch.

Caribbean Examinations Council. (2010), Caribbean Examinations Council Annual Report, 2010. St Michael: CXC. http://www.cxc.org/SiteAssets/CXCAR2010final.pdf (accessed 21 July 2012).

CARICOM. (2008), *Women and Men in the Caribbean, 1998–2005*. Georgetown: Guyana Caribbean Community Secretariat.

Chevannes, B. (2002), 'What you sow is what you reap: Violence and construction of male identity in Jamaica', *Current Issues in Comparative Education*, 2, 51–61.

Clarke, C. (2005), 'Socialisation and teacher expectations of Jamaican boys in school: The need for a responsive teacher preparation program', *International Journal of Educational Policy*, 5, 3–34.

Cobbett, M (2013) 'Being "nuff" and "scudding class": exploring girls' and boys' perceptions of popularity, gender and achievement in Antiguan secondary schools', *British Educational Research Journal*, DOI: 10.1002/berj.3027.

—— and Warrington, M. (2013), '"Sometimes it's fun to play with them first": Girls and boys talking about sexual harassment in Caribbean schools', *Culture Health and Sexuality*, 15.9, 1026–39.

—— and Younger, M. (2012), 'Boys' educational "underachievement" in the Caribbean: Interpreting the "problem"', *Gender and Education*, 24, 611–25.

Commonwealth Secretariat. (2011), *Consultancy for Boys' Underachievement Initiatives – Regional Strategy in the Caribbean*. London: Commonwealth Secretariat.

Crump-Russell, C. (2009), Taking boys out of risk in Antigua and Barbuda. Paper presented at the Boys at Risk: Raising Awareness Conference, October, St Johns.

De Lisle, J., Smith, P. and Jules, V. (2005), 'Which males or females are most at risk and on what? An analysis of gender differentials within the primary school system of Trinidad and Tobago', *Educational Studies*, 31, 393–418.

——. (2010), 'Evaluating the geography of gendered achievement using large-scale assessment data from the primary school system of the Republic of Trinidad and Tobago', *International Journal of Educational Development*, 30, 405–17.

Epstein, D., Elwood, J., Hey, V. and Maw, J. (1998), *Failing Boys? Issues in Gender and Achievement*. Buckingham: Open University Press.

Evans, H. (1999), *Gender Differences in Education in Jamaica, Education for All in the Caribbean: Assessment 2000 Monograph Series*. Kingston: UNESCO and Planning Institute of Jamaica.

Figueroa, M. (2000), 'Making sense of male experience: The case of academic underachievement in the English-speaking Caribbean', *IDS Bulletin*, 31, 68–74.

——. (2004), 'Male privileging and male "academic underperformance" in Jamaica', in R. Reddock (ed.) *Interrogating Caribbean Masculinities; Theoretical and Empirical Analyses*. Jamaica: University of the West Indies Press, 137–66.

——. (2010), Coming to terms with boys at risk in Jamaica and the rest of the Caribbean. www.cedol.org/wp-content/uploads/2012/02/66-69-2010.pdf (accessed 10 October 2012).

—— and Mortley, N. (2009), Is the hegemony of male political leadership at risk in the English speaking Caribbean? Paper presented to 10th Annual SALISES Conference, 25–27 March, Barbados, Navigating Risks and Building Resilience in Small States.

Fordham, S. (1993), 'Those loud black girls': (Black) women, silence and gender "passing" in the academy', *Anthropology and Education Quarterly*, 24, 3–32.

Francis, B. (2000), *Boys, Girls and Achievement: Addressing the Classroom Issues*. London: Routledge Falmer.

——. (2010), 'Re/theorizing gender: Female masculinity and male femininity in the classroom?', *Gender and Education*, 22, 477–90.

——, Skelton, C. and Read, B. (2009), 'The simultaneous production of educational achievement and popularity: How do some pupils accomplish it?', *British Educational Research Journal*, 36, 317–40.

Frank, B., Kehler, M., Lovell, T. and Davison, K. (2003), 'A tangle of trouble: Boys, masculinity and schooling – future directions', *Educational Review*, 55, 119–33.

George, P. (2009), Another foray into the boy-girl achievement debate: A Caribbean perspective. Paper presented at the Boys at Risk: Raising Awareness Conference, October, St Johns.

——. (2011), *Risk in OECS Education Systems*. Bridgetown: OECS/Caribbean Development Bank.

——. (2013), 'Fighting the wrong war? Gender, poverty and achievement in the Caribbean', in J. MacBeath and M. Younger (eds.) *A Common Wealth of Learning*. London: Routledge, 113–25.

Hey, V. (1997), *The Company She Keeps: An Ethnography of Girls' Friendships*. Maidenhead: Open University Press.

Jackson, C. (2006), 'Wild' girls? An exploration of "ladette" cultures in secondary schools', *Gender and Education*, 18, 339–60.

——, Paechter, C. and Renold, E. (2010), *Girls and Education 3-16: Continuing Concerns, New Agendas*. Maidenhead: Open University Press.

Jha, J. and Kelleher, F. (2006), *Boys' Underachievement in Education: An Exploration in Selected Commonwealth Countries*. London: Commonwealth Secretariat /Commonwealth of Learning.

Jóhannesson, I., Lingard, B. and Mills, M. (2009), 'Possibilities in the boy turn? Comparative lessons from Australia and Iceland', *Scandinavian Journal of Educational Research*, 53, 309–25.

Jules, V. and Kutnick, P. (1997), 'Student perceptions of a good teacher: The gender perspective', *British Journal of Educational Psychology*, 67, (no. 4), 497–511.

Kenway, J. and Willis, S, with Blackmore, J. and Rennie, L. (1998), *Answering Back: Girls, Boys and Feminism in School*. London: Routledge.

Kutnick, P., Layne, A. and Jules, V. (1997), *Gender and School Achievement in the Caribbean*. London: Department for International Development.

Layne, A., Jules, V., Kutnick, P. and Layne, C. (2008), 'Academic achievement, pupil participation and integration of group work skills in secondary school classrooms in Trinidad and Barbados', *International Journal Of Educational Development*, 28, 176–94.

Lindsay, K. (2002), 'Is the Caribbean male an endangered species?', in P. Mohammed (ed.) *Gendered Realities: Essays in Caribbean Feminist Thought*. Kingston: University of the West Indies Press, 56–82.

Lingard, B. (2003), 'Where to in gender policy after recuperative masculinity politics?', *Journal of Inclusive Education*, 7, 33–56.

——, Martino, M. and Mills, M. (2009), *Boys and Schooling*. London: Palgrave.

Mahony, P. (1998), 'Girls will be girls and boys will be first', in D. Epstein, J. Ellwood, V. Hey and J. Maw (eds.) *Failing Boys*. Buckingham: Open University Press, 37–55.

Majors, R. (2001), *Educating Our Black Children*. London: Routledge-Falmer.

Martino, W. (1999), '"Cool Boys", "Party Animals", "Squids" and "Poofters": Interrogating the dynamics and politics of adolescent masculinities in school', *British Journal of Sociology of Education*, 20, 239–63.

—— and Berrill, D. (2003), 'Boys, schooling and masculinities: Interrogating the "right" ways to educate boys', *Educational Review*, 55, 99–117.

—— and Pallotta-Chiarolli, M. (2005), *Being Normal is the Only Way to be: Adolescent Perspectives on Gender and School*. Sydney: University of New South Wales Press.

McRobbie, A. (2009), *The Aftermath of Feminism: Gender, Culture and Social Change*. London: Sage.

Miller, E. (1986), *Marginalization of the Black Male: Insights from the Development of the Teaching Profession*. Kingston: University of the West Indies Press.

——. (1991), *Men at Risk*. Kingston: Jamaica Publishing House.

Mills, M. (2003), 'Shaping the boys' agenda: The backlash blockbusters', *Journal of Inclusive Education*, 7, 57–73.

——, Francis, B. and Skelton, C. (2009), 'Gender policies in Australia and the United Kingdom: The construction of "new" boys and girls', in W. Martino, M. Kehler and M. Weaver-Hightower (eds.) *The Problem with Boys' Education: Beyond the Backlash*. Abingdon: Routledge, 36–55.

Morris, E. (2007), 'Ladies' or "loudies"? Perceptions and experiences of black girls in classrooms', *Youth and Society*, 38, 490–515.

Myhill, D. A. (2002), 'Bad boys and good girls? Patterns of interaction and response in whole class teaching', *British Educational Research Journal*, 28, 339–52.

—— and Jones, S. (2006), '"She doesn't shout at no girls": Pupils' perceptions of gender equity in the classroom', *Cambridge Journal of Education*, 36, 99–113.

Parry, O. (1996), In one ear and out the other: Unmasking masculinities in the Caribbean classroom. Sociological Research Online 1, unpaginated.

——. (1997), 'Schooling is fooling: Why do Jamaican boys underachieve at school', *Gender and Education*, 9, 223–32.

Plummer, D. and Geofroy, S. (2010), 'When bad is cool: Violence and crime as rites of passage to manhood', *Caribbean Review of Gender Studies*, 4, 1–17.

——, McLean, A. and Simpson, J. (2008), 'Has learning become taboo and is risk-taking compulsory for Caribbean boys? Researching the relationship between masculinities, education and risk', *Caribbean Review of Gender Studies*, 2, 1–14.

Rampersad, K. (2011), Good money after bad in male underachievement studies? Research Caribbean, 27 June. http://www.researchresearch.com/index.php?option=com_news (accessed 7 July 2011).

Reay, D. (2001), 'Spice girls, "nice girls", "girlies" and tomboys: Gender discourses, girls' cultures and femininities in the primary classroom', *Gender and Education*, 13, 153–66.

Reddock, R. (2009), Gender an achievement in higher education. Paper presented at the Conference of the Association of Caribbean Higher Education Administrators, 10 July, in Port of Spain, Trinidad.

Renold, E. (2005), *Girls, Boys and Junior sexualities: Exploring Childrens' Gender and Sexual Relations in the Primary School*. London: Routledge Falmer.

—— and Allen, A. (2006), 'Bright and beautiful: High achieving girls, ambivalent femininities, and the feminisation of success in the primary school', *Discourse: Studies in the Cultural Politics of Education*, 27, 457–73.

Ringrose, J. (2007), 'Successful girls? Complicating post-feminist, neoliberal discourses of educational achievement and gender equality', *Gender and Education*, 19, 471–89.

Roulston, K. and Mills, M. (2000), 'Male teachers in feminized teaching areas: Marching to the beat of the men's movement drum', *Oxford Review of Education*, 26, 221–37.

Skelton, C. (2001), *Schooling the Boys: Masculinities and Primary Education*. Buckingham: Open University Press.

——. (2010), 'Girls and achievement: Are girls the "success stories" of restructured education systems?', *Educational Review*, 62, 131–42.

——, Francis, B. and Read, B. (2011), 'Gender, popularity and notions of in authenticity amongst 12–13 year old school girls', *British Journal of Sociology of Education*, 21, 169–83.

UNESCO. (2011), *The Hidden Crisis: Armed Conflict and Education: EFA Global Monitoring Report 2011*. Paris: UNESCO.

Walkerdine, V. (1990), *Schoolgirl Fictions*. London: Verso.

Warrington, M. and Younger, M. (2006), 'Working on the inside: Discourses, dilemmas and decisions', *Gender and Education*, 18, 265–80.

——, Younger, M. and Williams, J. (2000), 'Student attitude, image and the gender gap', *British Educational Research Journal*, 26, 393–407.

Weaver-Hightower, M. (2003), 'The "boy-turn" in research on gender and education', *Review of Educational Research*, 73, 471–98.

World Bank. (2009), *Proceedings of Regional Caribbean Conference, 'Keeping Boys Out of Risk'.Montego Bay*. New York: World Bank/Commonwealth Secretariat.

Wright, C. (2005), 'Black femininities go to school: How young black females negotiate race, class and gender', in G. Lloyd (ed.) *Problem Girls: Understanding and Supporting Troubled and Troublesome Girls and Young Women*. London: Routledge Falmer, 103–13.

Youdell, D. (2005), 'Sex-gender-sexuality: How sex, gender and sexuality constellations are constituted in secondary schools', *Gender and Education*, 17, 249–70.

Younger, M. and Cobbett, M. (2012), 'Gendered perceptions of schooling: Classroom dynamics and inequalities within four Caribbean secondary schools', *Educational Review*, DOI:10.1080/00131911.2012.749218.

——, Warrington, M. and Williams, J. (1999), 'The gender gap and classroom interactions', *Reality and Rhetoric? British Journal of Sociology of Education*, 20, 325–41.

—— and Warrington, M., with McLellan, R. (2005), *Raising Boys' Achievement in Secondary Schools: Issues, Dilemmas and Opportunities*. Maidenhead: Open University Press.

Gender and Graduate Education in the United States: Women's Advancement in STEM Fields

3

Ann Mari May and Yana van der Meulen Rodgers

Chapter Outline

The importance of increased levels of education in improving the status of women and children throughout the world is well established. Although economists have traditionally argued that education is important for adding to human capital, we have come to understand that higher levels of education are also associated with lower birth rates (Breierova and Duflo, 2004) and lower rates of infant mortality.[1] Moreover, as Amartya Sen and Martha Nussbaum have demonstrated, education adds not only to human capital but also to human capability, enabling women to exercise their legal rights and strengthening their political and civic engagement as well (Sen, 1999; Nussbaum, 2003).

Diversity in higher education has a particularly strong social and economic rationale as well. Different perspectives nurture creative thought and creative thought is needed to solve the world's most challenging problems. As studies of group dynamics have shown, greater diversity in teams encourages individual team members to do more preparation for any exercise, results in a wider range of alternatives being debated and discussed and is more likely to generate better results (Phillips et al., 2011). Diversity, it seems, plays a crucial role in problem-solving, innovations and higher productivity (Rodgers and Woerdeman, 2006).

In the last third of the twentieth century, women have made particularly significant strides in gaining educational parity with men in many countries. For example, data from the United Nations Educational, Scientific and Cultural Organization (UNESCO) indicate that women's share of enrolment in higher education in Switzerland rose from 3 per cent in 1985 to 43 per cent in 2000 and in France from 50 per cent to 55 per cent. Women's share in Latin American colleges and universities over the same time period rose from 43 per cent to 47 per cent in Chile and from 44 per cent to 54 per cent in El Salvador. In India, women's share has risen from 30 per cent to 39 per cent.[2] While certainly not universal, this trend towards gender balance in student enrolment is remarkably similar in a large number of industrialized countries throughout the world (May, 2008b).

The increase in women's representation among university enrollees and degree recipients is beginning to reach the highest levels of educational attainment. The Nordic Research Board (NORBAL) reports that women received 45 per cent of doctoral degrees awarded by universities in the Nordic and Baltic countries in 2006 – up from 27 per cent in 1990 (NORBAL, 2008). In the United States, in 2002, for the first time in American history, more American women than American men received doctorates from US universities (Hoffer et al., 2003) and in 2009, for the first time, more women than men in the United States received doctoral degrees (Bell, 2010).

Although there has been substantial growth in the representation of women in graduate education in general, they continue to be significantly under-represented in so-called STEM fields (science, technology, engineering and mathematics). Because women with STEM jobs earn approximately 33 per cent more than women with non-STEM jobs, one barrier to reducing the gender wage gap remains the paucity of women in STEM fields (Beede et al., 2011).

Questions about how to diversify the scientific workforce have gained attention in recent years in academic circles, policy discourse and the media. A large literature, based mostly on US statistics, reveals numerous factors that influence women in scientific and technical disciplines and why far fewer reach high positions.[3] European countries exhibit the same pattern as women remain under-represented in Europe's professional scientific employment across the business sector and academia (European Commission, 2013).[4] The low female representation comes at a cost because women bring a distinct set of skills, work styles and attitudes to the table that can potentially affect productivity at all levels.

This study uses data from the National Science Foundation (NSF) to examine how the concentration of women graduate students in various fields in US graduate programmes has changed over time. The analysis will also compare women's representation among the faculty at different faculty ranks with women's representation among the graduate student body across fields. Finally, we are interested in better understanding a neglected aspect of women's graduate education in STEM fields – women students who are temporary residents receiving their education in the United States. Results will contribute to a better understanding of gender differences in institution and field of study among graduate students and faculty as well as the extent to which gender gaps have closed since 1995. These results will thus help to improve ongoing discussions of policy and institutional reforms that support diversity in academia and the labour market.

Closing the gender gap in US higher education

The American system of higher education has witnessed a considerable transformation during the twentieth century, as women were increasingly enrolled in colleges and universities, particularly at the undergraduate level and later at the graduate level. The percentage of both bachelor's and master's degrees awarded to women increased from approximately 20 per cent in 1900 to approximately 58 per cent by 2000. Although women received less than 20 per cent of all doctorates awarded from US universities for the first seventy years of the twentieth century, by the year 2000, they earned 45 per cent of all doctorates awarded in the United States.[5] Moreover, the growth in women's participation at the graduate level was concentrated in the last third of the twentieth century. Women steadily increased their participation in the early years of the century, but this progress stalled in the immediate post-war era with the influx of men into higher education brought about by the G.I. Bill – a bill that provided, among other benefits, cash payments of tuition and living expenses for returning veterans wishing to attend college. Still, the story of women's representation as students overall is one of significant progress (Jacobs, 1996).

Particularly interesting are changes in graduate education in the past ten years in the United States. According to data provided by the Council of Graduate Schools, we may be seeing a levelling out in the growth of women's representation in graduate education. From 2001 to 2011, total graduate enrolment in the United States grew at an average of 3 per cent per year, with women averaging 3.3 per cent growth over this period and men averaging 2.5 per cent growth. A more detailed breakdown of the data shows that men outpaced women by 2.4 per cent to 1.8 per cent average annual growth from 2006 to 2011. While overall graduate enrolment declined from 2010–2011 for both men and women, the decline was sharper for women (–1.3 per cent) than for men (–0.2 per cent) (Allum et al., 2012).

Between 2001 and 2011, growth in total enrolment in US universities was greater for temporary residents than for US citizens and permanent residents. Between 2006 and 2011, total graduate enrolment increased an average 2.9 per cent annually for temporary residents, compared with 2.4 per cent for US citizens and permanent residents (Allum et al., 2012).[6]

While we appear to see an overall levelling off of women's participation in graduate enrolments relative to men since 2006, the growth in enrolment of women foreign students shows increasing strength. The average annual growth in women temporary residents enrolled in US schools was 3.9 per cent over the period 2001–2011 while the average annual growth in men who are temporary residents enrolled in US schools over the same period was only 1.5 per cent. This may not be surprising given that women who are US citizens began this period with higher enrolment levels relative to their male counterparts (61.3 per cent to 38.7 per cent) than did women who are temporary residents to their male counterparts (42 per cent to 58 per cent) (Allum et al., 2012).

Trends in women's representation in STEM fields

These overall trends in women's participation in higher education in US institutions reveal that women now receive the majority of bachelor's, master's and doctoral degrees. However, the women students continue to be concentrated in particular fields of study (also referred to in this chapter as fields of inquiry) that tend to be non-STEM fields. In 2011, the majority of bachelor's degrees earned by women were in business, management and marketing, while the majority of doctoral degrees awarded to women were concentrated in health professions and related programmes and in law.[7]

Although women's representation in STEM fields in higher education is still disproportionately low relative to other fields, women have made progress in the past decade, especially in the sciences. Moreover, women's advancement in STEM fields has occurred at various levels, from graduate student enrolment rates to doctoral degree recipients to full-time faculty in research universities. Among fields of inquiry the overall drop in enrolments after 2010 came largely in fields such as education and from the arts and humanities while enrolments in the STEM fields continued to grow at positive rates for both women and men.

According to the NSF, by 2010, women comprised 43 per cent of all graduate students enrolled in STEM fields in US universities, out of a total of more than 550,000 students enrolled (see Table 3.1). This percentage increased slowly in the preceding decade, up from 41 per cent in 1999. These inroads have come from both scientific fields as well as engineering, where the base rate has historically been quite lower. In particular, while women made up slightly less than half of all graduate students in scientific fields in 1999, they had surpassed

Table 3.1: Graduate students enrolled in STEM fields in US universities: Total and per cent female, 1999–2010 selected years

	1999		2002		2006		2010	
All graduate students	**Total**	**% F**	**Total**	**% F**	**Total**	**% F**	**Total**	**% F**
Total enrolment	411,182	41.0	454,834	41.5	486,287	43.4	556,532	43.2
Science	309,491	48.0	335,166	48.8	363,246	50.4	407,291	50.6
Agricultural sciences	12,312	41.0	12,698	44.5	13,016	48.4	15,656	49.9
Biological sciences	56,959	52.0	61,088	54.7	69,941	56.3	74,928	56.8
Anatomy	749	46.1	906	49.8	961	50.7	849	50.9
Biochemistry	5,101	44.4	5,190	46.7	5,824	48.3	5,308	50.0
Biology	13,989	51.1	13,822	54.4	16,463	55.0	17,210	55.7
Biometry and epidemiology	3,704	62.7	4,071	62.7	4,789	62.3	6,398	58.6
Biophysics	710	30.0	953	32.1	1,203	33.7	1,072	35.1
Botany	1,974	49.7	1,973	51.6	1,850	52.0	1,863	52.5
Cell biology	4,637	50.9	5,375	51.9	6,553	53.9	7,047	54.3
Ecology	1,704	51.7	1,967	52.8	2,162	56.6	1,828	55.2
Entomology and parasitology	1,145	35.5	1,191	41.3	1,114	46.5	1,116	49.3
Genetics	1,783	57.0	1,909	58.3	2,154	61.1	2,333	58.9
Microbiology, immunology and virology	4,815	50.9	5,208	53.9	5,324	57.3	4,896	58.2

(continued)

All graduate students	1999 Total	1999 % F	2002 Total	2002 % F	2006 Total	2006 % F	2010 Total	2010 % F
Nutrition	4,508	76.1	4,539	77.4	5,042	78.2	5,548	80.7
Pathology	1,580	50.9	1,613	56.2	1,612	60.9	1,376	60.7
Pharmacology	2,757	48.7	3,234	54.8	2,985	55.7	3,101	56.6
Physiology	2,083	43.1	2,076	47.9	2,416	52.8	2,879	50.9
Zoology	1,523	44.0	1,349	47.3	1,145	51.2	896	56.7
Other biological sciences	4,197	49.8	5,712	54.0	8,344	54.8	11,208	54.9
Computer sciences	42,478	29.5	55,269	29.0	47,653	25.3	51,546	24.8
Earth, atmospheric and ocean sciences	14,083	40.7	14,240	43.9	14,920	46.9	15,655	46.0
Atmospheric	913	26.5	1,036	32.1	1,079	34.0	1,455	33.3
Earth	6,637	36.2	6,712	38.9	7,177	42.9	8,251	42.3
Ocean	2,624	46.6	2,618	50.0	2,770	54.0	2,556	55.7
Other earth sciences	3,909	47.6	3,874	51.4	3,894	52.9	3,393	53.1
Mathematics and statistics	16,257	37.2	18,163	37.9	20,815	37.0	23,136	35.1
Mathematics/applied mathematics	13,521	36.0	14,702	35.6	16,649	34.7	17,589	32.8
Statistics	2,736	43.2	3,461	47.6	4,166	46.1	5,547	42.5
Physical sciences	30,691	29.0	32,341	31.1	36,901	32.5	38,973	32.9
Astronomy	832	27.0	990	30.5	1,211	33.6	1,331	31.8
Chemistry	18,416	35.9	19,045	38.5	21,351	40.5	22,436	41.3
Physics	10,869	17.3	11,701	18.8	13,722	19.7	14,507	20.0
Other physical sciences	574	34.3	605	39.3	617	39.5	699	34.8
Psychology	51,727	72.1	51,152	73.7	57,653	75.8	53,419	75.3
Clinical	12,798	72.6	12,609	75.1	13,947	77.7	12,155	77.8
General	16,071	70.0	14,969	70.3	16,622	72.1	14,022	71.3
Nonclinical	22,858	73.2	23,574	75.2	27,084	77.1	27,242	76.3
Social sciences	84,984	51.0	90,215	52.8	102,347	53.8	109,220	53.7
Agricultural economics	2,014	35.5	2,187	38.6	2,158	42.1	2,180	42.5
Anthropology (cultural and social)	7,633	60.8	7,481	61.7	8,150	64.0	8,857	64.4
Economics	10,562	33.1	12,009	35.5	12,132	35.8	14,317	36.4
Geography	4,250	40.1	4,383	42.0	4,750	42.1	5,059	42.9
History and philosophy of science	557	38.1	663	45.4	968	44.2	705	44.8
Linguistics	2,799	65.5	2,875	65.8	3,074	64.6	3,132	60.3
Political science and public admin.	31,372	49.6	34,934	53.3	41,784	53.2	45,045	53.2
Sociology	9,707	64.0	9,665	64.4	9,872	64.2	9,883	64.0

(continued)

All graduate students	1999 Total	1999 % F	2002 Total	2002 % F	2006 Total	2006 % F	2010 Total	2010 % F
Other social sciences	16,090	55.6	16,018	56.4	19,459	59.4	20,042	60.6
Other sciences*	..	..	..	..	..	..	24,758	63.7
Engineering	101,691	19.6	119,668	20.9	123,041	22.7	149,241	23.1
Aerospace	3,349	12.6	3,685	14.0	4,482	15.8	5,540	14.2
Agricultural	986	27.3	952	30.3	1,073	32.6	1,457	34.9
Biomedical	3,069	32.1	4,338	34.9	6,482	38.4	8,497	36.9
Chemical	6,883	25.2	7,414	26.9	7,261	29.7	8,668	31.4
Civil	16,226	25.6	17,713	27.7	17,802	30.5	26,354	32.7
Electrical	31,822	16.1	39,948	18.2	38,265	18.4	41,336	17.4
Engineering sciences/ physics	1,627	19.6	2,121	20.3	2,046	22.0	2,071	21.1
Industrial/manufacturing	11,803	22.5	14,033	21.9	13,829	25.1	15,205	24.2
Mechanical	14,956	12.0	17,139	12.2	17,919	13.9	22,509	14.2
Metallurgical/materials	4,481	24.2	4,992	25.1	5,268	26.4	6,274	28.0
Mining	328	16.8	267	13.9	244	17.6	419	18.4
Nuclear	830	17.3	795	18.6	1,099	19.5	1,459	15.6
Petroleum	642	12.8	766	14.0	813	16.6	1,295	18.1
Other engineering	4,689	22.5	5,505	24.5	6,458	24.9	8,157	23.2

Note: *Other sciences includes communication, family & consumer science, interdisciplinary studies, and neuroscience. These fields were added in 2007 as part of the NSF's reclassification of eligible fields.

Sources: Calculated from NSF (2007, 2011, 2013).

the 50 per cent mark by 2006. In contrast, in engineering, women made up less than a fifth of graduate students enrolled in US universities in 1999, with an increase to 23 per cent by 2010. Also of note in Table 3.1, the overall number of graduate students in the STEM fields has grown consistently since 1999, at an average rate of about 3 per cent overall, with a slightly higher growth rate for women (3.2 per cent) than for men (2.2 per cent). These growth rates in enrolment in STEM fields are comparable to the growth rate for graduate students in all fields as reported in Allum et al. (2012).

Within the sciences, women have historically seen the greatest representation in psychology and in the biological sciences. About three quarters of all graduate students enrolled in US programmes in psychology are women, with a particularly strong increase since 1999 in clinical psychology as opposed to general or non-clinical areas in psychology. Within the biological sciences, women have a disproportionately high and growing representation in nutrition (81 per cent of graduate students in 2010, up from 76 per cent in

1999). Pathology, entomology, pharmacology, physiology and zoology are also increasingly popular fields of study for women in the biological sciences. In contrast, biometry/epidemiology is the only area within the biological sciences that has seen a decline in the relative representation of female graduate students – from 63 per cent in 1999 to 59 per cent in 2010. The reason for this decline is certainly not a lack of interest among women; women saw growth in their absolute numbers in this field, but the growth for men was considerably higher.

Just behind the biological sciences in terms of the representation of female graduate students are the social sciences, with a small increase of about 3 percentage points in the past decade to 54 per cent in 2010. Within the social sciences, sociology and anthropology remain the most popular areas for women, while women continue to be under-represented in economics, the most mathematically intense social science. Even in 2010, just 36 per cent of all graduate students in economics were women. A higher, and growing, representation of women was found in agricultural economics, a more applied field that women perhaps find more appealing. The increasing popularity of agricultural economics for women as compared to men is likely related to the very high representation of female graduate students in family and consumer science – a new field in 2010 as categorized by the NSF that uses similar analytical tools and frameworks. Also witnessing substantial growth in the past decade was the field entitled history and philosophy of science – a field in which women's enrolment increased from 38 per cent in 1999 to 45 per cent in 2010.

In contrast to psychology, biological sciences and social sciences, women have had very low representation in computer sciences, physical sciences, and mathematics and statistics. The percentage of graduate students who are female is lowest in computer sciences: just 25 per cent in 2010, down from 30 per cent in 1999. In the physical sciences, where one third of graduate students were women in 2010, the field of physics remains particularly low. In 2010, just one in five graduate students specializing in physics – a mathematically intensive field – were women. This imbalance is even more severe than in the field of mathematics, in which one third of graduate students were women in 2010. In comparison, women have seen a stronger increase in their relative presence in the fields of chemistry and astronomy.

The final set of results in Table 3.1 show women's representation in engineering, which is almost as low as in physics. In 2010, just 23 per cent of graduate students in engineering were women, up from 20 per cent in 1999.

Within engineering, women have relatively high rates of representation in biomedical and agricultural engineering but very low rates in aerospace, mechanical and nuclear engineering. Despite the very low presence of women in these fields, all fields within engineering have seen growth over time except for nuclear engineering. Progress for women was particularly strong in agricultural and civil engineering.

Thus far this discussion has focused on all graduate students in US universities, including US citizens, permanent residents and temporary residents (foreign students). For comparison purposes, it is interesting to examine US students and foreign students separately since foreign students have historically been predominantly male. According to data from the NSF, while 47 per cent of all US students enrolled in STEM fields in US universities in 2010 were female, only 35 per cent of foreign graduate students in STEM fields were female (see Table 3.2). However, these aggregate numbers mask some interesting patterns. Although women's representation among foreign graduate students is substantially lower in aggregate, their share has risen by a greater amount over time as compared to women US graduate students who are US citizens and permanent residents. Moreover, the representation of women among foreign graduate students is actually higher than it is among US citizens and permanent residents for several fields that traditionally have had trouble attracting and retaining women, including computer sciences, mathematics and statistics, physical sciences and engineering. In contrast, US women have a relatively higher representation as compared to their foreign counterparts in earth, atmospheric and ocean sciences (47 per cent versus 41 per cent in 2010) and in the social sciences (55 per cent versus 49 per cent).

Examining graduate student enrolment rates by gender presents only a partial view of the state of gender equality in higher education given the well-documented 'leaky pipeline' or 'gender filter' along the progression from graduate school enrolment to doctoral recipients to employment as tenure-track and tenured faculty.[8] Explanations for the leaky pipeline are numerous and include bias, discrimination, lack of mentoring, insufficient female role models, discouragement from secondary school teachers, insufficient family-friendly policies on campuses such as paid maternity leave and a flexible tenure clock and incompatibility of long working hours with family responsibilities. Hence, the increase in women graduate students in the past decade may not have produced a proportionate increase in the representation of women among doctoral degree recipients and university faculty.

Table 3.2: Graduate students enrolled in STEM fields in US universities: Total and per cent female by citizenship, 1999–2010

	1999		2002		2006		2010	
	Total	**%F**	**Total**	**%F**	**Total**	**%F**	**Total**	**%F**
Total US Citizens/ Permanent residents	301,254	45.0	309,119	46.7	343,603	47.7	390,403	46.9
Science	241,066	51.0	247,842	52.6	275,905	53.8	308,108	53.4
Agricultural sciences	9,774	42.9	10,085	46.0	10,341	49.9	12,416	50.4
Biological sciences	45,770	52.8	47,253	55.6	53,034	57.1	57,497	57.5
Computer sciences	25,323	29.3	28,203	29.1	26,675	25.3	26,170	23.1
Earth, atmospheric and ocean sciences	11,563	42.1	11,463	45.6	12,153	48.5	12,729	47.3
Mathematics and statistics	10,330	38.5	11,139	39.3	13,219	36.7	14,521	34.0
Physical sciences	19,559	30.0	19,251	32.1	22,144	33.3	23,652	32.6
Psychology	49,488	72.4	48,295	74.4	54,802	76.0	50,332	75.4
Social sciences	69,259	53.0	72,153	54.9	83,537	55.5	89,647	54.6
Other sciences*	..	..	..	..	..	..	21,144	64.2
Engineering	60,188	20.6	61,277	22.5	67,698	22.8	82,295	22.4
Total foreign students	109,928	30.0	145,715	30.5	142,684	33.1	166,129	34.6
Science	68,425	37.2	87,324	38.0	87,341	39.9	99,183	41.8
Agricultural sciences	2,538	33.7	2,613	38.7	2,675	42.7	3,240	48.3
Biological sciences	11,189	48.6	13,835	51.7	16,907	53.6	17,431	54.7
Computer sciences	17,155	29.9	27,066	28.9	20,978	25.4	25,376	26.6
Earth, atmospheric and ocean sciences	2,520	34.0	2,777	36.6	2,767	40.0	2,926	40.5
Mathematics and statistics	5,927	34.8	7,024	35.7	7,596	37.3	8,615	37.0
Physical sciences	11,132	27.4	13,090	29.7	14,757	31.4	15,321	33.3
Psychology	2,239	64.7	2,857	61.8	2,851	72.1	3,087	73.9
Social sciences	15,725	42.0	18,062	44.6	18,810	46.0	19,573	49.4
Other sciences*	..	..	..	..	..	..	3,614	61.3
Engineering	41,503	18.1	58,391	19.1	55,343	22.5	66,946	23.9

Note: *Other sciences includes communication, family & consumer science, interdisciplinary studies and neuroscience. These fields were added in 2007 as part of the NSF's reclassification of eligible fields.
Sources: Calculated from NSF (2007, 2011, 2013).

Figure 3.1 and Table 3.3 explore this question further with evidence on doctoral degrees awarded in US universities in the major STEM field categories from 1999 to 2010. While we expect the total number of doctoral

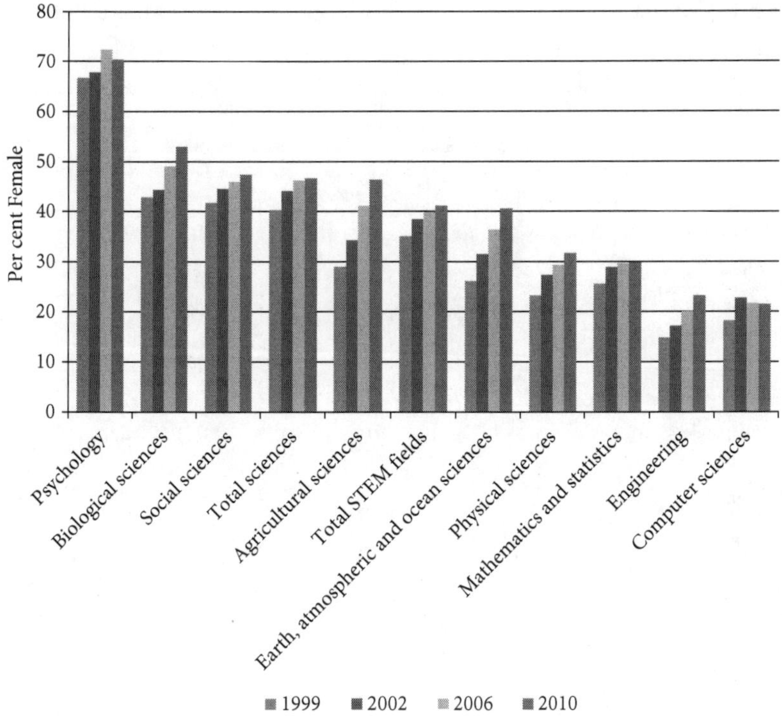

Figure 3.1 Doctoral degrees awarded in STEM fields in US universities: Per cent female, 1999–2010.

Sources: Calculated from data in NSF (2009, 2013)

degrees awarded to be smaller than the total number of individuals enrolled in graduate school, the data in Figure 3.1 and Table 3.3 indicates that the percentage of doctoral degree recipients who are female is lower in most fields than the percentage of enrolled graduate students who are female. In particular, for the STEM fields in aggregate, 41 per cent of doctoral degree recipients in 2010 were women as compared to 43 per cent of students enrolled in graduate school programmes in the same year. The gap between doctoral degree recipients is somewhat bigger for the sciences as an aggregate (47 per cent versus 51 per cent). This differential in the per cent female occurs for every broad field within the sciences and is especially pronounced for the social sciences (47 per cent of doctoral degree recipients versus 54 per cent female among enrolled graduate students) and for earth, atmospheric and ocean sciences (41 per cent of doctoral degree recipients versus 46 per cent female among enrolled graduate students). Fortunately, these losses in the pipeline from graduate school enrolment to awarding the doctoral decree are

Table 3.3: Comparison of per cent female among enrolled graduate students and doctoral degree recipients, 1999–2010

	1999		2002		2006		2010	
	Enrolments	**PhD Recipients**	**Enrolments**	**PhD Recipients**	**Enrolments**	**PhD Recipients**	**Enrolments**	**PhD Recipients**
Total STEM fields	41.0	35.0	41.5	38.4	43.4	39.8	43.2	41.1
Total sciences	48.0	40.3	48.8	44.2	50.4	46.2	50.6	46.7
Agricultural sciences	41.0	29.0	44.5	34.3	48.4	41.0	49.9	46.3
Biological sciences	52.0	42.9	54.7	44.4	56.3	49.1	56.8	52.9
Computer sciences	29.5	18.2	29.0	22.8	25.3	21.7	24.8	21.5
Earth, atmospheric and ocean sciences	40.7	26.1	43.9	31.5	46.9	36.3	46.0	40.5
Mathematics and statistics	37.2	25.6	37.9	28.9	37.0	29.6	35.1	29.9
Physical sciences	29.0	23.2	31.1	27.4	32.5	29.3	32.9	31.7
Psychology	72.1	66.8	73.7	67.8	75.8	72.4	75.3	70.4
Social sciences	51.0	41.7	52.8	44.6	53.8	46.0	53.7	47.4
Total engineering	19.6	14.8	20.9	17.2	22.7	20.0	23.1	23.2

Sources: Calculated from NSF (2007, 2009, 2011, 2013).

not as substantial as they were in 1999, with substantial shrinkage across many of the broad science categories in the gaps between women's representation among doctoral degree recipients versus enrolled graduate students. For example, in earth, atmospheric and ocean sciences in 1999, just 26 per cent of doctoral degree recipients were women compared to 41 per cent of enrolled graduate students. This gap of about 15 percentage points in 1999 had shrunk considerably by 2010. Note that these losses in the pipeline are no longer apparent in engineering in the most recent year for which the NSF report these data. In 2010, 23 per cent of graduate students and 23 per cent of doctoral degree recipients were women, a measure of equality not seen until after 2006.

Although the pipeline losses in the sciences still appear to be substantial as recent as 2010, Figure 3.1 does show a general increase in the percentage of doctoral degree recipients who are female, between 1999 and 2010. This increase in the percentage of women receiving doctorates is increasing both because there have been increases in the absolute number of women doctoral recipients from year to year and because these increases have outpaced those of men. Every STEM field across the board saw an increase over time in the percentage of doctoral degree recipients who were female, with an average increase of 6 percentage points for STEM fields as a whole and for the sciences and an increase of 8 percentage points for engineering. In most cases, both women and men received more doctorates over time in particular field areas and women's growth outpaced that of men. However, in a few fields, men saw declining absolute numbers while women continued to gain, including agricultural sciences and history of science. In fact, in agricultural sciences, a substantial drop in the absolute number of male doctoral degree recipients contributed to an increase in the per cent of female recipients from 29 per cent in 1999 to 46 per cent in 2010.

One of the most troubling issues for women in STEM fields concerns the lower than expected entry of women PhDs into tenure-track positions. While the proportion of women receiving doctoral degrees in STEM fields has increased, the National Academy of Sciences (2006) points out that women are more likely than men to report plans to keep post-doctoral positions, report lower satisfaction with their post-doctoral experience and are under-represented in the applicant pools for tenure-track faculty positions. This argument is supported with NSF data for 2010 in Figure 3.2, which reports the per cent of tenured/tenure-track faculty who are women plotted against the per cent of doctoral degree recipients who are women for each major category

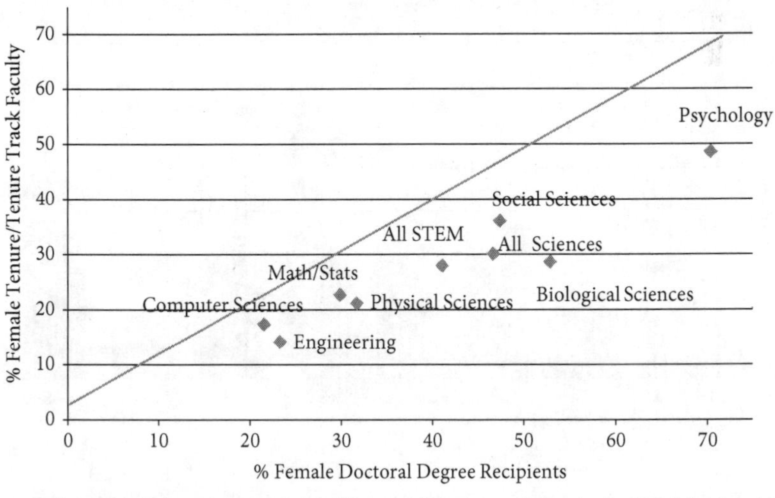

Figure 3.2 Doctoral degrees awarded and tenured/tenure track faculty in STEM fields in US universities: Per cent female, 2010.

Sources: Calculated from data in NSF (2013)

in the STEM fields. For example, in the social sciences, 47 per cent of doctoral degree recipients are women, while only 36 per cent of tenured/tenure-track faculty are women. As shown in the figure by the distance from the diagonal line, the gap between doctoral degree recipients and faculty in academia is largest in the biological sciences (a 24 percentage point gap) and smallest in computer sciences (a 4 percentage point gap).

The leaky pipeline does not stop at the assistant professor level and continues along the faculty ranks, as documented in Figures 3.3 and 3.4, which clearly shows that for every year depicted, the percentage of faculty who are women decreases across fields of inquiry in the move from lower ranked professor

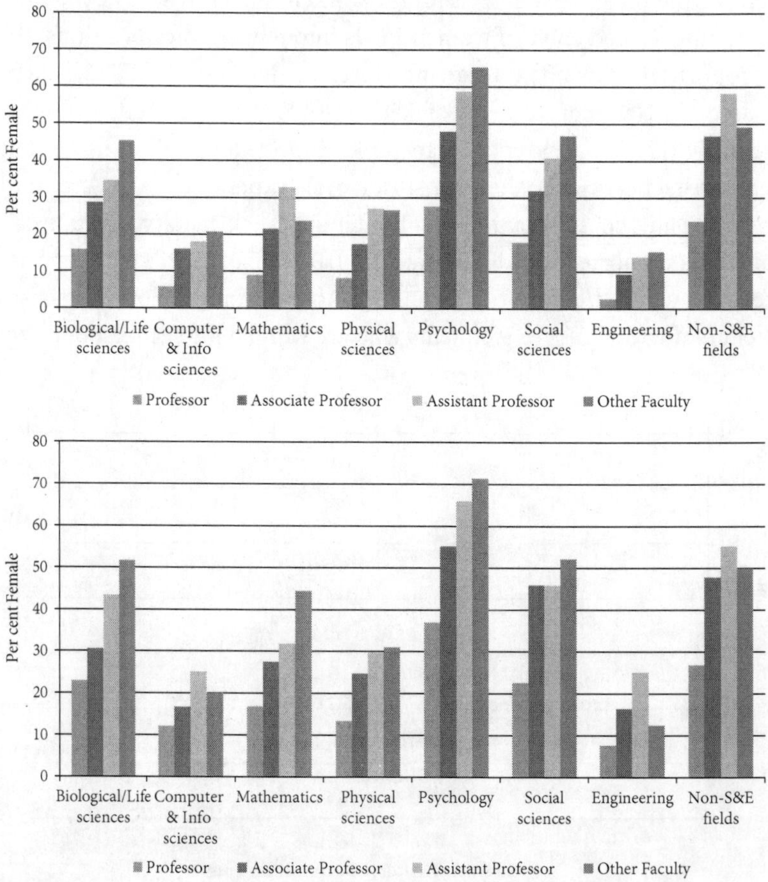

Figure 3.3 Female representation among faculty with doctorates in science, engineering, and health, by faculty rank and field, 2001–2010.

Sources: Calculated from data in NSF (2004, 2013)

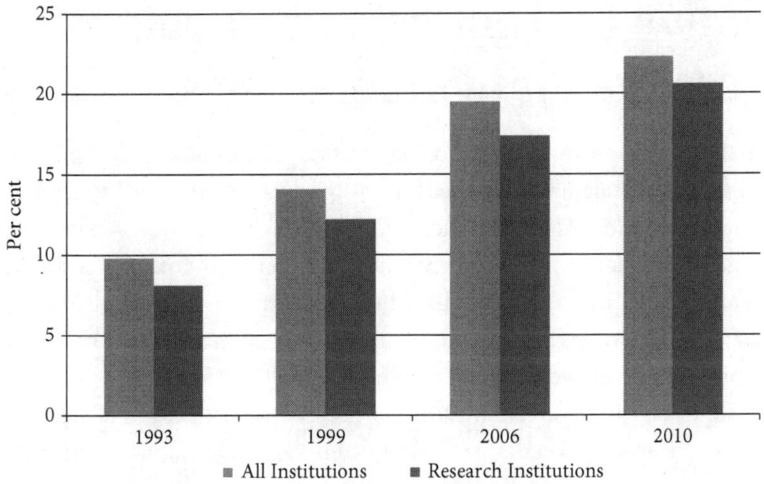

Figure 3.4 Female representation among full professors with doctorates in science, engineering, and health: 1993–2010.

Sources: NSF (2013)

positions to higher ranked professor positions. For example, in 2010, 52 per cent of non-tenured/non-tenure-track faculty in the biological and life sciences were women, compared to 43 per cent of assistant professors, 31 per cent of associate professors and 23 per cent of full professors. The per cent of female among full professors was the lowest for engineering (8 per cent) and computer and information sciences (12 per cent) – numbers that had risen very little since 2001. Similar to the concentration of female graduate students in psychology, Figure 3.3 also shows that in 2010, the highest concentrations of female faculty members at every faculty rank were in psychology, a pattern that has not changed since 2001.

Figure 3.4 shows that in 2010, women made up just 22 per cent of full-time, full professors with science, engineering and health doctorates in all US universities and 21 per cent in US research universities. By way of comparison, in 2002, when today's younger full professors were obtaining their doctoral degrees, 38 per cent of doctoral degree recipients in all STEM fields were women. This decline between receipt of the doctorate and advancement to full professor in the STEM fields is substantial. That said, there is some good news in the large jump over time in women's representation among the highest ranks of university faculty. In 1993, just 8 per cent of full professors in research universities and 10 per cent in all universities were women; hence the per cent female has more than doubled in a seventeen-year period.

Relative concentration of women across graduate programmes

To further examine the relative concentration of women's representation in STEM fields, we calculate two measures – the Dissimilarity or Duncan Index (DI) and the Gender Concentration Quotient (GCQ). The DI is a commonly used index for examining the segregation between two groups. As discussed in greater detail in the Appendix, the DI describes in a single value the proportion of men or women who would have to change fields for there to be equal proportions of women and men in each field of inquiry.

While the DI is a convenient tool for measuring the degree of segregation of men and women in academia, it does not reveal much about the underlying nature of that segregation. That is, the DI may become smaller over time, but the reduction could result from different forces, including the introduction of more women to male-dominated fields, the entrance of more men in female-dominated fields or a growth in integrated fields. The GCQ has the advantage of providing a continuous measure of the degree to which women are under- or over-represented in a particular field (May and Watrel, 2000). This measure allows us to identify male-dominated, female-dominated and integrated fields of inquiry within the context of variations in graduate school enrolments and faculty employment by sex.

Results in Figure 3.5, Panel A for graduate student enrolment rates indicate that the DI for all graduate students in STEM fields has increased slightly since 1999, indicating that sex segregation across STEM fields has not diminished. Specifically, the data show that as of 2010, about 34 per cent of men and women would need to change fields for there to be equal proportions of men and women in each field, up slightly from 33 per cent in 1999. Patterns in the DI for all graduate student enrolments are closely mirrored by the pattern for graduate students who are US citizens and permanent residents. In contrast, the DI for foreigners enrolled in US students is considerably lower, at about 0.28 in 2010 as compared to 0.35 for US citizens. The DI for graduate students from abroad enrolled in STEM fields shows less segregation by gender than that of US citizens and permanent residents. Just as the DI has risen slightly for US students, foreign students have also seen a slight rise in sex segregation across fields.

While the average level of the DI for doctoral degree recipients in STEM fields (Figure 3.5, Panel B) is comparable to the average level for all graduate

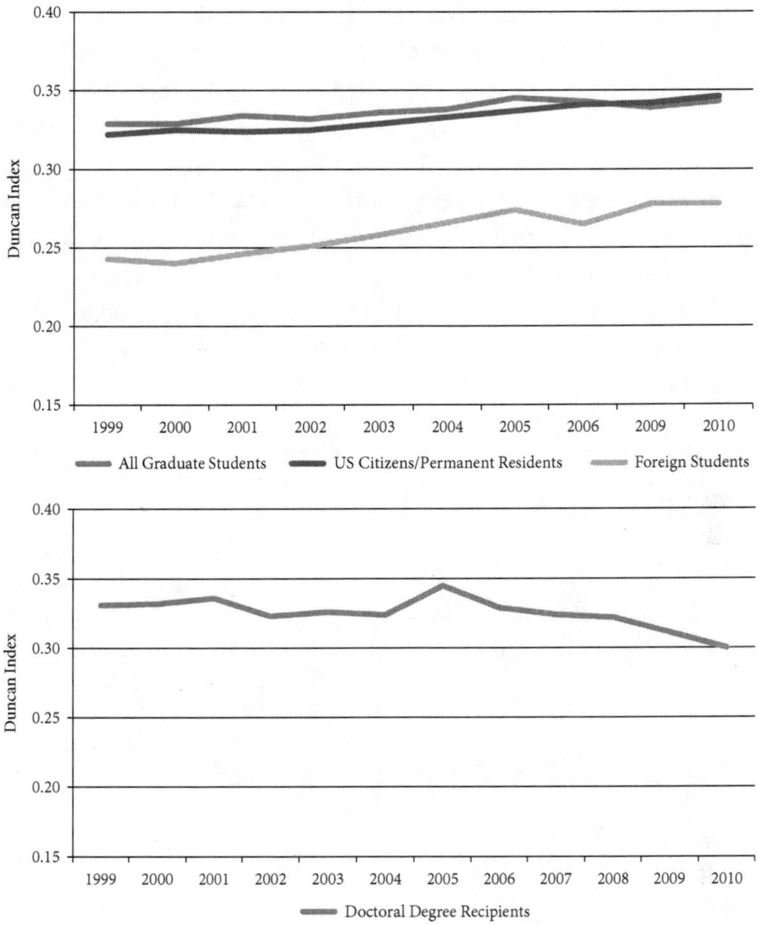

Figure 3.5 Duncan index of dissimilarity for graduate students in STEM fields, 1999–2010.

Sources: Calculated from data in NSF (2007, 2011, 2013)

student enrolments, there is more variability by year in the DI for doctoral degree recipients than for enrolled graduate students. During the 1999–2010 period, the DI for all graduate students enrolled in STEM fields averaged 0.34, which is very close to the average of 0.32 for doctoral degree recipients. However, segregation exhibited larger fluctuations from year to year for doctoral degree recipients. Moreover, the DI for doctoral degrees awarded shows a downward trend after 2005, in contrast to the increase for all graduate student enrolments.

Finally, the GCQ allows us to better identify those particular STEM fields in which women appear to be under- or over-represented among enrolled graduate students given male enrolment patterns. Figure 3.6, Panel A shows the 'top-ten' STEM fields in which women are over-represented among enrolled graduate students. Any field with a GCQ greater than one shows that women are over-represented given male enrolment patterns. As we can see, women are most over-represented in family and consumer science and in nutrition, with a number of the remaining top-ten fields in the social sciences. In contrast, Figure 3.6, Panel B shows the ten fields in which women are most under-represented given male enrolment patterns. Specifically, fields where women are most under-represented are concentrated in engineering and physics. Clearly, more effort is required in these fields to promote and produce greater gender balance.

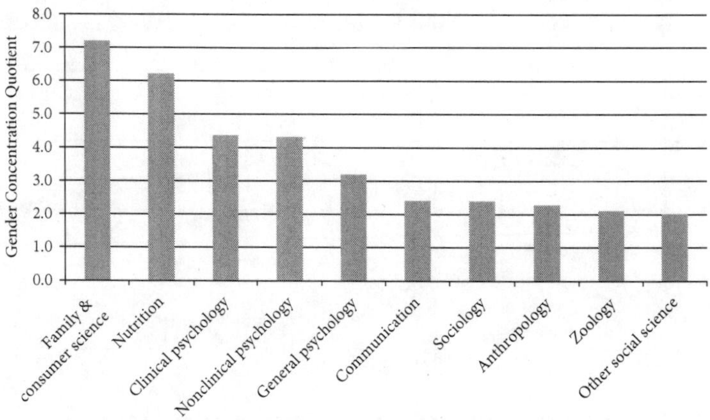

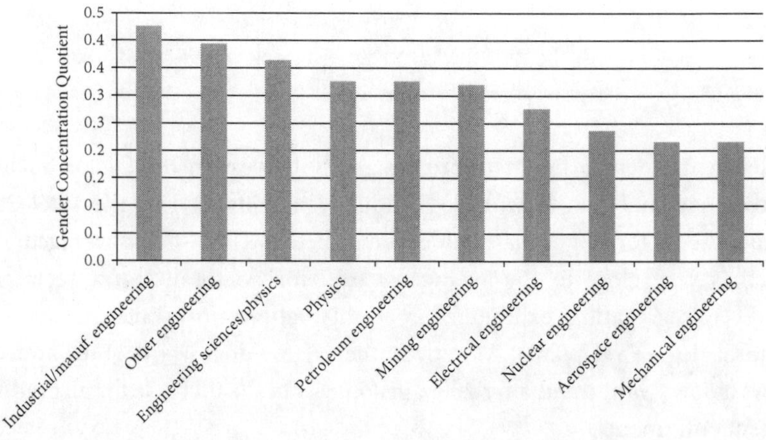

Figure 3.6 Ranking of fields of inquiry by the gender concentration quotient, 2010.

Sources: Calculated from data in NSF (2007, 2011, 2013)

Overcoming barriers for women in STEM fields

As we have seen, while women have made substantial progress in terms of their representation in graduate education in general in the last third of the twentieth century, they continue to be significantly under-represented in the STEM fields of science, technology, engineering and mathematics. Given the slow progress of women into many of the STEM fields, it is important to examine some of the potential barriers in these areas as well as possible policies to bring women into parity with men in these fields.

Much work has been done to chronicle our changing image of what a scientist looks like – images that prevent girls from choosing courses, majors and careers in STEM fields and often serve as a foundation for biases and implicit barriers. Historically, when asked to 'draw a scientist', 98 per cent of school-age children drew males (Kahle, 1987, Figure 1.1). Although this number fell in the 1990s to around 70 per cent, there continues to be an implicit bias associating science with men (Rahm and Charbonneau, 1997).

In related research, psychologists have found widespread implicit bias, on the part of both men and women, associating men with science and careers and women with liberal arts and family. In their well-known exercise, participants are asked to sort series of male and female names and words associated with family and career (Greenwald et al., 2002). The results suggest that both women and men are more likely to associate women with family and men with careers and to associate women with liberal arts and men with science.[9]

Virginia Valian explains these biases in terms of 'gender schemas' – hypotheses we often unknowingly make about what it means to be male or female and hypotheses that place individuals into social groups with particular characteristics – women as nurturing and men as independent, for example. While gender schemas may be our brain's way of sorting an immense amount of information, they also affect our judgements on competence, ability and worth (Valian, 2008).

Gender schemas may explain why it is that although in elementary school, boys and girls are equally interested in science, as children move on to their middle-school years, girls have become significantly less interested in science than boys (Simpson and Oliver, 1990; Jones et al., 2000). In a study of high school students, women were less likely to take advanced math classes than boys due to their perceived lack of ability (Pedro et al., 1981) – despite the fact that studies shows no actual gender differences in average math and science achievement (Coley, 2001). This trend carries on into college, where fewer women enter degree programmes in STEM fields.

Reasons for the dearth of women in STEM fields include the smaller proportion of women majors in these fields as undergraduates as well as attrition at all career transition points (Xie and Shauman, 2003). This attrition may in part reflect the lack of women role models for women students in STEM fields. In their study of the top 50 STEM research universities, Nelson and Rogers (2003) find that there are few female full professors in STEM fields and that the percentage of women doctoral recipients is much higher than the percentage of women assistant professors. In some disciplines, a woman can get a bachelor of science degree without being taught by a female professor in that discipline. Still other studies have focused on women's disadvantage in developing mentoring relationships with largely male faculty members. According to this view, women may be disadvantaged in the sponsorship processes (advising, mentoring, collegial) because most tenured professors are male and maintaining a professional, cross-sex relationship can be difficult. For example, Nettles and Millet (2006) suggested that female graduate students interact less frequently with male professors than do male graduate students and perceive their relationships with their mentors as less relaxed and friendly.

Studies have also shown that variations in family responsibilities between men and women may play a role. According to Xie and Shauman, marriage per se does not seem to matter, but women are disadvantaged if they have children. These women are less likely to pursue careers in science and engineering after completion of a science and engineering education and are less likely to be promoted (Xie and Shauman, 2003).

Finally, at the faculty level, studies have shown that women are held to a different standard. For example, in their now famous study of Sweden higher education, Wenneras and Wold (1997) showed that women need 2.5 more publications than men to be awarded post-doctoral fellowships. Experiments examining the evaluation of research in the United States showed that when the identical article was scored with various gendered fictitious names – male, female, and gender neutral names – both men and women rated the article with the male name for the author superior to the article with the female name (Goldberg, 1968; Paludi and Strayer, 1985). Moreover, studies examining identical dossiers for hiring showed similar results depending upon the gendered nature of the name on the dossier (Steinpreis et al., 1999). All of these biases create barriers for women in moving successfully in this transition from student to faculty member and affect the ability of women to be promoted.

In addition to these barriers for women, institutional barriers sometimes work to prevent women from successfully negotiating their careers in higher education. As academics, information on the processes surrounding tenure and promotion are especially important and studies have shown that male faculty report that they have a clearer understanding of their tenure prospects and standards than do women faculty (Trower and Bleak, 2004). Given these reported gender differences, institutions such as faculty unions may play an especially important role for women in formalizing tenure and promotion procedures and providing faculty with greater opportunities to pursue grievances (May et al., 2010).

Moreover, excess service demands on women faculty have been shown to take time away from research efforts. With so few women faculty in STEM fields, women may be called upon to serve on committees to make committees more diverse and may have more demands for mentoring other female students. The diversion of effort out of research and into service activities creates additional barriers for women faculty (Fogg, 2003).

Conclusion

This growing gender diversity within graduate student and faculty populations has indeed transformed knowledge. Yet women faculty members continue to be concentrated in less prestigious universities and in lower academic ranks, and they are increasingly found in non-tenure-track instructional positions.

Particularly difficult is the movement of women into the so-called STEM fields. Although there has been some improvement in the representation of women faculty and graduate students into these fields over time, our data reveal the stubborn nature of change in these fields as well as the need to examine in more detail differences between US citizens and permanent residents and temporary residents in terms of women's representation.

Efforts have been made by important agencies such as the NSF to provide programmes such as the ADVANCE programme (Increasing the Participation and Advancement of Women in Academic Science and Engineering Careers) aimed at development of a more diverse science and engineering workforce.

Universities with significant STEM faculty and research have, along with other universities, instituted a number of programmes to assist in the recruitment of women faculty including targeted hiring, dual career programmes, tenure extensions, and easier access to childcare facilities. However, along with these important initiatives, one of the most important changes that we believe will also assist in promoting greater gender balance in these fields is the movement to formally value and encourage interdisciplinary research and research teams within the university community and in the important area of grant awards by granting agencies. Specifically, university administrators need to provide incentives and reward structures that encourage and value interdisciplinary research.

Institutional discrimination theorists argue that dominant status groups engage in practices to maintain their privileged positions (Tomaskovic-Devey, 1993; Kulis, 1997). Field specific values, mores, and so-called production practices are themselves chosen in order to maximize the returns to individuals already involved in the production process. Along with these practices also come elaborate screening mechanisms to control access to particular jobs. In academe, this form of institutional discrimination is reflected in the standards and rituals of scholarly conduct that affect hiring, promotion and performance evaluation (May et al., 2010).

The barriers engrained in this type of institutional discrimination will greatly diminish by fostering interdisciplinary and trans-disciplinary work – or, as Elinor Ostrom, winner of the Nobel Memorial Prize in Economic Sciences puts it – when the 'silos' created by narrowly defined disciplinary structures are replaced by 'meadows' (May and Summerfield, 2012). Broadening the criteria for tenure to include interdisciplinary journals, valuing manuscripts in addition to journal articles in so-called 'top journals' and providing opportunities through institutional grants for collaborative cross-disciplinary research would all help to change the silo culture and promote the inclusion of women in fields where they have been under-represented while enriching current research output.

Finally, with increased pressure on finances particularly for public universities, granting agencies such as the NSF and NIH as well as a growing cadre of NGOs can play a pivotal and crucial role in providing incentives for women's inclusion in STEM fields while improving science and solving problems. Encouraging gender balance and cross-disciplinarity in research teams on grants, reporting gender of principle and co-principle investigators in statistics on grant awards, would be especially important means of documenting and encouraging greater gender balance. As our research shows, there is much work to be done to achieve greater gender balance in the STEM fields but creative and workable solutions are indeed possible.

Notes

1 Although it has generally been argued that greater education for women results in lower infant mortality, it is not clear that education for mothers has a different effect than education for fathers in this regard. See Duflo (2012).

2 These descriptive statistics were calculated from the Global Education Database maintained by UNESCO's Institute for Statistics, available at http://www.uis.unesco.org.

3 For comprehensive reviews about women in science, see Di'Tomaso and Farris (1992), Sonnert and Holton (1995), Xie and Shauman (2003) and Preston (2004).

4 Papers about the status of women in the sciences in Europe and policy reforms to advance European women's careers in the sciences include Dewandre (2002), ETAN (2000), Glover (2001) and Osborn (1994).

5 These descriptive statistics are from NCES (2002).

6 Growth in graduate enrolment of foreign students has received growing attention and is not without controversy, as noted in Clotfelter (2010).

7 Statistics on bachelor's and doctoral degree recipients by field are found at NCES (2011).

8 There is a large literature on the 'leaky pipeline' in STEM fields in higher education in the United States and in other countries. See, for example, Blickenstaff (2005), Bystydzienski and Bird (2006), Adamuti-Trache and Andres (2008) and May (2008a).

9 See also the implicit association test available at http://www.understandingprejudice.org/iat/index2.htm.

Questions for reflection

a) Which fields in the sciences have historically seen the greatest representation of women among enrolled graduate students? Which field in the social sciences has seen the lowest representation of women among enrolled graduate students?

b) How does the per cent female of US graduate students compare with the per cent female of foreign graduate students enrolled in STEM fields in US universities, and how have these shares been changing in recent years?

c) What is meant by the 'leaky pipeline' along the progression from graduate school enrolment to doctoral recipients to employment as a tenured/tenure-track faculty member, and what are some of the reasons for this leaky pipeline?

d) What is the Duncan Index, how has it been changing in terms of graduate student enrolments in STEM fields, and what does this mean for sex segregation across STEM fields?

Further Reading

Glass, Christy and Minnotte, Krista Lynn. (Dec 2010), 'Recruiting and hiring women in STEM fields', *Journal of Diversity in Higher Education*, 3 (4), 218–29.

Using a unique data set of the entire pool of applicants to tenure-track STEM faculty positions over a six-year period at a large public research university, this article identifies strategies that universities and academic departments can use to increase women's representation in tenure-track positions, including placing greater emphasis on increasing the number of women applicants and placing advertisements in venues that specifically target women.

Shapiro, Jenessa R. and Williams, Amy M. (2012), 'The role of stereotype threats in undermining girls' and women's performance and interest in STEM fields', *Sex Roles*, 66, (3–4), 175–183.

This article draws on the Multi-Threat Framework to explore gender-related math attitudes and how they put girls and women at risk for stereotype threats.

Lott, Joe L., Gardner, Susan and Powers, Daniel A. (2009), 'Doctoral student attrition in the STEM fields: An exploratory event history analysis', *Journal of College Student Retention: Research, Theory and Practice*, 11, (2), 247–66.

This study utilizes discrete-time event history analysis to model doctoral attrition for 10,088 individuals, in fifty-six STEM departments, at one research-extensive institution, located in the South, over a 20-year period. Results show that the odds of attrition are the greatest in the first year. Additionally, the odds of attrition are greater for females, Asians and for those who belong to a hard-applied science major (versus a hard-pure major).

Price, Joshua. (2010), 'The effect of instructor race and gender on student persistence in STEM fields', *Economics of Education Review*, 29, (6), 901–10.

This study determines if minority and female students are more likely to persist in a science, technology, engineering and math (STEM) major when they enroll in classes taught by instructors of their own race or gender. Results indicate that black students are more likely to persist in a STEM major if they have a STEM course taught by a black instructor, and female students are less likely to persist when more of their STEM courses are taught by female instructors.

Bibliography

Adamuti-Trache, M. and Andres, L. (2008), 'Embarking on and persisting in scientific fields of study: Cultural capital, gender, and curriculum along the science pipeline', *International Journal of Science Education*, 30, (12), 1557–84.

Allum, J., Bell, N. and Sowell, R. (2012), *Graduate Enrolment and Degrees: 2001 to 2011*. Washington DC: Council of Graduate Schools.

Beede, D., Julian, T., Langdon, D., McKittrick, G., Kahn, B. and Doms, M. (2011), 'Women in STEM: A gender gap to innovation', US Department of Commerce, Economics and Statistics Administration. Available at http://www.esa.doc.gov/sites/default/files/reports/documents/womeninstemagapto innovation8311.pdf.

Bell, N. (2010), *Graduate Enrolment and Degrees: 1999–2009*. Washington, DC: Council of Graduate Schools.

Blickenstaff, J. (2005), 'Women and science careers: Leaky pipeline or gender filter?', *Gender and Education*, 17, (4), 369–86.

Breierova, L. and Duflo, E. (2004), 'The impact of education on fertility and child mortality: Do fathers really matter less than mothers?' National Bureau of Economic Research Working Paper No. 10513.

Bystydzienski, J. and Sharon Bird, S. (eds.) (2006), *Removing Barriers: Women in Academic Science, Technology, Engineering, and Mathematics*. Bloomington, IN: Indiana University Press.

Clotfelter, C. (2010), *American Universities in a Global Setting*. Chicago, IL: University of Chicago Press.

Coley, R. J. (2001), *Differences in the Gender Gap: Comparisons Across Racial/Ethnic Groups in Education and Work*, Policy Information Report. Princeton, NJ: Educational Testing Service. http://www.ets.org/Media/Research/pdf/PICGENDER.pdf.

Dewandre, N. (2002), 'European strategies for promoting women in science', *Science*, 295, (5553), 278–79.

Di'Tomaso, N. and Farris, G. (1992), 'Work and career issues for women scientists in industrial research and development in the U.S.', *Berlin Journal of Sociology*, 2, 91–102.

Dulfo, E. (2012), 'Women empowerment and economic development', *Journal of Economic Literature*, 50 (4), 1051–79.

European Commission. (2013), Women and Science: Statistics and Indicators. Available at http://ec.europa.eu/research/science-society/women/wssi/index_en.html.

European Technology Assessment Network (ETAN). (2000), *Science Policies in the European Union: Promoting Excellence Through Mainstreaming Gender Equality*. Brussels: European Commission.

Fogg, P. (2003), 'So many committees, so little time', *Chronicle of Higher Education*, 50, (17), A14.

Glover, J. (2001), 'Targeting women: Policy issues relating to women's representation in professional scientific employment', *Policy Studies*, 22, (2), 69–82.

Goldberg, P. (1968), 'Are women prejudiced against women?', *Transaction*, 5, 28–30.

Greenwald, A., Banaji, M., Rudman, L., Farnham, S., Brian Nosek, B. and Mellott, D. (2002), 'A unified theory of implicit attitudes, stereotypes, self-esteeem, and self-concept', *Psychological Review*, 109, (1), 3–25.

Hoffer, T., Sederstrom, S., Selfa, L., Welch, V., Hess, M., Brown, S., Reyes, S., Webber, K. and Guzman-Barron, I. (2003), *Doctorate Recipients from United States Universities: Summary Report 2002*. Chicago: National Opinion Research Center.

Jacobs, J. A. (1996), 'Gender inequality and higher education', *Annual Review of Sociology*, 22, 153–85.

Jones, G., Howe, A. and Rua, M. (2000), 'Gender differences in students' experiences, interests, and attitudes towards science and scientists', *Science Education*, 84, 180–92.

Kahle, J. (1987), 'Images of science: The physicist and the cowboy', in B. Fraser and G. Giddings (eds.) *Gender Issues in Science Education*. Perth: Curtin University of Technology, 1–11.

Kulis, S. (1997), 'Gender segregation among college and university employees', *Sociology of Education*, 70, (2), 151–73.

May, A. M. (ed.) (2008a), *The 'Woman Question' and Higher Education: Perspectives on Gender and Knowledge Production in America*. Cheltenham, UK and Northampton, MA: Edward Elgar Publishing.

—— (2008b), 'Gender and the political economy of knowledge', in F. Bettio and A. Veraschangina (eds.) *Frontiers in the Economics of Gender*. London and New York: Routledge, 267–85.

——, Moorhouse, E. and Bossard, J. (2010), 'Representation of women faculty at public research universities: Do unions matter?', *Industrial and Labor Relations Review*, 63, (4), 699–718.

—— and Summerfield, G. (2012), 'Creating a space where gender matters', *Feminist Economics*, 18, (4), 25–37.

—— and Watrel, R. (2000), 'Occupational segregation of women on the great plains', *Great Plains Research*, 10, 169–88.

National Academy of Sciences, National Academy of Engineering, and Institute of Medicine. (2006), *Beyond Bias and Barriers: Fulfilling the Potential of Women in Academic Science and Engineering*. Washington, DC: National Academies Press.

National Center for Education Statistics, U.S. Department of Education (NCES). (Various Years), *Digest of Education Statistics*. Available at http://nces.ed.gov/Programs/digest/.

National Science Foundation, National Center for Science and Engineering Statistics. (Various Years), *Women, Minorities, and Persons with Disabilities in Science and Engineering: 2013*. Special Report NSF 13-304. Arlington, VA: National Science Foundation. Available at http://www.nsf.gov/statistics/wmpd/.

National Center for Education Statistics, U.S. Department of Education (NCES). (Various Years), *Digest of Education Statistics*. Available at http://nces.ed.gov/Programs/digest/

Nelson, D. and Rogers, D. (2003), *A National Analysis of Diversity in Science and Engineering Faculties at Research Universities*. Washington, DC: National Organization for Women.

Nettles, M. and Millet, C. (2006), *Three Magic Letters: Getting to PhD*. Baltimore, MD: Johns Hopkins Press.

Nordic Research Board (NORBAL). (2008), 'Statistics on Awarded Doctoral Degrees and Doctoral Students in the Baltic Countries'. Available at http://www.nordforsk.org/en/news/new-norbal-statistics-slight-decrease-in-awarded-doctoral-degrees-753.

Nussbaum, M. (2003), 'Women's education: A global challenge', *Signs: Journal of Women in Culture and Society*, 29, (2), 325–55.

Osborn, M. (1994), 'Status and prospects of women in science and Europe', *Science*, 263, (5152), 1389–91.

Paludi, M. A. and Strayer, L. A. (1985), 'What's in an author's name? Differential evaluations of performance as a function of author's name', *Sex Roles*, 12, 353–61.

Pedro, J. D., Wolleat, P., Fennema, E. and Becker, A. D. (1981), 'Election of high school mathematics by females and males: Attribution and attitudes', *American Educational Research Journal*, 18, 207–18.

Phillips, K. W., Kim-Jun, S. Y. and Shim, S. (2011), 'The value of diversity in organizations: A social psychological perspective', in David De Cremer, Rolf van Dick and J. Keith Murnighan (eds.) *Social Psychology and Organizations*. New York: Routledge, 253–71.

Preston, A. (2004), *Leaving Science: Occupational Exit from Scientific Careers*. New York: Russell Sage Foundation.

Rahm, J. and Charbonneau, P. (1997), 'Probing stereotypes through students' drawings of scientists', *American Journal of Physics*, 65, (8), 774–78.

Rodgers, Y. and Woerdeman, D. (2006), 'Work styles, attitudes, and productivity of scientists in the Netherlands and United Kingdom: A comparison by gender', *Management Revue*, 17, (2), 184–202.

Sen, A. (1999), *Development as Freedom*. New York, NY: Knopf Publishing.

Simpson, R. D. and Oliver, J. S. (1990), 'A summary of the major influences on attitude toward and achievement in science among adolescent students', *Science Education*, 74, 1–18.

Sonnert, G. and Holton, G. (1995), *Who Succeeds in Science? The Gender Dimension*. New Brunswick, NJ: Rutgers University Press.

Steinpreis, R. E., Anders, K. A. and Ritzke, D. (1999), 'The impact of gender on the review of the curricular vitae of job applicants and tenure candidates: A national empirical study', *Sex Roles*, 41, 509–28.

Tomaskovic-Devey, D. (1993), *Gender and Racial Inequality at Work: The Sources and Consequences of Job Segregation*. Ithaca, NY: ILR Press (an imprint of Cornell University Press).

Trower, C. and Bleak, J. (2004), *Study of New Scholars, Gender: Statistical Report*. Cambridge, MA: Harvard Graduate School of Education.

Valian, V. (2008), 'Women in science – and elsewhere', in A. M. May (ed.) *The 'Woman Question' and Higher Education: Perspectives on Gender and Knowledge Production in America*. Cheltenham, UK and Northampton, MA: Edward Elgar Publishing, 93–101.

Wenneras, C. and Wold, A. (1997), 'Nepotism and sexism in peer-review', *Nature*, 387 (22 May), 341–43.

Xie, Y. and Shauman, K. (2003), *Women in Science: Career Processes and Outcomes*. Cambridge, MA: Harvard University Press.

Appendix: Duncan Index and gender concentration quotient

The Duncan Index (DI) describes the proportion of all women or men in the sample who would have to change fields of inquiry in order to equalize the distributions of fields between men and women. The DI, which is commonly used to describe the extent of occupational segregation in the workforce, is defined as:

$$DI = \tfrac{1}{2} \Sigma_i \left| \alpha_{mi} - \alpha_{fi} \right|$$

where α_{mi} is the share of male graduate students in the sample enrolled in field i, α_{fi} is the share of female graduate students in the sample enrolled in the same field i, and i sums across all fields of inquiry. The DI ranges from zero (complete integration) to one (complete segregation). For example, if women make up 46 per cent of all graduate students, an index of zero would mean that women make up 46 per cent of the graduate students in any given field of inquiry. Alternatively, an index of one would indicate total enrolment segregation by sex; and an index of 0.75 would mean that three quarters of women would need to change fields for an equal representation of women and men by field.

The Gender Concentration Quotient (GCQ) in each field *i* is:

$$GCQ_i = F_{i\,/}\,F_i^*,\ where\ F_i^* = \alpha_{mi} \times TF.$$

In this case, F_i is the actual number of female graduate students enrolled in field *i* and F_i^* is the expected number of female graduate students enrolled in field *i* if women were enrolled in field *i* in the same proportion that men are enrolled in field *i*. Thus, F_i^* is derived by taking the proportion of male graduate students enrolled in field *i* (α_{mi}) multiplied by the total number of female graduate students in all fields of study. The GCQ allows us to examine the actual number of women enrolled in a field, compared to the expected number of women who would be enrolled if women were distributed among fields in the same proportions that men are distributed among fields. As such, the GCQ utilizes what economic historians refer to as a counterfactual framework – a framework that compares actual female enrolment patterns with a hypothetical pattern that would exist if women were enrolled in fields in the same proportions as men.

The GCQ can be interpreted in the following manner. If the GCQ in a particular field is greater than one, then more women are enrolled in that field than would be expected on the basis of men's enrolment patterns. If the GCQ is equal to one, then the number of women that are enrolled in that field equals the number expected on the basis of men's enrolment patterns. And, if the GCQ is less than one, then fewer women are enrolled in that field than would be expected on the basis of men's enrolment patterns. Thus, a GCQ greater than one represents a female-dominated field; less than one represents a male-dominated field; and equal to one represents a field in which men and women are roughly equally represented given their overall enrolment in graduate school. The GCQ provides information about whether a particular field retains more women than would be expected, given the enrolment patterns of men. The GCQ allows us to identify fields which are male-dominated (those with a low GCQ), female-dominated (those with a high GCQ), or integrated (those in with GCQ equal to one). In addition to allowing us to identify these three categories of fields, the GCQ has the advantage of providing a continuous measure of the degree of segregation across fields in graduate school.

4 Nineteenth-Century Social Reform, Gender Politics and the Contemporary Indian Education System

Rumina Sethi

Chapter Outline

The issue of education exists not outside the ambit of sexual politics but within it. Feminist criticism attempts to dismantle the unsettled debates of the gendered subject caught in the crossfire of patriarchal traditions and policy change. This chapter uses a historical lens to examine the issue of women's education in India. Analysing how debates on women's education were first framed in the nineteenth century, a period of intense political awakening and rapid social transformation during colonialism, in which centuries old traditions relating to the subordination of minorities were being interrogated, the chapter will trace the links between the nationalist agenda of the nineteenth century and contemporary educational frameworks.

The upliftment of women through education was among the priorities of social reformers, a cause that was linked with the history of India's struggle for freedom. A free India could hardly have contained disempowered women. I have argued here that the initiation of women's education and the designing of a curricula have been conceptualized within the nationalist stereotypes that were being fashioned at that time. From Rammohan Roy to Mahatma Gandhi, nationalist ideology focused on the symbology of the maternal woman, leading to a pattern of education that would safeguard such role playing. Education strategically had to reflect the nationalist agenda. The nationalist patriarchy intended women's education to serve as a means to create educated mothers who could, in turn, produce educated sons. It may be noted that reform movements were operational only in British India, mainly Bengal, which is my focus in the first part of the chapter. My analysis works its way through women's subversive literature in nineteenth-century Bengal to a confrontation with distinguished commissions and committees operating in free India that set the guidelines for preparing school and university syllabi sensitive to the putative need to empower women.

British initiatives and women's education

Early nineteenth-century writing by missionaries reveals how 'Hindoos' perceived women would become presumptuous and proud or engage in 'clandestine correspondence' and 'most certainly become ... widow[s]' if they were afforded an education (Ward, 1818, p. 598). An educated woman would not only bring disrepute to her family by the loss of her 'feminine' qualities but also develop the desire to exercise her rights in choosing a husband. Education was sure to create disharmony with tradition and disrupt the domain of domesticity by encouraging women to disregard, in the words of Bal Gangadhar Tilak, their 'rightful place' (qtd. in Basu, 2005, p. 184). Education was thus virtually taboo for the nineteenth-century Indian woman, leaving the way open for the British to make the initial efforts in promoting it. The ingress of the British system of education was not intended as such to initiate social reform as much as it was to introduce evangelism and the 'english-medium' in Indian society, both of which would serve hegemonically as 'tactical maneuver[s] in the consolidation of power' (Viswanathan, 1989, p. 2).

In the early nineteenth century, there was thus hardly any enrolment of girls in the local schools of Bengal, although there existed *pathshalas*, or schools, for young boys. In 1835, Rev. William Adam recorded that some form of education for women was initiated in Calcutta by a certain Calcutta Female Juvenile Society, later called the Calcutta Baptist Female Society (1835). He recounts that there were other schools also in Chitpore and Sibpore enrolling up to 120 girl students who were taught reading, spelling and geography and, of course, religious instruction.[1] Adam goes on to write that six of the 'Christian girls' had begun to learn English, implying thereby that Hindu girls from upper castes did not attend school (Adam, 1835, p. 51). He adds, however, that '[n]ative ladies of the most respectable caste in society have themselves expressed anxiety to obtain instruction. The system of instruction pursued is also stated to have met the express concurrence and approbation of some of the most distinguished among the native gentry and religious instructors'. But in actual fact, '[t]he majority of the more respectable natives... still continue[d] to manifest great apathy concerning the education of their daughters' (Adam, 1835, p. 53). In another report written a year later, Adam states that the 'notion of providing the means of instruction for female children never enter[ed] into the minds of parents' (Adam, 1836, p. 64).

In 1853, it was reported by Colonel Jacob that not 'a single female ha[d] come under the government system of education yet' although John Bethune, the President of the Council of Education, had set up a girls' school in Calcutta in 1849 to encourage the education of women (qtd. in Basu, 2005, p. 187). Bethune's Hindu Female School, with Ishwarchandra Vidyasagar notably as its secretary, did manage to recruit the daughters of several social reformers. Though 'respectable' people still frowned upon educating their daughters, by the 1860s, prominent voices in Bengal, such as those of Keshub Chander Sen, had begun to uphold the importance of women's education. Sen was a leader of the Brahmo Samaj, a reformist society among the Hindus that was institutionalized by early social reformers such as Debendranath Tagore and Rammohan Roy. Even as education was a means to enlightenment, assurances had to be offered to the patriarchy that the end of women's education would be that of fostering better mothers and wives. Thus, we see from the very beginning that the proposal to educate women was caught between two irreconcilable positions: the sheer modernity of one was contradicted by the traditionalism of the other.

The rationale of nationalism

The 1860s witnessed intense speculation about the status of women in Indian society, particularly relating to social evils like *sati*, or self-immolation, by women; *purdah*, or veil; child marriage and the oppression of widows. In their debates on social reform, Ishwarchandra Vidyasagar and, earlier, Rammohan Roy, argued endlessly about these issues, although women's education and the curricula in schools and colleges were debated too. Yet, it was India's national struggle, with its tentative beginnings in the late nineteenth century, that may be linked to the so-called 'coming out' of women. It was the progressive face of nationalism that urgently required enlightened thinking in what had so far been a feudal society.

In the environment of flux characterizing the nineteenth century, the burden of epitomizing the concept of change lay with women (Chatterjee, 1993, p. 135). Like everything else, a 'new' woman had to be fashioned. Education for women was included in the agendas promoted by men with the express purpose of creating such a woman. Yet, she could not be the embodiment of change because nationalism, and with it, the promotion of education, was a modern movement that would have to be accepted as one of the 'gifts of civilization' accorded by a 'material' West. National identity had to retain the strength of antiquity for the sake of national pride as much as to vaunt its new-fangled modernity. Women were to become the expression of this dichotomy – an aspect within cultural nationalism that was inherently regressive.

The ideology relating to the 'new' woman was concomitant with the cultural construction of a free India as essentially spiritual. Women as the image of the quintessential spiritual component of national culture worked conjointly with the Hindu discourse of woman as the chaste, nurturing mother. References have often been made to the status of women as 'Container' in the nationalist discourse and as 'the repository of Indian (Hindu) tradition, the essence, the "inner" side, the spirituality and greatness of Hindu civilization'.[2] The link between woman-as-mother and Mother India serves the important function of staking claim to the land of one's birth, which has been forcibly controlled by foreigners.[3] Nationalist discourse, thus, capitalizes on the symbol of Mother India. [4] Gandhi, of course, perpetuated this bourgeois notion to the hilt. Even as he sought social reform, his gaze remained fixed on the symbology of the mother so that women entered public life primarily to play maternal roles. His image of the Indian woman remained an essentialized one, an unchanging and passive picture of womanhood that undoubtedly possessed freedom but only within 'narrow parameters and well defined boundaries' (Kishwar, 1985, p. 1692). The pointers are towards the traditional, upper-caste Hindu woman who is represented as sacrificing, passive and eternally giving.

The dichotomy of the material/spiritual corresponded with the outer/inner worlds of being: since the material lay outside, it was unimportant. What was important was the inner world, the *ghar* (home) as opposed to the *bahir* (outside/the world) (Chatterjee, 1993, p. 120). Since women traditionally stayed at home, they began to symbolize the *ghar*, whereas men, who dirtied their hands in the outer material world, came to represent the *bahir*. Such was the tenacity of belief in traditional gender roles.[5]

Within such a terrain of nationalist culture, what could the 'new' woman hope to be? The 'new' woman would be the cause of enormous lament since she would turn out to be considerably westernized. Male patriarchy, undoubtedly, would relate women's current 'laziness' and 'refinement' to the fancy ideas imbibed from 'western' education.[6] As Chatterjee writes, modernity would have to be made 'consistent with the nationalist project' (1993, p. 121). In other words, the 'new' woman had to be first constructed, and then derided, since she appeared to have abandoned the traditional principles of faith, hospitality and charity.

There was thus a prodigious amount of 'normative' literature that was written during these years, concentrating on the 'making' of women through what was constituted 'fit' behaviour (Tharu and Lalitha, 1991, pp. 164–65). Modernization was certainly not on the agenda. And yet, paradoxically, education was. This was probably the origin of the equation that would be created between modernization and westernization. Education, therefore, had to be tempered with a kind of reform that was not modern. The only way out was to 'Indianize' the curriculum and make it representative of the spiritual potential of India, as exemplified through its womankind (Bhog, 2002, p. 1639).

Feminine subjects: Faithful wives and chaste mothers

In an essay about the education of women in pre-independence India, Karuna Chanana links the curriculum designed for women with the roles that they were intended to assume and perform. Just as education trained boys for certain types of jobs, homemaking and mothering skills took precedence in education for women. Since they were 'only going to get married', an education in domestic science, to advance such talents, was the order of the day. All other kinds of education for girls were considered a 'wastage' (Chanana, 1988, p. 96). Although most reformers argued that educated women would educate society, underlying such proclamations was the view that women were, at best, domestic props of the family structure. Such a view bespeaks of the intention (conscious or otherwise) to perceive womanhood as 'an asserted or desired, not an actual, cultural continuity' (Sangari and Vaid, 1989, p. 17). That is why, in spite of promoting women's education, the curriculum could not but bolster such 'role socialization' (Chanana, 1988, p. 118).

The reformist arguments about the kind of education that would be imparted to women was also related to the zeal with which British missionaries were promoting their *cause célèbre* – proselytization – which could only be advanced through the education of both men and women. The fear of conversion would prevent many a reformer from pressing for more schools for girls or even insist upon some kind of conservative, orthodox curriculum, which would impart to girls lessons in music, nursing, midwifery, needle work and home science. There was very little variance in this regard between Hindus and Muslims, except for the teaching of the Quran. As Sir Sayyid Ahmad Khan, who founded the Aligarh Muslim University, declared to the Indian Education Commission in 1882:

> The question of female education much resembles the question of the oriental philosopher who asked whether the egg or the hen were first created. Those who hold that women should be educated and civilized prior to the men are greatly mistaken. The fact is that no satisfactory education can be provided for Muhammadan females until a large number of Muhammadan males receive a sound education. The present state of education among Muhammadan females is, in my opinion, enough for domestic happiness. (qtd. in Minault, 2012, p. 113)

The reformist initiative to educate women, though only in a certain way, was considered necessary for the upbringing of children because only those women who were educated would be able to impart discipline and moral goodness. In all of this, *purdah* would not be questioned, since education could be brought to the veiled woman and yet disseminated to coming generations (Minault, 2012, p. 126). Secular Muslim novelists of the nineteenth century, like Nazir Ahmad and Khwaja Altaf Husain Hali – the latter especially known for creating Zubaida Khatun, an exceptional woman character in his novel *Majalis un-Nissa* – would ultimately promote the conservative view that women were to become better wives and mothers and good practitioners of their religion through education. Significantly, the books of both Ahmad and Hali were approved as textbooks for girls by the British Indian government. Reform was thus institutionalized to an extent.

Tradition versus modernity

The desire for a need-based curriculum for girls first surfaced in 1882. This may well be the start of the academic differentiation between 'masculine' and 'feminine' subjects, the former including mathematics, physics and chemistry while the latter consisted of a host of household skills (Chanana, 1988, p. 117).[7] It appears that women were being trained to play the roles of wives and mothers concomitantly with the nationalist reconstruction of motherhood in that very period. Thus, although there were raging debates on the construction of the 'new' woman through new educational curricula, its subject matter could not be allowed to destabilize and derail the prevailing power equations that existed in the nineteenth-century family structure. There would have to be, then, the induction of 'feminine' subjects in fashioning an ideal woman suited to the national sensibility.

Significantly, this affords a confrontation between the 'ideals of education' and the 'ideals of womanhood' (Karlekar, 1988, p. 133). Education, which is intended to establish egalitarianism and a freedom of the mind, had to be balanced with a division of labour between men and women, acceptable within Indian society. Since education for a career, involving examinations, would be an arduous undertaking for a woman who had to perform her primary duties first, a syllabus that adapted well with their prescribed roles appeared to be better suited. A *zenana* education conducted by women tutors within the home, involving the rudiments of home science, would do very well indeed.

So compulsive was the ideology relating to women's education that reformers themselves reacted strongly to any radical attempt to create equality between men and women. In her exhaustive study of curriculum reform, Karlekar recounts the acerbic, even hysterical, reaction of men belonging to Keshub Chander Sen's free-thinking Brahmo Samaj when Dwarkanath Ganguly, a high-caste Brahmin from Bengal, tried to put several women through the education system (1988, pp. 135–40). Among them was Kadambini, one of the first women graduates of Calcutta University in 1882, who was later to become his wife. Kadambini became a successful doctor, who was also inducted into the Indian National Congress in 1885 when Ganguly pressed for women's representation in politics. Judging from our standpoint today, Kadambini must have been a remarkable role model for the nineteenth-century woman. It turns out, however, that her efforts were perceived to be a defiance of all norms of respectability, since she had not only breached the limits set for women's studies by venturing successfully into medicine but also diminished the virtues of homemakers. Such women were likely to desecrate the social fabric of Indian womanhood with their 'free' ideas of modernity. In other words, women like Kadambini were a threat to the chastity of Indian women. Croft's *Review of Education* reports that so great was the apprehension to 'native gentlemen' if 'the women of the country [began] to be educated and [learn] independence' that they feared it would lead to 'harassing times' involving the 'loosening of social ties, the upheaval of customary ways, and by prolonged and severe domestic embarrassment' (Croft, 1888, p. 278).[8]

The thirty years from 1860 to 1890 were rent with conflicting voices as reformers pursued their own protocols: while Dwarkanath Ganguly and his associate, Sibnath Sastri, argued for equal opportunities, those like Keshub Chander Sen and other Brahmos maintained the need to study separate subjects and limit levels of education for women to stall the deleterious effects of a higher education.[9] The nineteenth-century woman, particularly the Bengali *bhadramahila* (genteel Bengali woman), had to conform to 'the stereotype of the well-educated yet unquestioning docile girl' to minimize the 'liberating potential of education' (Karlekar, 1988, p. 145). Two of Rabindranath Tagore's novels, *Nashta Neer* (The Broken Nest) (1901) and *Ghare Baire* (The Home and the World) (1916) are testimonies of women seeking higher education, resulting in the breakdown of their married lives and families.[10] Both heroines, Charulata and Bimala, wives of men who are encouraged to step beyond conservatism, are products of the uncertainty of those times. An educated woman bore the risk of becoming all-powerful, as she would carry the possibility of trampling upon *purusha,* or man. The use of the 'new' woman in conceptualizing a new nation thus became both fascinating and terrifying, fruitful and disrupting, because while a transformatory model could dispel a disappointing history and posit an India free from foreign representation, it also presupposed a changed social order. On the one hand, national identity could be claimed by mobilizing representations and memories of a mythical and timeless past based on ideological representations; on the other, these very representations would '[militate] against the restlessness of modernity' (Zutshi, 1993, pp. 135–36).

The absence of any form of politicization in the issue of women's education for almost a hundred years is related to the easy manner in which they were spoken for and appropriated by the reformers of both pre- and post-independent India, including a large number of women like Sarojini Naidu and Annie Besant.[11] It is here that the categories of 'thematic' and 'problematic' in a nation-state, which Partha Chatterjee describes in *Nationalist Thought and the Colonial World*, can be evoked (1986, p. 38). The 'thematic', in our context here, may be identified with the construction of the maternal Hindu woman, a mother of sons, whereas the 'problematic' would be constituted by the urgent need for 'progress', 'reason' and 'modernity' – principles imbibed from the West. The latter would eliminate the possibility of the nation's thematic agenda that carried the symbology of women-as-mothers, unless the former was maintained and protected at all costs. It is thus that the question of women's education can neither be liberated from, nor resolved within, the reformist agendas of nationalism.

It is striking that throughout the period of social reform, it was generally assumed that women were an inert category that needed the existing patriarchy to decide ways of alleviating their problems. These were largely identified to be the evils of *purdah* and child marriage and those relating to the degraded state of widows and lack of education. But perhaps social reformers were out of touch with what women really wanted, since 'except for child marriage the other problems taken up by the reform movement meant nothing to them' (Mazumdar, 1976, p. 64). This was mainly because the focus of social reform – widow remarriage, and the end of *purdah* and *sati* – did not predominantly affect the majority of Indian women.[12] As Tharu and Lalitha report, these were problems of a very small percentage of women that comprised the upper caste (1991, pp. 150–1). Sati was practiced among the Rajputs, though later it was known to have been also followed by the Brahmins of Bengal. Again, as far as the plight of widowhood was concerned, non-Brahmin women were better off than Brahmin women as they did not have to observe diet restrictions and practice self-control to absurd limits. Widow remarriage, too, was a problem pertaining to the upper- and middle-class groups, not just with the Hindus but also among people of other religions.[13] This makes one wonder where the focus of social reform lay. Clearly, it was upper-caste women whose difficulties and disabilities were addressed.[14] The same pattern is perceived when the question of education among women is concerned: 'it was the education of these women from the upper strata that was at issue' (Tharu and Lalitha, 1991, p. 151).[15] As for girls belonging to the lower castes, it was not difficult to induce them to come to school (Croft, 1888, p. 279). It was for this reason that the issue of women's education remained 'rather flat' all through the nineteenth century (John, 2008, p. 305). Although women's education was part of the agenda of the social reformers, it was really the radical *shudra* leader Jyotiba Phule who pioneered the earliest school for lower caste girls (*shudra* and *atishudra*) in the 1840s in Maharashtra. He had to struggle to overcome the hostility of upper-caste orthodox Brahmins.

Against the grain: Subversive writings by women

Critics have often pointed out that while the discourse of nineteenth-century reform was about women, women themselves scarcely spoke about their equality or freedom (Chatterjee, 1993, p. 133). Social reform initiated by men was more in the nature of moral policing. This is evinced from the mushrooming of a number of writings by women who denounced and transformed male agendas. While the reformists had deplored the atrocity of custom that could be so unfavourable to women, the texts that women produced turned to education as a means of autonomy and self-dependence in contrast to the condemnation of other barbarous practices that had conspired to subordinate them. In fact, the assertion of widow remarriage or the illegitimacy of *sati* was low in priority in comparison with the desire to educate themselves: 'In the women's journals . . . purdah was seen more as an obstacle to education, and as part of a larger oppressive system, than as a blot on a nation's self-respect' (Tharu and Lalitha, 1991, p. 168).

In such a claustrophobic environment, women had to learn to read and write in secrecy, through what Rashsundari Debi calls 'jitakshara', or 'mastery over the word', in her autobiography *Amar Jiban* (My Life) (1876; Sarkar, 1999, p. 4). Rashsundari (1809–1900), an upper-caste woman, had to abandon her schooling owing to an early marriage and teach herself through the recognition of the alphabet learnt long ago in childhood. Despite household chores and the demands of the many children she bore, she succeeded in writing her autobiography. *Amar Jiban*, perhaps the first autobiography ever to be written in the Bengali language and certainly the first by a Bengali woman, recounts the household experiences of Rashsundari, and as such, is hardly eventful. A close reading, however, exposes the transgressions, desire for freedom and misery of having to bring up children – all of which may be discovered by uncovering its subtleties.

Rashsundari declares at the outset of her narrative: 'I have spent such a very long time in this Bharatbarsha since I came here. This body, this mind, this very life of mine, have taken on several different forms' (Sarkar, 1999, p. 140). One might ponder over the possible ironic and wry implications of Rashsundari's use of 'Bharatbarsha', or 'India', which imposes a tradition of nurturing and mothering upon her that becomes the cause of her endless suffering. She appears to be implying that the India where she spent almost a century already existed, but the world she inhabited was not the one in which she lived. She lived, on the other hand, in a world of her own, a forbidden space of dreams and fantasies. Her reference of living in a more generalized place – 'India' – removes her from precise locations and local time, creating a spatial abstraction, for Rashsundari does not mention any outdoor locales or even homely settings in this 'self-absorbed' chronicle (Sarkar, 1999, pp. 8–9). At the same time, 'Bharatbarsha' may refer to the new political reality of a united India after the uprising of 1857 – an historic event never mentioned by Rashsundari – succeeding which Queen Victoria assumed the title of 'Empress of India' (1877). Taking recourse to a fluid image of India, Rashsundari's focus on time, which is not 'real' worldly time, her indifference to politics and to other events – all indicate her determination to free herself from the concept of 'Indian' motherhood, at least in the world of imagination.

Despite being fortunate to have a reasonably kind husband and mother-in-law, not least because she had begotten many sons, Rashsundari was fettered to the miseries of a restrictive domestic life: 'I was [a] caged bird. I was now shut up in a cage and I won't ever be free again for the rest of my life' (Sarkar, 1999, p. 154). Like multitudes of upper-caste women, she slogged through household duties without a moment to herself to have her meals, quite apart from finding the leisure to read. She would often wonder why she could not have the freedom to become educated so as to be able to read religious manuscripts. In her autobiography, she registers her anguish at not having the liberty to meet her mother even as she lay dying:

> I … tried desperately to pay her a last visit, but I had no luck, it was not to be. This was not an ordinary grief! … Why was I born a woman? Shame on my life! … Had I been her son, I would fly like a bird to reach her side when I got news of her end. What was I to do, I was behind bars, I was shut up in a cage. (Sarkar, 1999, p. 167)[16]

Notwithstanding her distress, Rashsundari internalized the work ethic, which was part of the sexual division of labour of those times, and accepted patriarchal ideology without question. But at the age of twenty-five, she began to harbour a desperate desire to read and write. Perhaps this yearning arose in order to overcome the wretchedness of her life within which she was imprisoned? Acknowledging that women were despised for wanting to learn, this sensitive woman speaks of how she would 'die of shame' if she were discovered with a piece of paper in her hands (Tharu and Lalitha, p. 199). Yet, she dreams one night of having read the *Chaitanya Bhagabat*, which fills her with delight. To have dreamt of reading! The joy of subsequently finding her husband's copy, stealing a page from it, attempting to revive her memory of the alphabet learnt long ago in primary school and finally to have read it at a much older age seems to her to be nothing short of a miraculous act of God.

Rashsundari's reiteration that her inspiration seems to be coming from divine quarters leads one to speculate whether she had read any contemporary literature on reform relating to women's education (Sarkar, 1999, p. 73) or, indeed, whether social reform had succeeded in making a departure from the existing patriarchal tradition.[17] From her autobiography, she appears to be unaffected by social reform and reformists even when her thinking matches their postures (Sarkar, 1999, p. 67). Unlike Tarabai Shinde, who candidly proclaimed her condemnation of Indian nationalist social reform in her book *Stri-Purush Tulna* (A Comparison between Women and Men) (1882), Rashsundari remained outside nationalist discourse. If hers was an instance of women's education, then it predates the nationalist agenda: 'the intervention of nationalist male reformers was not required to set Rashsundari's consciousness into motion' (Chatterjee, 1993, p. 144). Her story uncovers that the 'new' woman was scarcely the creation of a nationalist agenda for social reform.

Rashsundari speaks only of a few sacred texts that she had read, such as the *Chaitanya Bhagabat*, which may have been a 'tactical' move to assert her womanly virtues of obedience and humility (Sarkar, 1999, p. 73). For the public that read her autobiography, it would probably have been a compendium of noble qualities *bhadramahilas* should possess. But Rashsundari could not have been completely oblivious to the modernity of mid-nineteenth century Bengal in which newspapers and periodicals were household items. She lets slip in her writing that 'times were very different then' (Sarkar, 1999, p. 170), since present-day Bengal was ostensibly championing the cause of education for women unlike the days of yore.[18] The printed book had come to Bengal during her lifetime. Even so, in keeping with her status as a woman, she repeatedly refers to herself as 'lowly' and 'ignorant' and yet, succeeds in producing this 'audacious act of writing about her life', exposing through an autobiography – a genre of self-revelation, which is anything but a sign of supreme humility – her life as a woman (Sarkar, 2001, p. 110).

Post-independence: A role reversal?

Until about 1921, girls were educated differently from boys: they went to separate girls' schools, were tutored by women teachers and read special textbooks for girls called *Kanya Vachan Malas* (Sharma et al., 1995, p. 277). Female literacy rose to 7.93 per cent in 1951 and then to 24.82 per cent in 1981 (National Policy on Education, 1986, p. 322). Yet, the ideology of the earliest post-independence University Education Commission of 1948–1949 did not vary much from the attitudes of nineteenth-century and early twentieth-century ideologues. In the year following India's independence, its members – all male – believed that although 'men and women are equally competent in academic work, ... it does not follow that in all things men's and women's education should be identical' (Report 1948–1949, 1963, p. 344). In a chapter curiously entitled 'Importance of Women's Education for National Life', it is reported:

> In every country, no matter how far the 'liberation' of women has gone, husbands and wives commonly play different parts. In general the man provides the income and the woman maintains the home. For many women who crave to achieve standards of excellence, the home provides an excellent setting. For a woman to give the home design, beauty, order and character, without being herself a slave to home-keeping ... is a high art. It will not be acquired by chance, and for many women its acquisition will be impossible, except through education. (Report 1948–1949, 1963, p. 344)

The 'ideals of womanhood', no doubt, were still uppermost in the minds of stalwarts like S. Radhakrishnan and Zakir Hussain – members of this committee – who felt that the essentials of education must meet the national needs. The Report goes on to list the inventory necessary for 'practical "laboratory" experience' since a woman 'is' and will 'continue to be' a homemaker: a baby home, a nursery school, a club for school children and adolescents, a home for convalescents, a small home for the old, and so on.[19] The subjects that would be taught in school, accordingly, would be Home Economics, Nursing, Teaching and Fine Arts (Report 1948–1949, 1963, pp. 344–9).

The Commission of 1948–1949 was followed by the National Council for Women's Education on the Differentiation of Curricula for Boys and Girls in

1962. For the first time, perhaps, this committee, presided over by Hansa Mehta, clarified that there was no such factor as the 'female aptitude' that could determine the division between a 'masculine' and a 'feminine' syllabus (Sharma et al., 1995, pp. 296–7, 306). Yet, certain 'hard realities' based on social and psychological differences were taken for granted in the 'transitional phase', since a change in thinking was not possible imminently (Sharma et al., 1995, p. 311). The Kothari Commission (1966) made similar ambiguous statements soon after; though it asserted equality between the sexes and declared women's education to be more important than men's, it also emphasized that women were duty-bound to undertake the 'dual role of home-making and following a suitable career' (Kothari, 1970, p. 224). It was urged that they should be schooled in 'teaching, nursing and social service' where they could play 'useful' roles (Kothari, 1970, p. 225). The coming-of-age of Indian women was tantamount to holding a dual responsibility: she would not only provide financial stability but also bring up children. Although educated, like men, she would have to inhabit both the *ghar* and the *bahir*. The 1975 Report of the Committee on the Status of Women in India chaired by Phulrenu Guha went on to suggest that women should have 'full opportunity', yet make their choices according to their 'local conditions, needs and aptitudes' (Sharma et al., 1995, p. 360). Ten years later, the Commission for Planning of Higher Education in West Bengal indulged in unparalleled conformity when it urged the institutionalization of Home Science colleges which, it was stressed, was the need of the hour (Karlekar, 1988, pp. 154–5).

Recent trends in education are pretty much a representation of patterns laid out by commissions and committees. It is evinced that fewer women choose to become engineers, mathematicians and scientists, as science subjects are often not taught after matriculation in girls' schools; in sports, girls are seldom encouraged to play games like football; most women who do not succeed in entering engineering colleges resort to arts and humanities. There seems to be an imperceptible profiling of both sexes that leads women to be less competitive than men, which may be the result of prioritizing housekeeping over employment.

It must be added that even during primary and secondary schooling, when girls and boys are less likely to behave prescriptively, school curricula sets standards of behaviour. Literature textbooks, particularly, are full of stories of 'adventurous' and 'courageous' boys and 'frail' and 'defenseless' girls. The class VII English textbook taught in Indian schools has ten chapters, of which nine contain stories about men. Men harvest crops, invent things, climb trees or fight fires – as such, they are 'doers' – whereas 'the wife' plays second fiddle by handing the man his tools or bustling about the house (Honeycomb, 2006). These stories are accompanied by illustrations that reinforce the written word. In the Hindi textbook for the same class of students, there are four chapters on heroic men – Mahatma Gandhi, the father of the nation; Rahim Das, famous for his couplets; 'Veer' (Brave) Kunwar Singh, champion of the 1857 insurrection against the British; and Dhanraj Pillai, former captain of the Indian hockey team – against one small poem on women entitled 'Kathputli' (puppet) by Bhawaniprasad Mishra. The female puppet wonders why she is tied up with strings instead of being supported on her feet (Basant, Part 2, 2006, p. 19). One look at the Contents reveals that with the exception of two authors – Mahadevi Verma and Mirabai – the rest are all male. In *Basant*, Part 3 (2007), which is prescribed for class VIII students, Ismat Chugtai is the only female author among seventeen male authors.

Essays on female warrior figures like Rani Lakshmibai of Jhansi, which are also part of school textbooks, are exceptions that go against the stereotype, but even the Rani, who fought valiantly against the British in 1858, is customarily featured with an infant son tied tightly on her back while she brandishes her sword on horseback, clearly not forsaking her duties as a mother.[20] The Rani is also given to spirituality: we are told she prays a great deal. Unlike the men whose stories are related in school textbooks – Mahatma Gandhi, Jawaharlal Nehru, and so on – women heroines are plagued by self-doubt, which they overcome by saying their prayers (Bhog, 2002, p. 1641). School children are thereby fed notions of gendering through such pedagogy. One of the fallouts of such indoctrination is the gravitation of women towards 'safe' jobs such as teaching, typing or secretarial work, which are 'suitable' for women and which allow them to perform a 'dual role'. There tend to be fewer men in such professions because men favour engineering, business, management or architecture according to the 'masculine' roles into which they are socialized.

In the last fifty years, education has been the fulcrum around which reform in the status of women has been initiated. The National Perspective Plan for Women (1988–2000) on women's education states unequivocally:

> In order to neutralize the accumulated distortions of the past, there will be a well-conceived edge in favour of women. The National Education System will play a positive interventionist role in the empowerment of women. It will foster the development of new values through redesigned curricula, textbooks, training and orientation of teachers, decision-makers and administrators. (p. 177)

In sheer contrast, the National Curriculum Framework (NCF) of 2000 constituted by the National Council of Education, Research and Training (NCERT), an organization that sets the standards for academic text books in Indian schools, exhibits a 'deep anxiety' about the direction that education has been taking (Bhog, 2002, p. 1639). The NCF document claims that the 'discontinuities' introduced by Western education have betrayed India's 'religio-philosophic ethos', since British education ushered in the trend of 'single parents' and 'unmarried relationships' through the demolition of the traditional extended family structure, commonly known as the 'joint family' system (NCF, 2000, p. 5). The consummate design of the NCF, through its introductory pages, sets the tone for the creation of an 'Indian' education system inclined towards a traditional, agrarian society, in contrast to a Western education system, where the latter is 'defined simply as a challenge to established authority' (Bhog, 2002, p. 1639).

So it is that students' 'SQ' (Spiritual Quotient) will be put to test alongside their 'IQ' (Intelligence Quotient), since a 'constant erosion of the essential social, moral and spiritual values' (NCF, 2000, p. 13) has been witnessed since independence. To inculcate this kind of value education, students have to be tutored in all religions. Considering that nineteenth-century liberalists and revivalists alike insisted upon the value of spirituality, the new curriculum might perhaps be perpetuating a narrow nationalism that underwrites gender-specific identities.

In the 'Education of Girls' section of the NCF, the phrase 'Education for Women's Equality and Empowerment' is privileged over 'Equality of Educational Opportunity', as advanced by the National Policy on Education in 1968, thereby attempting to remove all kinds of gender bias in school textbooks. Yet, it states the need 'to recognize and nurture the *best feature of each gender in the best Indian tradition*' (NCF, 2000, p. 8, my emphasis). The directive boasts of India giving its women 'the right to vote without any prolonged battle for it unlike in the west' (NCF, 2000, p. 8). These statements that besmirch British education, which allegedly tears down family values, must be placed side by side with the narcissistic politics of an earlier nationalism. Here, in India, the NCF seems to suggest, there is a complementarity of roles that men and women play according to ancient tradition, roles that are best suited to their station as men and women. Thus, Indian women, unlike their Western counterparts, will not need to protest, because like the right to vote, the patriarchy would grant them 'their legitimate dues in the natural course' (Bhog, 2002, p. 1639). A new kind of education, then, for the next generation's 'new' woman, is on the anvil.

Conclusion: Changing a shared value system

Under the University Grants Commission (UGC), sixty-seven centres for Women's Studies have been established in universities and colleges in India since 1986 to bring gender consciousness to educational institutions. The *Guidelines for the Development of Women's Studies* for the IX Plan, drawn by the UGC, uses the phrase 'feminist identity', perhaps, for the first time (1997–2002, p. 11). In the UGC *Guidelines* for the XI Plan, the desire to initiate a 'gender perspective' is proposed by linking women's studies with the curriculum of other departments (2007–2012, p. 6). Concurrently, it is recommended that women's studies be introduced at the master's level with core courses in feminist theory, in which debates and discussions on patriarchy, family and gender would be initiated (*Guidelines*, 2007–2012, pp. 8–9).

Further changes in the curriculum are now underway in an endeavour to change the male 'mindset', first in the educational sphere and thereafter among the general populace. This is so because of the enormous increase in crimes committed against women. For instance, in a country where rape has increased by 875 per cent since the beginning of records relating to rape forty years ago, it may be claimed with some certainty that there exists a correlation between the gendered nature of our education system, which I have attempted to trace from the nineteenth century, and the status of our women. I write this keeping in mind the recent rape and death of Jyoti Singh Pandey, a twenty-three year old Delhi-based student, who was raped and diabolically brutalized by six men in a moving bus she had boarded with a male friend after a pleasant evening at the cinema. The crime resulted in national outrage where the youth of Delhi, and virtually every other Indian city, galvanized in unprecedented support of the victim, clamouring for justice. Thereafter, the Indian government set up the Justice Verma Committee in December 2013 to make amendments to Criminal Law, after re-examining existing laws on rape. Although the men (excluding one juvenile) have been sentenced to death, there is the need to address the deeper malaise in a society where women are punished for the outrageous act of enjoying their new-found freedom. Soon after the rape, several prominent male leaders voiced their thoughts: among the usual reiteration of gender stereotypes, the remark made by Mohan Bhagawat, supreme chief of the Rashtriya Swayamsewak Sangh, a right-wing Hindu organization, played on the tradition-modernity debate. He claimed that rapes took place in 'India', not in 'Bharat', implying as though the India of the golden era (Bharat) which boasted of mythical superwomen like Sita and Savitri, was one in which women observed their limits and thus prevented crimes against themselves.[21] 'India', on the other hand, signifying urbanity – and thus Westernization – is viewed as promiscuous because of the loss of 'actual Indian values', a place where women no longer exhibit the chastity inherent in motherhood (Bhagawat, *India Today*).

This 'mindset' is arguably the result of a system of education as much as it is a consequence of various other retrogressive social factors such as caste, illiteracy and traditionalism. Curriculum change, as proposed by the Verma Committee, may be among the long-term measures that would make a departure from this shared value system. A gender-equitable curriculum in schools might bring a change in the way we bring up young boys. Keeping in mind that crimes against women are committed by men who are 'deeply uncomfortable with women displaying their independence, receiving education and joining the workforce' (Desai, 2013, p. 11), the Verma Committee has recommended that an evaluation of the education system be made, whereby 'replication and consensus' would be resisted (Verma et al., *Report*, p. 383). While centres for women's studies are set up in colleges and universities, it is in schools, both at primary and secondary levels, that 'femininity' and 'masculinity' are reinforced.[22] The act of merely admitting more girls to schools is not the panacea; rather, filtering the 'language of sexism' from reading material and checking the lopsided representation of men and women in school textbooks would be a productive method of checking gender bias (Verma et al., *Report*, p. 402). Gender sensitivity amounts to both including stories about heroic women as much as correcting the skewed representation of women authors, so that young children recognize that women are active agents and are also academically skilled. Article 21A of the Indian Constitution, which defines the fundamental right to a free and compulsory education for children, would have to incorporate 'the right to gender mainstreaming' so that education can promote a 'transformative potential' in the true sense (Verma et al., *Report*, p. 410).

The feminist analytical practice attempts to expose the site as well as the mode of enunciation of dominant ideologies such as patriarchy, colonialism and nationalism that masquerade as the social and political consciousness of the state. Before feminist politics establishes itself into a recognizable and substantial theoretical field, its inherent interrogation of 'who speaks for whom', or in other words, 'the discovery of representation itself' is an effective way forward (John, 1989, p. 63). The journey of women's education that I have charted speaks predominantly about the patriarchal agendas fashioned out of the dilemmas posed by tradition and modernity. In spite of the ambivalence that postpones the departure of a masculinist state politics, the need for an articulation of a multitude of women's voices, which largely remain unheard in the interstices of history, cannot be undermined.

Acknowledgements

I am indebted to Ranjini Mendis for editing and proofreading this paper and offering many insightful suggestions.

Notes

1 It is not clear what kind of religious instruction was taught but it must have been Christianity (in mission schools).

2 Pandey (1993, p. 260). Pandey also quotes from Swami Shraddhanand, an Arya Samaj reformer and militant nationalist in the 1920s, on the status of women in Hindu discourse: 'Every child of the Matri-Bhumi [Motherland] may daily bow before the Mother and renew *his* pledge to restore *her* to the ancient pinnacle of glory from which she has fallen!' The child, Pandey ironically notes, is apparently male (p. 259).

3 See also Bankimchandra Chatterjee's early nationalist text, Anandamath (1882).

4 This is represented, for instance, by Dadabhai Naoroji, who said:

> The time will come when natives generally will see the benefit of female education as a great social necessity to rise in civilization and to advance social happiness and progress; and will understand that women had as much right to exercise and enjoy all the rights, privileges and duties of this world as man .... *But that time has not come yet ... Good and educated mothers only will raise good and educated sons.* (qtd. in Bhog, 2002, pp. 1638–9)

5 In spite of being an enlightenment rationalist, even Rammohan Roy had declared that Hindu women were 'infinitely more self-sacrificing than men' as they possessed 'exemplifying wifely devotion and spiritual strength' (qtd. in Bhog, 2002, p. 1639).

6 Partha Chatterjee here alludes to a famous 1870 essay, *Prācīnā ebam nabīnā*, by the distinguished Bengali novelist of the times, Bankimchandra Chatterjee, in which modern and traditional women are contrasted. Using the medium of self-irony, Bankim deplores the way in which self-centred men have used women for their own ends. The subsequent issue of the same journal in which Bankim's essay was published carries three letters – purportedly rejoinders by women to the said article – criticizing men. Partha Chatterjee concludes that the discourse that produced this writing was entirely hegemonic and male, in that it tried 'to appropriate discordant, marginal and critical voices' (1993, p. 136).

7 It could be argued that men too were being 'role socialized', in that they were being groomed for the roles they were meant to play, the only difference being that whereas the social role for women was primarily maternal, that for men was never paternal (Chanana, 1988, pp. 122–3).

8 Croft writes further: 'The people of India at large encourage or tolerate the education of their girls only up to an age and in standards at which it can do little good or, according to the point of view, little harm' (1888, p. 279).

9 The prevalent practices of *purdah* and child marriage necessitated the seclusion of women at an age when their education had scarcely begun. Girls often left school before the age of ten in order to get married. See Croft (1888, p. 278).

10 *Nashta Neer* is set in the 1880s, while *Ghare Baire* is in the early twentieth century.

11 Naidu's famous phrase, 'The hand that rocks the cradle rules the world' bestows power to women through eulogizing motherhood (1906; Kumar, 1993, p. 50).

12 John refers to these three evils as the 'privileged issues' taken up by reformers (2008, p. 305).

13 As Mazumdar writes, 'Even Muslim reformers complained that re-marriage of widows had become "strictly taboo among the respectable classes"' (1976, p. 51).

14 In Pushpa Joshi's collection of Gandhi's writings and speeches on women, it is surprising that Gandhi has not referred even once to peasant women (1988).

15 Tharu and Lalitha go so far as to claim that it is 'not useful to consider social reform as the framework from which to write a cultural history of gender in nineteenth-century India' (1991, p. 152).

16 Many women of that time use the imagery of the caged bird. Sarkar refers to Soudamini Debi from Bakarganj who wrote in 1865:

> Why have men kept us in such a low state? Are we not the children of the Great Father? … How much longer do we stay chained to our homes?' Another anonymous woman Sarkar quotes, writes (1868): 'Must we live in chains all our lives? … Alas! Were we born in this land only to perform low tasks? … Why must we live all our lives like caged birds within the home? (1999, pp. 72–3)

17 Ghosh, through her examination of several autobiographies written by women of Bengal, believes that reform scarcely touched the life of upper-caste women (Ghosh, 1986).

18 Rashsundari also adds: 'It is good to see women having an easier time of it now. Even if someone has a daughter these days, he educates her carefully. We suffered so much just to learn to read' (Sarkar, 1999, pp. 171–2).

19 The Report of 1948–1949 echoes one of Annie Besant's statements: '[T]he *national* movement for the education of girls must be one which meets the national needs, and India needs nobly trained wives and mothers, wise and tender rulers of the household, educated teachers of the young, helpful counsellors of their husbands, skilled nurses of the sick, rather than girls [*sic*] graduates, educated for the learned professions (1904; Sen, 2008, p. 199).

20 Loomba writes that Lakshmibai has been 'vigorously celebrated as a model of female – as opposed to feminist – valour' (1991, p. 167). The Rani has also been lauded for being '*mardani*', translated as 'masculine woman' or, in this context, a woman who fought 'like a man'.

21 Sita, however, did cross the 'Lakshman Rekha' or the threshold beyond which she should not have stepped and was abducted by Ravana, the evil king of Lanka. This led to a battle between good (symbolized by her husband, Lord Rama) and evil, which is the subject of the epic *Ramayana*. Needless to say, good triumphed over evil and Sita's honour was restored.

22 For gender constructs in primary schools, see Das (2003).

Questions for reflection

a) Was the British system of education introduced to initiate social reform or was the purpose hegemonic?
b) What was the manner in which the nationalist intelligentsia used the tradition versus modernity debate in outlining the agendas of women's education in the nineteenth century?
c) Why did it become important for the nationalist patriarchy to emphasize a certain role-playing in the construction of women?
d) Do you think the various committees and commissions set up after independence helped change the shared value system that has profiled women of India?

Further Reading

Radha Kumar. (1993), *The History of Doing*. London: Verso.

This is an excellent account of the history of Indian women and their political movements, both on the personal and the national level, from the nineteenth century to the end of the twentieth. It traces women's agency and their involvement in movements against dowry, price rise, *sati* and so on.

Mani, Lata. (1987), 'Contentious traditions: The debate on sati in colonial India', *Cultural Critique*, 7, 119–56.

This article examines the legislation against *sati* in 1829, imposed by the British and impressed upon by the social reformers. Mani argues that the lengthy dialogues between the British and the reactionary opponents of the legislation focused more on the subject of the correct interpretation of Hindu tradition rather than on the issue of the widow's burning.

Radhakrishnan, R. (1992), 'Nationalism, gender, and the narrative of identity', in Andrew Parker, Mary Russo, Doris Sommer and Patricia Yaeger (eds.) *Nationalisms and Sexualities*. New York and London: Routledge.

Radhakrishnan analyses how the women's question has never been politicized owing to the easy manner in which the homogeneous discourse of nationalism appropriates the heterogeneity of their existence.

Spivak, Gayatri Chakravorty. (1988), 'Can the subaltern speak?', in Cary Nelson and Lawrence Grossberg (eds.) *Marxism and the Interpretation of Culture*. London: Macmillan, 271–313.

In this theoretical essay, Spivak controversially contends that the gendered subaltern cannot speak because both the colonial and the national discourse render women silent. In her endeavour to recover subaltern voice, she finds that elite approaches tend to appropriate any positionality of the subaltern.

Bibliography

Adam, Rev. William. (1835), *Report on the State of Education in Bengal.* Calcutta: G. H. Huttman, Bengal Military Orphan Press.

—— (1836), *Second Report on the State of Education in Bengal.* Calcutta: G. H. Huttman, Bengal Military Orphan Press.

Basant: Part 2. (2006), *Hindi Textbook for Class VII.* New Delhi: NCERT.

Basant: Part 3. (2007), *Hindi Textbook for Class VIII.* New Delhi: NCERT.

Basu, Aparna. (2005), 'A century and a half's journey: Women's education in India, 1850s to 2000', in Bharati Ray (ed.) *Women of India: Colonial and Post-Colonial Periods.* New Delhi: Sage, 183–207.

Besant, Annie. (1904), 'The education of Indian girls', in Indrani Sen (ed.), (2008) *Memsahibs' Writings: Colonial Narratives on Indian Women.* Hyderabad: Orient Longman, 197–202.

Bhagawat, Mohan. (2013), 'RSS chief Mohan Bhagawat at it again, says women should be just housewives and husbands should be the breadwinners', *India Today*, 6 January. Available at http://indiatoday.intoday.in/story/rss-mohan-bhagwat-at-it-again-says-women-should-be-just-housewives-and-husbands-should-be-the-breadwinners/1/241008.html.

Bhog, Deepta. (2002), 'Gender and curriculum', *Economic and Political Weekly*, 37, (17), 1638–42.

Chanana, Karuna. (1988), 'Social change or social reform: The education of women in pre-independence India', in Karuna Chanana (ed.) *Socialisation, Education and Women: Explorations in Gender Identity.* Hyderabad: Orient Longman and New Delhi: Nehru Memorial Museum and Library, 96–128.

Chatterjee, Bankimchandra. (1882), 'Anandamath', in Jogshchandra Bagal (ed.) *Bankim Rachanavali (1953–69).* Calcutta: Sahitya Samsad.

Chatterjee, Partha. (1986), *Nationalist Thought and the Colonial World – A Derivative Discourse?* London: Zed.

——. (1993), *The Nation and Its Fragments: Colonial and Postcolonial Histories.* New Jersey: Princeton University Press.

Croft, Sir Alfred. (1888), *Review of Education in India in 1886.* Calcutta: Superintendent of Government Printing.

Das, Shilpa. (2003), 'Gender constructs in primary school textbooks: A critique', in Ranjana Harish and V. Bharathi Harishankar (eds.) *Shakti: Multidisciplinary Perspectives on Women's Empowerment in India.* Jaipur: Rawat, 164–78.

Desai, Kishwar. (2013), 'Skimming the surfaces of sexism isn't enough', *The Indian Express*, 3 January, 11.

Ghosh, Srabashi. (1986), '"Birds in a Cage": Changes in Bengali social life as recorded in autobiographies by women', *Economic and Political Weekly*, 21, (43), 88–96.

Guidelines for Development of Women's Studies in Indian Universities and Colleges during Ninth Plan. (1997–2002), New Delhi: University Grants Commission. Available at http://www.ugc.ac.in/oldpdf/ixplanpdf/womenstudiesindianuni.pdf.

Guidelines for Development of Women's Studies in Indian Universities and Colleges during Eleventh Plan. (2007–2012), New Delhi: University Grants Commission. Available at http://www.ugc.ac.in/oldpdf/xiplanpdf/womenstudies.pdf.

Honeycomb: Textbook in English for Class VII. (2006), New Delhi: NCERT.

John, Mary E. (1989), 'Postcolonial feminists in the western intellectual field: Anthropologists and native informants?', *Inscriptions*, 5, 49–73.

——. (ed.). (2008), *Women's Studies in India: A Reader*. New Delhi: Penguin.

Joshi, Pushpa. (1988), *Gandhi on Women: Collection of Mahatma Gandhi's Writings and Speeches on Women*. New Delhi: Centre for Women's Development Studies and Navajivan.

Karlekar, Malvika. (1988), 'Women's nature and the access to education', in Karuna Chanana (ed.) *Socialisation, Education and Women: Explorations in Gender Identity*. Hyderabad: Orient Longman and New Delhi: Nehru Memorial Museum and Library, 129–65.

Kishwar, Madhu. (1985), 'Gandhi on women', *Economic and Political Weekly*, 20, (40), 1691–702.

Kothari, D. S. (1970), *Education and National Development: Report of the Education Commission, 1964–66*. New Delhi: National Council of Educational Research and Training. Available at http://www.teindia.nic.in/Files/Reports/CCR/KC/KC_V1.pdf.

Loomba, Ania. (1991), 'Overworlding the "third world"', *Oxford Literary Review*, 13, (1–2), 164–91.

Mazumdar, Vina. (1976), 'The social reform movement in India – from Ranade to Nehru', in B. R. Nanda (ed.) *Indian Women: From Purdah to Modernity*. New Delhi: Nehru Memorial Museum and Library, 41–66.

Minault, Gail. (2012), 'Educated Muslim women: Real and ideal', in Charu Gupta (ed.) *Gendering Colonial India: Reforms, Print, Caste and Communalism*. Hyderabad: Orient Blackswan, 109–35.

Naidu, Sarojini. (1906), 'What we want: Speech to the Indian social conference', in Radha Kumar (ed.) (1993), *The History of Doing*. London: Verso.

National Curriculum Framework for School Education. (2000), New Delhi: NCERT. www.eledu.net/rrcusrn_data/NCF-2000.pdf.

National Perspective Plan for Women. (1988–2000), in K. B. Powar (eds.) (1999) *Education and Women's Empowerment*. New Delhi: Association of Indian Universities, 177–92.

National Policy on Education. (1986), in Mary E. John (ed.), (2008) *Women's Studies in India: A Reader*. New Delhi: Penguin, 322–28.

Pandey, Gyanendra. (1993), 'Which of us are Hindus?', in Gyanendra Pandey (ed.) *Hindus and Others: The Question of Identity in India Today*. New Delhi: Viking, 238–71.

Report of the University Education Commission. (1948–49, 1963), Vol. 1. New Delhi: Ministry of Education, Government of India. Available at http://www.teindia.nic.in/Files/Reports/CCR/Report%20of%20the%20University%20Education%20Commission.pdf.

Sangari, Kumkum and Vaid, Sudesh (eds.). (1989), *Recasting Women: Essays in Colonial History*. New Delhi: Kali for Women.

Sarkar, Tanika (trans.). (1999), *Words to Win: The Making of Amar Jiban: A Modern Autobiography*. New Delhi: Kali for Women.

——. (2001), *Hindu Wife, Hindu Nation: Community, Religion and Cultural Nationalism*. New Delhi: Permanent Black.

Sharma, Usha and Sharma, B. M. (eds.). (1995), *Committees and Commissions on Women Education*. New Delhi: Commonwealth.

Tharu, Susie and Lalitha, K. (eds.). (1991), *Women Writing in India: 600 BC to the Present*, Vol. 1. Oxford: Oxford University Press.

Verma, J. S., Seth, Leila and Subramanium, Gopal. (2013), Report of the Committee on Amendments to Criminal Law. Available at http://www.prsindia.org/uploads/media/Justice%20verma%20committee/js%20verma%20committe%20report.pdf.

Viswanathan, Gauri. (1989), *Masks of Conquest: Literary Study and British Rule in India*. New York: Columbia University Press.

Ward, Rev. William. (1818), *A View of the History, Literature, and Mythology of the Hindoos Including a Minute Description of their Manners and Customs*, Vol. 1. Serampore: Mission Press.

Zutshi, Somnath. (1993), 'Women, nation and the outsider in contemporary Hindi cinema', in Tejaswini Niranjana, P. Sudhir and Vivek Dhareshwar (eds.) *Interrogating Modernity: Culture and Colonialism in India*. Calcutta: Seagull, 83–142.

5 The Gender and Education Agenda in the United Kingdom, 1988–2013: The Ever-Turning Wheel

Mike Younger

Chapter Outline

Tracing the evolution of a theme in education over the time scale of twenty-five years is always a fascinating experience, since there is frequently a feeling of déjà vu, a sense that we have been here before and are returning to a recurring theme, perhaps with a new emphasis or angle. So it is with the gender agenda in the United Kingdom.

Equal opportunities for girls?

The concern with gender equality, and with equal opportunities for boys and girls, is not new. In the United Kingdom, the implementation of the Sex Discrimination Act (SDA) in 1975–1976 generated an intense debate about the contrasting experiences of girls and boys in schools. Studies by feminist educators reiterated the extent to which girls and young women were disadvantaged in education, from early childhood education to higher education, with underachievement of certain groups, lower aspirations, and unequal and discriminatory experiences of girls both at school and subsequently within the labour market. The debates of the 1970s and 1980s, well-documented by researchers such as Sandra Acker, Miriam David, Kate Myers and Jean Rudduck, give fascinating insights of the concerns of the time:

- A concern with classroom dynamics, where studies suggested that teachers devoted significantly more time to boys than to girls, directing more questions to boys, responding more to comments and issues raised by boys, offering more praise and giving more rebukes; teachers, too, frequently claimed that they enjoyed teaching boys more, since boys raised more challenges, offered more stimulation and were more interesting to teach; time and again, classroom observations suggested that boys dominated the ethos of classrooms, the style and the tone of interactions.
- A concern with the use of space in classrooms and in play spaces around the school, as girls avoided areas where there were robust and dominant boys, for fear of intimidation, particularly in playgrounds where boys frequently dominated the physical space through active, physical games such as football, with girls reduced to circulating around the peripheries.
- A concern with the curriculum where – even in primary schools – there seemed to be very clear stereotypical expectations from many teachers, that girls were unable to understand and excel in Maths and science, that boys could not write stories which were as vibrant, interesting, language rich and as well-crafted as girls.
- A concern with the sexist language and images of many textbooks and curriculum materials, with the assumption that there were set roles for men and women, that gender exclusive language ('he', 'man', 'mankind', 'chairman') was acceptable to describe all people regardless of gender.

'Equal opportunities' became an issue as research revealed that both the formal curriculum and the hidden curriculum were structured along gendered lines (Sharpe, 1976; Deem, 1980). Girls tended to avoid subjects such as mathematics and science, which were socially constructed as masculine (Walden, 1991), and opted for careers such as nursing or primary school teaching, which were traditionally associated with the so-called feminine qualities of caring. Similar concerns were not only high profile in the United Kingdom, but in parts of Europe, particularly in the Benelux countries and Scandinavia, where sex role stereotyping was under extreme pressure; in the United States and Canada where single-sex education for girls began to be considered; and in Australia and New Zealand where a series of government commissions were established to address gender equity issues for girls. These concerns were associated not only with a commitment to natural justice and equal opportunities for girls and women but a disquiet that primary and secondary education was not preparing girls well enough for the modern world, that expectations and aspirations were too low and narrowly confined, that there was a glass ceiling in post-sixteen education and employment that restricted opportunities in the workplace and reduced the scope of women's earning power.

The subsequent equal opportunities movement of the 1970s and 1980s which developed in England following the SDA attempted to address many of these issues. Certainly through to 1992, it appeared that there had been some significant success in asserting opportunity and entitlement for girls and opening up equity of access. Despite significant difficulties and open hostility from some sections of the media, the work of the Equal Opportunities Commission did effectively challenge many inequalities both within and outside in the classroom. Campaigns such as *Women into Science and Engineering, Girls Into Maths Can Go, Girls into Science and technology*; gender equality work in some innovative local education authorities such as Brent, Croydon and Sheffield; the work of pioneering groups of feminist teachers and emerging femocrats in women's education groups – all combined to force equal opportunities on to the agenda of schools, teacher education institutions, local authorities and the local and national advisory and inspectorate bodies. In the same period, the introduction of the National Curriculum in 1988 ensured that girls and boys followed the same basic curriculum throughout the years of compulsory schooling, so that girls were no longer able to cease their study of science subjects at the age of fourteen, or to take a 'softer' scientific subject such as human biology, rather than a 'hard' science subject such as physics.

There is, indeed, much to celebrate in this period of the seventies and eighties, ironically, despite an entrenched and conservative national education policy. As Kate Myers points out, 'much of what we now take for granted is due to pioneers who went before. Newfangled ideas that work are adopted and adapted until they become the norm and their, perhaps controversial, origins long-forgotten' (Myers, 2000, p. 218). By 2000, Macrae and Maguire could assert that the picture for women's educational achievement in the West had never been brighter or better and that there were now many positive aspects to life for the twenty-first century girl. In many respects, there was considerable evidence to support this: examination performances both at General Certificate of Secondary Education (GCSE) level and at A-level showed that girls outperformed boys in almost every subject; participation in higher education was rising more quickly for females than for males such that by 2004, 57 per cent of first-time entrants in the age group of 17–30 was female; women accounted for 56 per cent of graduates in 2002/2003; and 58 per cent of women obtained a first or upper-second class degree, compared with 51 per cent of men. The National Curriculum for all students above sixteen, an outcome of the 1988 Education Reform Act, appeared to have wiped out gender stereotyping in subject choices (Stables, 1990; Walden, 1991); career choices were now apparently more open (Myers, 2000) and the glass ceiling of occupational opportunity broken (McDowell,1997; Walby, 1997); and teachers were now more alert to the dangers of boys dominating classroom interactions and spaces (Mahony, 1985; Stanworth, 1981; Warrington and Younger, 2000).

A triumph for equal opportunities, then? Certainly the evidence seemed to suggest that the equal opportunities policies of the 1970s and 1980s had been successful, and that the position of girls in school, and as they left school and participated more fully in wider society, was no longer problematic. Indeed, some commentators claimed that gender had been 'done', even that gender reforms had gone too far and had pandered too much to the desire for political correctness that – in the words of the then Education Secretary Gillian Shephard at the annual meeting of the Girls' Schools Association in 1994 – 'although girls' academic advances were a cause for pride, there was a danger of *going too far*' (Gold, 1995, my emphasis). Indeed, the effects of girls' achievements, some sections of the media suggested, were to provoke a situation that has 'reached crisis point across the country' (Bright, 1998), making 'grim reading for males' (anon, 1998). It is suggested that boys were being systematically disadvantaged (Sommers, 2000) to the extent that there was an urgent need to refocus equal opportunities policies so as to redress the balance for *boys*.

Changing focus in the gender equity agenda: Disadvantaged boys?

Thus it was that the two decades of the 1990s and 2000s saw a dramatic reorientation of the gender equity debate, as concerns about equal opportunities for girls (Stanworth, 1981; Mahony, 1985; Arnot and Weiner, 1987) were superceded by a preoccupation with boys (Myers, 2000; Weaver-Hightower, 2003). Within the United Kingdom, the emphasis of successive governments upon performativity and standards (Arnot and Miles, 2005) put the focus centrally upon the apparent 'underachievement' of boys in national assessments at the ages of seven, eleven, fourteen and sixteen, as the focus of political and media attention similarly shifted to a concern with boys as the new disadvantaged, whether in literacy, economic opportunity, self-esteem or a dislocated sense of manhood. To Ailwood (2003) and Lingard (2003), the boys' lobbies silenced the debate for girls in schools (Ailwood, 2003, p. 26), with some commentators arguing that many young men were engaging in 'self-sabotage, … resisting school through disengagement and disruptiveness, acting up in the classroom in order to display their masculinity and get respect' (Kleinfeld, 2005, unpaginated). It was as though the very successes of girls were seen as threatening, as undermining for boys in schools and for men generally, a threat to the group which for so long was dominant in Western societies; in effect, a backlash developed against the feminist successes of the equal opportunities movement. There were clearly societal and power relationships involved here, then, in these emerging concerns, but it was also true that the emphasis in the United Kingdom upon testing and performance, of schools competing within a market economy for pupils and being judged by parents on the basis of performance in local and national league tables, served to highlight the issue.

It was within this context in the United Kingdom that discussions about *'lost boys', 'boys in terminal decline', 'the failing sex'* became the prevailing theme, driven by what amounted to a re-discovery of notions of 'the gender gap' and by the moral panic generated by the common perception that boys were failing at schools. At different times, fears were aired that a critical mass of boys were not well-equipped, through their schooling, to meet the changing labour needs of post-industrial society and that social unrest might arise through frustration/anger of disenchanted groups of unemployed young men. 'Is the future female?' became a common preoccupation of the media. The gaze of the media and the preoccupation of government with issues of male achievement ought not to surprise us, since the whole structure and ethos of the English educational system has always enshrined a preoccupation with boys (Weiner et al., 1997; Arnot, 2002), and these were exacerbated as the increasing demands of a post-industrial economy for a well-educated and skilled workforce (McDowell, 2003) exposed the apparently inadequate educational levels of some students. Indeed, in the United Kingdom the scale of the gender gap in the achievements in English become a particular concern: in 2005, for example, one in three boys did not achieve the expected level in the 2005 National Curriculum tests (compared to one in five girls), and only 50 per cent of the school population gained a higher level pass (grade C or above), compared to 65 per cent of girls. There emerged, then, a prevailing sense of a moral panic (Epstein et al., 1998; Gilbert and Gilbert, 1998; Weiner et al., 1997) about much of this debate about boys and their schooling, and the media onslaught and subsequent public anxiety clearly had a profound effect upon educational policymakers and administrators (Titus, 2004).

In the United Kingdom, then – and indeed in many other countries of the Western world – organizational and pedagogic responses by national governments, local educational authorities and schools were developed within a framework of recuperative masculinity politics (Lingard and Douglas, 1999), recognizing boys as being disadvantaged in their schooling by feminist approaches and policies and attempting to rectify this through 'male-repair' agendas. Thus the concern with the apparent underachievement of boys was constructed within the 'poor boys' discourse (Epstein et al., 1998) – seeing boys as victims in a feminized world within schools and denying the biological constructs of maleness and boyhood. The consequence of this, most starkly evident in Australia as well as in the United Kingdom, was the development of a focus on short-term essentialist policies related to boy-friendly pedagogies (Biddulph, 1997; Pollack, 1998; Hannan, 1999), affirmative-action for boys programmes (critiqued by Martino and Berrill, 2003) and the advocacy of teaching strategies which apparently favoured boys and 'guy-ify' schools (Pollack, 1998, p. 250). These approaches, emphasizing pedagogic strategies which were supposedly 'boy-friendly', and the emphasis on competitive activities in the classroom rather than collaborative ones which apparently favoured girls, together with a demand for more male teachers (critiqued by Skelton, 2003; Mills et al., 2004), typified a backlash against girls, such that now 'girls were regularly washed out of considerations about equity and education' (Mills, 2003, p. 59). This 'male repair' agenda was based around the notion that – since the 1980s – schools had developed teaching styles and approaches which favoured girls and that schools generally had become more feminized environments in terms of staffing, curricula and assessment. As a consequence, it was argued, schools had opened up opportunity to girls but boys had suffered as a result, and what was now needed was a programme which incorporated approaches which emphasized men's rights, their interests and their needs.

There are some concerns, however, about the extent to which the complexity and nuanced nature of the debate was recognized and identified by national governments and policymakers. In England, for example, DfES[1] promoted major curriculum initiatives, as evident, for example, in the *National Healthy School Standard to Raise Boys' Achievement* (DfES, 2003) and the *National Education Breakthrough Programme for Raising Boys' Achievement in Secondary Schools* (DfES/NPDT, 2003), which developed strategies and approaches to gender issues which were more readily located within contexts of recuperative masculinity. Equally, the emphasis of successive governments upon performativity and standards meant that the gender agenda continued to be addressed through somewhat simplistic solutions which problematized boys' learning in essentialist ways. This approach was summed up in a speech given by the then Prime Minister, Gordon Brown, in the Donald Dewar memorial lecture, 12 October 2006:

> We need a personalisation of boys' needs to include greater use of computers, ... more sport and community service to encourage discipline and personal responsibility, ... a 'father's revolution' where dads take greater involvement in schooling and upbringing, ... to tackle the gender gap in educational achievement and avert the prospect of a wasted generation of boys.

In the government-funded *Raising Boys' Achievement Project (2000–2005)*, we challenged this approach not only because we saw it as reinforcing dominant versions of hegemonic masculinity, reinforcing male stereotypes, and assuming a homogeneity among boys, which is difficult to recognize except at the most superficial of levels, but also because we felt that the effectiveness of such strategies is unproven by research or in practice (Younger and Warrington 2005; Warrington and Younger, 2006) and attempted to promote a position which was neither based upon short-term men's rights approaches nor based on pro-feminist perspectives but which was gender-relational, incorporating notions of difference and agency and placing the emphasis on boys *and* girls. Intervention strategies evolved through discussion and subsequent trialling, evaluation and modification with teachers, strategies which supported teachers in developing research-based knowledge about the ways in which gender – and the construction of gender by boys but also by girls – affected schooling and the quality of learning opportunities for both girls and boys. Intervention strategies were developed – pedagogic, individual, organizational and socio-cultural – which attempted to change images of laddish masculinity held by the peer group or perhaps the family and community, and to develop an ethos which helped to eradicate the 'it's not cool to learn' attitude among boys and which recognized the diversity and the fluidity of gender without reinforcing dominant versions of masculinity and femininity or reinstating dominant versions of hegemonic masculinity in more subtle and sophisticated ways.

The debates of the 1990s and 2000s: Invisible girls?

The moral panic which characterized the two decades of the 1990s and 2000s led inevitably to a growing invisibility of girl's learning needs in national and school policies, at a time when in UK schools, there still persisted hidden underachievement of girls, often of white working-class girls. The continuing constructions of the debate around boys' learning needs meant that those of girls frequently went unrecognized, simply because girls were often perceived as being more cooperative, less insistent, more quietly diligent and less intolerant of poor teaching. Frequently, too, off-task behaviour of such girls was subtle and disguised, carefully cloaked under a mask of normal working and participation in learning and far less likely to be confrontational. The underachieving girl remained a shadowy figure, rendered invisible and rarely challenged in terms of work level or achievement (Jones, 2005). Some teachers, furthermore, were predisposed to see boys rather than girls as underachievers, despite the existence of an increasing number of disengaged girls in high school, who were uncooperative and monosyllabic, challenging rather than passive and demanding rather than diligent (Jones and Myhill, 2004) – closer indeed to the picture that teachers painted of underachieving boys, being in various degrees confrontational, disruptive and challenging of the school ethos. At its extreme, these behaviours find their expression in the ladette culture so negatively reviewed in the British media (Jackson, 2006), in terms of some girls' adoption of hedonistic, binge drinking and drugs, behaviours which transgress normative femininity and represent a threat to the prevailing gender order (Jackson and Tinkler, 2005).

There remained, too, a continuing alienation of some girls from traditional 'male' subjects, particularly science. Despite the compulsory nature of some aspects of the National Curriculum, girls' subject choices for A-level study stubbornly conformed to stereotypes, such that a highly gendered pattern in post-compulsory subject choice remained. In 1999, Delamont reiterated the familiar complaint about the fear of mathematics among young women and girls, reluctance to choose science A-levels, borne out by the 2002 entries, which showed that only 23 per cent of physics, 29 per cent of computing and 37 per cent of mathematics A-level entries were female. By 2010, the physics figure stood at 21.5 per cent, computing at 9 per cent and mathematics at 41 per cent, whereas 75 per cent of sociology entries, 73 per cent of psychology entries, 70 per cent of English entries and 69 per cent of French entries were from girls. Unsurprisingly, these patterns were evident in the proportions of students in higher education (2007–2008), where 16 per cent of men followed courses in business and administration (compared to 11 per cent of women), 11.8 per cent studied engineering and technology (the comparable figure for women was 1.7 per cent), 7.8 per cent computer sciences (1.4 per cent of women) and 4.9 per cent physical sciences (2.6 per cent of women). Such choices affect students' careers later in life, frequently excluding women from well-paid jobs in business and in the scientific and technological professions. Warrington and Younger's (2000) research suggested that girls still felt alienated from traditionally 'male' subjects, therefore, and that career aspirations remained highly gendered. There is evidence here, then, to support Walby's notion of gender polarization (1997), for, while *some* women – those with higher educational attainments, in high status careers such as investment banking, the media, consultancy and medicine, usually younger women free of family 'ties' – have seen their economic opportunities transformed, others remained trapped by family commitments and family locality in part-time, less-well paid, less stable employment,and form a 'more flexible' labour force for employers. While it *is* true that over the period 1998 to 209, the gender pay gap did fall, from 27 per cent to 22 per cent (ONS, 2010), a pay gap of this magnitude can hardly be said to reflect success.

To some degree, this emphasis on boys' underachievement marginalized girls at a time when, while they appeared to be achieving more success at school such that the gender gap seemed to have been eliminated and indeed reversed, this level of achievement had not yet translated into the wider society. Any assumption that the battle for gender equality had been won needed to be treated with extreme caution. As early as 2001, for example, Lois Weiss was reiterating this point:

> What exactly does it mean that women and men have virtually closed the gender gap in educational attainment? Do they obtain equivalent jobs in the paid labour force? Are women able to negotiate equal labour in the home and family sphere? Are women's lives free from the haunting physical abuse that surrounds us now? ... It is important that we do not assume that this closing (of the educational gap) alone will translate into broader egalitarian outcomes. (Weiss, 2003, p. 120)

As Treneman pointed out in 1998, 'the statistical under-achievement of boys in schools is nothing compared with the statistical over-achievement of men in life', a point reiterated by David Bell, then Her Majesty's Chief Inspector of Schools in a speech to the Fawcett Society to mark International Women's Day in March 2004 (Bell, 2004), when he reiterated the point that the success that girls enjoy at school was all too often not mirrored in later life:

> Some girls' self esteem is affected from an early age. Others suffer problems more quietly than boys and so don't receive help and support. Boys are encouraged to be rougher, tougher and stand up for themselves: behaviour which is often discouraged in girls. Even careers choices differ. More girls choosing to study arts and humanities, so are unable to benefit from more lucrative science and technological careers. All of these areas of concern must be addressed. (Bell, 5 March, 2004)

Reflecting on an Australian perspective which was, nonetheless, equally valid in the United Kingdom, Lingard and Douglas (1999) argued that while girls stayed longer at school, and had higher participation rates in higher education, this

> does not convert into more equal post-education options in terms of career opportunities and income for women when compared to men ... (because of) a host of reasons to do with subject choices, coherence and vocational relevance of that choice, and the gendered character of labour market and careers. (Lingard and Douglas, 1999, p. 97)

Similarly, Aveling (2002), reflecting on her longitudinal study of a group of female academic achievers, suggested that:

> the discourse of equality of opportunity had failed these women in a number of respects. While they have demonstrated that they can succeed on male terms, the culture of the workplace ensured that despite equal opportunity strategies, and despite these women's hopes that their lives would be substantially different from those they had seen their mothers leading, their work patterns essentially replicated the employment patterns of women of an earlier generation.... It would be naive to assume that gender equity has been achieved.

The essence of the argument here, quite clearly, was that there had not occurred any radical shift in emphasis as to who did the parenting and domestic work, stressing the need for educators to move beyond merely encouraging girls into non-traditional occupations and to be more aware that the curriculum, for the most part, continued to be silent about women as mothers and men as fathers. Thus, rather than focusing on ways in which boys were 'disadvantaged' through past equal opportunities strategies, policymakers needed to shift the focus to ask, for example, why boys had low levels of participation in the domestic sciences and why they had low levels of self-discipline, socialization and relationship skills (Foster, 1992).

Revisiting gender equity issues in English secondary schools

It might be argued that some of the persistent gender inequalities in English society which are outlined above simply reflect an inevitable time lag as the educational achievements of girls in school work through into their enhanced positions in the labour force. There is some merit in this argument, although to assume it is simply a case of 'being patient' (Howard, 2005) is both demeaning and complacent. Within the realm of educational policy and practices, however, there is an evolving consensus which challenges the 'underachieving boys' debate, and a growing awareness of the complexity and the multi-faceted nature of the debate about boys' and girls' engagement, motivation and achievement. There is a growing resistance to the 'poor boys' discourse (Epstein et al., 1998; Francis, 2000) and to 'male repair' agendas (Younger and Warrington, 2005); to interpretations which see boys as being disadvantaged in their schooling by feminist approaches and policies; to recuperative masculinity approaches which seek to confirm commonality and identity among men (Lingard and Douglas, 1999); and a reaction against short-term essentialist policies related to boy-friendly pedagogies. Instead, there is an increasing recognition of the diversity and variety of gender constructions (Frosh et al., 2002; Renold, 2004) and a re-emerging emphasis on inclusivity and diversity (Warrington et al., 2006). Similarly, attempts have been made to take a more nuanced discussion of gender into schools (Ailwood, 2003) and a fundamental questioning of the contemporary key debates around gender and achievement (Francis and Skelton, 2005; Younger et al., 2005).

Thus it is that the gender discourse is beginning to re-engage with the needs of girls. As early as 2006, an ESRC seminar series, 'Girls and Education 3-16', had focused attention on the then current concerns about girls' education in the United Kingdom, and considered new research agendas, policy imperatives and ways forward for practice. This had reviewed some of the issues identified above, their 'disempowering experiences in schooling, their avoidance of high-status, masculine-labelled subjects such as mathematics and physical sciences', but also focused upon 'newer concerns emerging around the numbers of girls formally and informally excluded from schooling, and increases in drug and alcohol use, particularly in the 12–16 age group' (ESRC, 2006). There were emerging concerns that girls in the early teenage years (ages 11–14) had been largely ignored by researchers in gender and education, although alcohol, tobacco and drug use, as well as first sex, are likely to begin for many girls during this period (Jackson et al., 2010). Similarly, World Health Organization (WHO) data suggested, for example, that 8.1 per cent of eleven-year old girls in England drink alcohol weekly; this rises to 24.8 per cent at age thirteen and 48.6 per cent at fifteen (Currie et al., 2004).

Furthermore, while it was accepted that – within any one cohort – more girls than boys 'succeeded' academically in terms of attaining the benchmark five A*-C grades in GCSE examinations (including English and Mathematics), nonetheless, there were many girls who did not attain this level; thus in 2011, for example, although 61.9 per cent of girls achieved the benchmark compared to only 54.6 per cent of boys, this meant that 38.1 per cent did not, and this proportion is significantly higher if one considers ethnicity and social class, with more girls from white, working-class English backgrounds and of Caribbean, African and Pakistani heritage failing to 'succeed'.

These concerns have been exacerbated by the backlash which many girls and women have experienced in recent years in some parts of the media and from some men within society. Levels of misogyny have – if not risen – certainly been sustained with online abuse 'creating a sewer for anonymous prejudice and hate' (Jenkins, 2013) and social media exposing prominent campaigning women and some of their male supporters to gender-based bigotry and vitriol. The recent proliferation of mobile phones and twitter accounts have posed significant threats within young people's networks, too, with girls (and boys) exposed at times to merciless online bullying and character assassination which in some schools have led to significant increases in eating disorders, truancy and pressures for girls to be involved in sexual relationships at an early age. In June 2013, for example, *The Guardian* reported on the hostility which girls reported facing from boys within their own state grammar school, when they brought up the idea that girls and young women face disadvantage at school and in careers:

> What I hadn't anticipated on setting up the feminist society was a massive backlash from the boys in my wider peer circle. They took to Twitter and started a campaign

> of abuse against me. I was called a 'feminist bitch', accused of 'feeding [girls] bullshit', and in a particularly racist comment was told 'all this feminism bull won't stop uncle Sanjit from marrying you when you leave school'. Our feminist society was derided with retorts such as, 'FemSoc, is that for real? DPMO' [don't piss me off] and every attempt we made to start a serious debate was met with responses such as 'feminism and rape are both ridiculously tiring'. The more girls started to voice their opinions about gender issues, the more vitriolic the boys' abuse became... Any attempt we made to stick up for each other was aggressively shot down with 'get in your lane before I par [ridicule] you too', or belittled with remarks like 'cute, they got offended'. (http://www.theguardian.com/education/mortarboard/2013/jun/20/why-i-started-a-feminist-society: accessed 30 July 2013)

This young woman reflects that it has been *over a century since the birth of the suffragette movement* and yet, there is a 'whole new battleground opening up online where boys can attack, humiliate, belittle us and do everything in their power to destroy our confidence before we even leave high school... If you thought the fight for female equality was over, I'm sorry to tell you that a whole new round is only just beginning'.

At a different level, there has been increasing concern, too, that even in the second decade of this century, the glass ceiling is still very much a reality in the United Kingdom. *Sex and Power 2013: Who Runs Britain?*, a report from the Centre for Women & Democracy on behalf of the Counting Women in Coalition (CfWD, the Electoral Reform Society, the Fawcett Society, the Hansard Society and Unlock Democracy), argues powerfully that women are still too often missing from politically powerful positions in the United Kingdom and that Britain is still a country run largely by men. The report outlines

> how women make up only 22.5% of MPs; 12.3% of council leaders (in England); and 17.4% of the cabinet. Only a third of public appointments are female, as are 15.6% of high court judges and 5% of editors of national daily newspapers. In many areas, progress has shifted into reverse, such as in the devolved regional political bodies, where fewer women have been returned at recent elections.

This is reinforced by the fact that, although the government has set a target of 25 per cent female representation in FTSE 100 boardrooms by 2015, recent evidence has suggested that progress towards that goal is stalling, with just 5.6 per cent of FTSE 100 directors being women.

> The report shows a shocking absence of women from powerful roles in Britain. We're told that change doesn't happen overnight; well, this is proving to be a very long night. (Nan Sloane, of the Centre for Women and Democracy: 2013)

This is not simply a matter for schools, of course, but schools are representative of the societies in which they sit and need to recognize and respond to these persisting and recurring power inequalities. Recently, the Chief Executive of the Girls Day School Trust (GDST), which has a long history – stretching back over 140 years – of pioneering innovation and academic excellence in girls' education (although regrettably only outside the state sector), has responded, arguing that women need to be more assertive in the workplace, be less embarrassed when they excel at work and be less reticent at drawing attention to their own achievements. In what she has dubbed as the 'tiara syndrome', Helen Fraser asserts that 'the "tiara syndrome" explains why girls do better at school, university, first jobs, even early management posts, but between 30 and 50 often face two lost decades when men take over' (Times, 8 June 2013). She argues that this is related not to career breaks to have children (as is often maintained) but to women's professional modesty, lack of self-promotion of work-based achievements and lack of explicit encouragement and praise from employers:

> The 'hurly burly' of working life with its setbacks, politics, and often its essential unfairness, is nothing like the 'educational escalator' which young women have become so adept at riding. It is important that girls understand the necessity and value of failing, of having the resilience to pick themselves up and have another go and of the need to be vocal about their own individual successes and achievements. There is an interesting tension between our desire for happiness and success for the girls and the need for them to learn that failing, being independent and sometimes (dare I say it?) being subversive and challenging will hold them in good stead in their future. (Fraser, 2013).

To some extent, the government has recently recognized this in the commitment to produce information packs for the parents of daughters to help them bring up 'aspirational young women' and to support them in making subject choices at school which open up, rather than close down, career options and opportunities. But clearly, a much more proactive and determined approach is needed to make girls more resilient and to risk failure, to empower girls to be more assertive and to help girls identify with powerful, appropriate women role models. Ironically, too, this might mean that girls should be challenged to be more subversive in their behaviour in school. This theme is taken up by Stannard (2013):

> Do schools reflect and reproduce gender differences or do they subvert them? Being disruptive is not something we would appear to value in our schools but

> experts say that disruption is a proven path to success. It's about subverting gender stereotypes and encouraging positive disruptive tendencies. Girls have to learn to challenge authority, find effective forms of self-promotion, go for being respected, not just liked. Schools should teach pupils to question and debate. We should not just praise girls who conform. We should not just work with the grain, with what we think girls do.

There are three different perspectives here, then, all of which are perplexing and give cause for concern:

- a significant minority of girls, close to 40 per cent, continue to fail if failure is defined as not achieving 5 A*-C grades (including English and Maths) at GCSE; furthermore, the fact that many of these girls are from specific ethnicities and social classes cautions us yet again against assuming that girls are a homogenous group and alerts us to the need to be aware of diversity and heterogeneity within gender constructions;
- girls report that they are increasingly being subject to online misogynist abuse, often from boys within their own schools; although this is under-reported, interviews with girls (and boys) in many schools confirm that gender-related cyber-bullying is indeed part of the reality of schooling and that acrimonious debates about looks, clothing and image are causing significant distress to some girls, and some boys, in some schools today;
- some successful girls do not translate their own academic successes at school and University to the workplace and need encouragement to be less risk-averse, to be more resilient in accepting failure and to be more robust in their approaches to their own education, both at school and in their own professional development.

Final words

Reviewing the gender agenda in schools in England in the twenty-five-year period between 1988 and 2013 reveals causes for celebration and frustration – celebration in that the equal opportunities movement of the 70s and 80s generated more debate and awareness of gender inequalities in schooling, and helped to reduce some of the more glaring inequalities which girls experienced; celebration in that the focus on boys' apparent underachievement in the 1990s and 2000s did generate a vigorous and robust debate which contributed to raising levels of academic achievements for both girls and boys, whatever critics assert; celebration because constructions of gender are becoming, however tentatively, more fluid, more negotiable, more openly discussed and recognized. But, frustrations exist, too, because the glass ceiling is still very much a reality for many women and girls today; misogynist abuse continues to be prevalent, almost encouraged indeed in parts of the media; underachievement at schools continues to exist, for both girls and boys, and governments – of whatever composition – continue to beat teachers and schools about their failures without recognizing the huge successes. Hence, the ever-turning wheel, and the sense of *déjà vu*, as we revisit, refine, reassert our beliefs, policies and practices and develop new moves to take us forward within the gender agenda: to quote – out of context – Martin Luther King, 'Change does not roll in on the wheels of inevitability, but comes through continuous struggle' – so it has been, and remains, with the gender agenda in UK schools.

Note

1 DfES: the Department for Education and Skills which administered education policy in England until June 2007, when it was replaced by the Department for Children, Schools and Families (DCSF) and subsequently by the Department for Education (DfE).

Questions for reflection

a) How far do you agree that the equal opportunities movement in the United Kingdom over the last three decades has effected a 'triumph for equal opportunities' for girls in school and in the wider society ?
b) What evidence suggests that boys continue to be disadvantaged during their secondary school?
c) What issues must schools' gender equity policies address over the next decade, and how might these policies be put into practice?

Further Reading

Jackson, C., Paechter, C. and Renold, E. (2010). *Girls and Education 3–16: Continuing Concerns, New Agendas*. Maidenhead: Open University Press.

This book examines girls' experiences in education and some of the concerns that continue to haunt education policy and praxis despite prevalent claims of gender equality. The chapters explore issues such as girls' complex relationship with achievement, the influence of social networks on education, negotiations of body image and power, gendered demands of time, experiences of digital literacies and more.

McDowell, L. (2003), *Redundant Masculinities?* Oxford: Blackwell.

This book investigates the relationship between working-class men, the social construction of masculinity and the changing demands of the labour market.

Younger, M. and Warrington, M. with R. McLellan, (2005), *Raising Boys' Achievements in Secondary School: Issues, Dilemmas and Opportunities*. Maidenhead: Open University Press.

Drawing upon empirical research and bringing together theoretical as well as practical issues related to gender and achievement, this book offers insights on how the achievement of boys and girls can be raised. It demonstrates the respective roles of teaching and learning, of school culture and other factors such as the diverse needs of different boys and the continuing invisibility of some girls. The authors evaluate different approaches and advocate evidence-based strategies to promote boys' as well as girls' educational achievements.

Bibliography

Ailwood, J. (2003), 'A national approach to gender equity policies in Australia: Another ending, another opening?', *Journal of Inclusive Education*, 7, 19–32.

Anon. (1998), 'Grim reading for males', *The Guardian*, Editorial, 6 January.

Arnot, M. (2002), *Reproducing Gender? Essays on Educational Theory and Feminist Politics*. London: RoutledgeFalmer.

—— and Miles, P. (2005), 'A reconstruction of the gender agenda: The contradictory gender dimensions in new labour's educational and economic policy', *Oxford Review of Education*, 31, 173–89.

—— and Weiner, G. (1987), *Gender and the Politics of Schooling*. London: Hutchinson.

Aveling, N. (2002), ' "Having It All" and the discourse of equal opportunity: Reflections on choice and changing perceptions', *Gender and Education*, 14, 265–80.

Bell, D. (2004), The Achievement of Girls. Speech to the Fawcett Society, London, 8 March.

Biddulph, S. (1997), *Raising Boys: Why Boys Are Different – and How to Help Them Become Happy and Well-balanced Men*. Sydney: Finch.

Bright, M. (1998), 'Girls really are better than boys – official', *The Observer*, 4 January.

Brown, G. (2006), *The Donald Dewar Memorial Lecture, reported in The Guardian*, 12 October.

Centre for Women and Democracy. (2013), *Sex and Power 2013: Who Runs Britain?* London: Counting Women in Coalition Democracy, available at http://www.countingwomenin.org/wp-content/uploads/2013/02/Sex-and-Power-2013.pdf (Executive Summary, p 2; accessed 31 July, 2013).

Currie, C., Roberts, C., Morgan, A., Smith, R., Settertobulte, W., Samdal, O. and Barnekow Rasmussen, V. (2004), *Young People's Health in Context: Health Behaviour in School-aged Children (HBSC) Report from the 2001/2001 Survey*. Copenhagen: World Health Organization.

Deem, R. (1980), *Schooling for Women's Work*. London: Routledge and Kegan Paul.

Delamont, S. (1999), 'Gender and the discourse for derision', *Research Papers in Education*, 14, 3–21.

DfES. (2003), *Using the National Healthy School Standard to Raise Boys' Achievement*. London: DoH/DfES.

DfES/NPDT. (2003), *National Education Breakthrough Programme for Raising Boys' Achievement in Secondary Schools*. Manchester: National Primary Care Development Team.

ESRC. (2006), Girls and Education 3–16: Continuing Concerns, New Agendas Seminar Series. Available at http://www.lancs.ac.uk/fass/events/girlsandeducation/ (accessed 30 July 2013).

Epstein, D., Elwood, J., Hey, V. and Maw, J. (1998), *Failing Boys? Issues in Gender and Achievement*. Buckingham: Open University Press.

Foster, V. (1992), 'Different but equal? Dilemmas in the reform of girls' education', *Australian Journal of Education*, 36, 53–67.

Francis, B. (2000), *Boys, Girls and Achievement: Addressing the Classroom Issues*. London: Routledge/ Falmer.

Fraser, H. (2013), *Chief Executive's Address to the Annual GDST*, Conference, 12 June. London: GDST.

Frosh, S., Phoenix, A. and Pattman, R. (2002), *Young Masculinities*. Basingstoke: Palgrave.

Gilbert, P. and Gilbert, R. (1998), *Masculinity Goes to School*. London: Routledge.

Gold, K. (1995), 'Hard times for Britain's lost boys', *New Scientist*, 4 February.

The Guardian (2013), What Happened When I Started a Feminist Society at School. Available at http:// www.theguardian.com/education/mortarboard/2013/jun/20/why-i-started-a-feminist-society.

Hannan, G. (1999), *Improving Boys' Performance*. London: Folens.

Howard, S. (2005), *Women Are on the Way Up: Just Be Patient*. London: The Sunday Times, 27 November.

Hurst, G. (2013), 'What's really holding women back at work? It's "tiara syndrome"', *The Times*, 8 June.

Jackson, C. (2006), *Lads and Ladettes in School: Gender and a Fear of Failure*. Maidenhead: Open University Press/McGraw-Hill.

——, Paechter, C. and Renold, E. (2010), *Girls and Education 3–16: Continuing Concerns, New Agendas*. Maidenhead: Open University Press.

—— and Tinkler, P. (2005), *'Ladettes' and 'Modern Girls': Girls behaving badly? So what!*. Paper presented at Gender and Education International Conference: Gender, Power and Difference, Cardiff, March.

Jenkins, S. (2013), 'How to make this misogynist sewer fit for debate? Simple', *The Guardian*, 31 May, 32.

Jones, S. (2005), 'The invisibility of the underachieving girl', *International Journal of Inclusive Education*, 9, 269–86.

—— and Myhill, D. (2004), 'Seeing things differently: Teachers' constructions of underachievement', *Gender and Education*, 16, 531–46.

Kleinfeld, J. (20 May 2005), 'Culture fuels boys' learning problems', *Alaska Daily News*.

Lingard, B. (2003), 'Where to in gender policy after recuperative masculinity politics?', *Journal of Inclusive Education*, 7, 33–56.

—— and Douglas, P. (1999), *Men Engaging Feminisms: Pro-feminism, Backlashes and Schooling*. Buckingham: Open University Press.

Macrae, S. and Maguire, M. (2000), 'All change, no change: Gendered regimes in the post-sixteen setting', in J. Salisbury and S. Riddell (eds.) *Gender Policy and Educational Change*. London: Routledge.

Mahony, P. (1985), *Schools for the Boys? Co-education Reassessed*. London: Hutchinson.

Martino, W. and Berrill, D. (2003), 'Boys, Schooling & Masculinities: Interrogating the "Right" ways to educate boys', *Educational Review*, 55, 99–117.

McDowell, L. (1997), *Capital Culture: Gender at Work in the City*. Blackwell: Oxford.

—— (2003), *Redundant Masculinities*? Oxford: Blackwell.

Mills, M. D. (2003), 'Shaping the boys' agenda: The backlash blockbusters', *International Journal of Inclusive Education*, 7.1, 57–73.

Mills, M., Martino, W. and Lingard, B. (2004), 'Attracting, recruiting and retaining male teachers: Policy issues in the male teacher debate', *British Journal of Sociology of Education*, 25, 355–69.

Myers, K. (2000), *Whatever Happened to Equal Opportunities in Schools? Gender Equality Initiatives in Education*. Buckingham: Open University Press.

ONS. (2010), *Social Trends, No. 40, 2010 Edition*. London: Office for National Statistics.

Pollack, W. (1998), *Rescuing Our Sons from the Myths of Boyhood*. New York: Random House.

Renold, E. (2004), 'Other boys': Negotiating non-hegemonic masculinities in the primary school', *Gender and Education*, 16, 247–66.

Sharpe, S. (1976), *Just Like a Girl: How Girls Learn to be Women*. London: Penguin.

Skelton, C. (2003), 'Typical boys? Theorising masculinity in educational settings', in B. Francis and C. Skelton (eds.) *Investigating Gender: Contemporary Perspectives in Education*. Buckingham: Open University Press.

Sommers, C. H. (2000), *The War Against Boys: How Misguided Feminism is Harming our Young Men*. New York: Simon and Schuster.

Stables, A. (1990), 'Differences between pupils from mixed and single-sex schools in their enjoyment of school subjects and in their attitudes to science and to school', *Educational Review*, 42, 221–30.

Stannard, K. (2013), 'Teach girls to disrupt, subvert and challenge authority – don't always praise their attentiveness', *The Times Educational Supplement Online*, 13 June. Available at http://www.tes.co.uk/article (accessed 31 July 2013).

Stanworth, M. (1981), *Gender and Schooling*. London: Century Hutchinson.

Titus, J. (2004), 'Boy Trouble: Rhetorical Framing of boys' underachievement', *Discourse*, 25, 145–69.

Treneman, A. (1998), 'Will the boys who can't read still end up as the men on top?', *The Independent*, 5 January.

Walby, S. (1997), *Gender Transformations*. London: Routledge.

Walden, J. (1991), 'Gender issues in classroom organisation and management', in C. McLaughlin, C. Lodge and C. Watkins (eds.). *Gender and Pastoral Care*. Oxford: Blackwell.

Warrington, M. and Younger, M. (2000), 'The other side of the gender gap', *Gender and Education*, 12, 493–508.

——, with Bearne, E. (2006), *Raising Boys' Achievement in Primary Schools: Towards an Holistic Approach*. Maidenhead: Open University Press/McGraw-Hill.

Weaver-Hightower, M. (2003), 'Crossing the divide: Bridging the disjunctures between theoretically oriented and practice-oriented literature about masculinity and boys at school', *Gender and Education*, 15, 407–21.

Weiner, G, Arnot, M. and David, M. (1997), 'Is the future female? Female success, male disadvantage, and changing gender patterns in education', in A. Halsey, H. Lauder, P. Brown and A. Wells (eds.). *Education: Culture, Economy and Society*. Oxford: Oxford University Press.

Weiss, L. (2003), 'Gender, masculinity and the new economy', *The Australian Educational Researcher*, 30, 111–28.

Younger, M. and Warrington, M., with McLellan, R. (2005), *Raising Boys' Achievements in Secondary School: Issues, Dilemmas and Opportunities*. Maidenhead: Open University Press.

6

Unlearning Gender and Sexuality: The Pedagogical Work of LGBTTT Organizations in Mexico City

Anahi Russo Garrido

Chapter Outline

On a Saturday afternoon of summer 2010, I attended a meeting of Grupo Lésbico Universitario (GLU), a lesbian-feminist organization in Mexico City. About fifteen women, mostly in their twenties and a few in their thirties, had gathered together. The meeting took place at a café for women; so we began by ordering sodas, beers, sandwiches, chips and other items on the menu. One of the main items on the agenda for the day was to determine who was going to participate in a brigade to put posters all over Ciudad Universitaria (the campus of the National University) to announce the second *Semana lésbica*

(Lesbian Week). Most of the posters were going to be displayed on campus, but other brigades were going to put posters in different parts of the city in order to invite the general population to take part in these activities. Mona[1] commented that she would put up posters in markets. As an ex-housewife herself, she said she knew that many of them felt very alone and were not necessarily aware of these kinds of activities taking place in the city. The group concluded that it would be a good idea to have posters near campus and in places where they would not necessarily be expected.

The Saturday afternoon meeting might be seen as part of a larger historical continuum of activities meant to transform dominant discourses on gender and sexuality in Mexico City, spearheaded by lesbian, gay, bisexual, transgender, transsexual and travestite (LGBTTT), feminist and youth groups since the late 1960s. The first openly gay and lesbian groups in Mexico surged in the 1970s (Lumsden, 1991; Mogrovejo, 2000; de la Dehesa, 2010). The ground had been opened by the 1968 student movement which gave rise to newer Mexican social movements such as the urban popular, the feminist and the gay and lesbian movement. According to Lumsden (1991), the first organization, the *Frente de Liberación Homosexual,* was formed in 1971 by a group of students and artists that had taken part in the 1968 youth movement. The group dissolved the following year, but shortly afterwards, activist Nancy Cardenas appeared on TV as an open-lesbian in 1973. According to Mogrovejo (2000), Lesvoz, a lesbian-feminist organization, was founded in 1977. Lesbian groups such as Lesvoz and Oikabeth emerged in the late 1970s and early 1980s in Mexico City; since then, a few lesbian organizations have existed in the city. The work of various organizations is documented in the research of mostly Mexican scholars (Mogrovejo, 2000; Alfarache Lorenzo, 2003; Espinosa Islas, 2007; Friedman, 2007). Most of these authors write of same-sex sexuality, depicting Mexico as historically permeated by 'silence' on women's sexuality. Mogrovejo's book title on Mexico and the Latin American lesbian movement, *Un amor que se atrevió a decir su nombre* (A love that dared to say its name) (2000), exemplifies this vision that prevailed at the time of its publication. Movements are now operating in a different context where societal debates on gender, sexuality and intimacy are changing. Recent discussions in Mexico City on same-sex marriage, anti-discrimination laws and urban planning of lesbian and gay zones, all signal to an ongoing public discussion on the forms of intimacy to be legitimated in the city. Lesbian organizations operate nowadays in a context where the administration of the Federal District tends to be supportive of LGBTTT rights. Homophobic discourses remain nonetheless widespread in lay right wing organizations and in the Catholic Church that exercise an important influence. It is in this new field of forces and meanings that I carried out my fieldwork in 2009–2010.

This chapter examines the ways in which lesbian and queer[2] women's organizations challenge heteronormativity through some of their pedagogical activities. While formal workshops formed part of the pedagogical tools to destabilize dominant norms on gender and sexuality that prevail in Mexico City, informal networks and conversations threaded through activities also hold this potential. This chapter principally focuses on the work of Grupo Lésbico Universitario (GLU) and also considers some activities carried out by the group Musas de Metal. I chose to focus on these two groups because, having participated in their meetings opened to the public the most, I have a broader view on how these two groups, and the social networks created through them, challenged the dominant norms on gender and sexuality that prevailed in Mexico City.

This chapter draws on participant observation at GLU and Musas de Metal at the time I conducted ethnographic fieldwork in Mexico City in 2009–2010. It is derived from a larger research project that investigates the transformation of intimacy in the lives of three generations of women participating in queer communities in Mexico City, at a time during which sexual citizenship is being redefined in Mexican society. For this research, I also attended some of the events of other lesbian or queer women's groups: Mujeres Mayores de 30, Shakti Les (a yoga group) and Joti Family. I also conducted participant observation in other queer spaces such as bars, women cafés and in everyday life circles of friendship. Additionally, I did forty interviews and the review of articles on LGBTTT issues in three newspapers of major circulation. Interviews were conducted with women, between the ages of twenty-two to sixty-five years old, who participate in contemporary queer spaces. Most of them identified as middle class, although some claimed to be part of the working class and all of them except for one had been born and raised in Mexico City. The chapter is also influenced by previous fieldwork conducted in 2000, as well as seven years of intermittent life spent in Mexico City.

The first part of the chapter focuses on the two organizations, GLU and Musas de Metal, while the second part discusses some of the dominant norms on gender and sexuality in Mexico City. The chapter then goes on to examine how these dominant gender norms are challenged through some of the pedagogical activities led by these two organizations.

Grupo Lésbico Universitario (GLU)

When I conducted fieldwork in Mexico City in 2009–2010, one of the first groups I connected with was the lesbian university group at the National University (UNAM) named Grupo Lésbico Universitario (GLU). A student in the seminar 'Borders and Citizenship' that I was attending in Gender studies at UNAM invited me and other friends for dinner. At that small gathering I met Nadia and Gabriela, two of the central organizers of the group at the time. The activist pair invited me to one of their meetings.

At the meeting I attended a week later in February 2010, most participants were undergraduate university students. However, the meeting was open to everyone and the group had been successful in promoting and advertising their activities among individuals who were not students at UNAM. The group met twice a month on the second floor of the Café Ellas/Nosotras[3] located in a central area in the southern part of Mexico City.

As stated on their webpage, the main goal of GLU is to generate spaces of support, visibility and empowerment for the young lesbian community in the Federal District and on campus[4] (GLU, 2013). While GLU has gone through different phases, the group considers itself to have maintained four principles over the years. First, it considers itself an autonomous group; the group plans their own activities and does not accept funding from institutions that challenge their principles. Second, the group self-claims its own identity (*revindicativo*). It recognizes that young lesbians in the Federal District are discriminated against and made invisible as lesbians, women and youth. The group believes that young lesbians should define and claim their own identities, something no one else is in a position to do for them. Third, the group has always worked with the principle of inclusiveness. While the group focuses on young lesbians, individuals with other identities who support the goals of the organization are welcome to participate in it. Finally, the group defines itself as feminist. Their web page recognizes that there are many feminisms, but GLU works from basic principles articulated through a youth perspective of feminism (self-definition, equity, empowerment, sisterhood and refusal to subjugate).

GLU's pedagogical approach is simultaneously activist, academic and artistic. At the time I was doing fieldwork in 2009–2010, one of the main activities that was being organized was the *Semana lésbica* (Lesbian week), where panels, performances, exhibits and various presentations take place on campus. During bi-monthly meetings, the group often offered workshops. For example, on a Saturday afternoon, a psychologist from the group Musas de Metal was invited to conduct a workshop on violence among lesbian couples, which I discuss in detail in the next section. On other occasions, the bi-monthly meetings were used to discuss the planning of activities such as *La Semana Lésbica*. While some women were specifically present for the planning of activities, many others participated in the meetings to get to know other women who took part in queer spaces. The prospect of forming new friendships or partnerships spoke of the few spaces available to young lesbians in Mexico City.

After the meetings, we often went to the colonial plaza of Coyoacán to get ice cream, coffee or esquites. We hung out by the fountain, laughed and talked while looking at people walk by. About five women attended every meeting during the time that I was there, while others attended less regularly. A few participants participated just once and never came back to the group. On an average, ten to twenty women were present during meetings. About half were students at UNAM (mostly undergraduates). Most women were in their twenties, although occasional visitors were in their thirties or forties. GLU was an independent group that did not enjoy the status of *Asociación Civil* (AC) at the time of fieldwork, which is necessary to receive state funding in Mexico.

Musas de Metal: Grupo de Mujeres Gay A. C.

In 2010, I returned to the meeting of the group Musas de Metal, which I had previously visited in 1998 and 2000. The organization was founded in 1995 and became an AC in 2002. According to their webpage, the mission of Musas de Metal is to 'contribute to the construction of diverse sexual identities of men and women with the goal of promoting auto-acceptation in a respectful environment to the right of difference, promoting the development of social and political subjects' (Musas de Metal, 2013).[5] The group was formed after the founders realized in 1995 that there were very few spaces for lesbian women to form friendships and congregate. At their first meeting, only ten women showed up; after three meetings, however, around thirty women began to gather regularly to take part in the activities. The group has been meeting every three weeks for the past seventeen years now.

In 2010, meetings were taking place at a rented locale in the Condesa neighbourhood. The meetings were mainly based on discussion, serving as a support group for women with diverse sexual preferences (but mostly subscribing to female same-sex sexuality). As in other discussion groups, themes related to same-sex sexuality were discussed. For example, in the first meeting that I participated, the theme was 'Is it important to be in a relationship?' Women explored the question and an organizer facilitated the dialogue, asking new questions, introducing a guest or taking part in workshop activities. Women of different ages attended, but the majority seemed to be in their thirties. A core group attended almost every meeting, but an important floating population attended the group occasionally. While participants take part in workshops and consciousness-raising activities, group organizers also lead research and artistic programmes. Coordinators also participate in various social justice coalitions with other organizations, working particularly to transform dominant gender and sexual norms in Mexico City. I discuss these norms in the following section.

Female sexualities in Mexico City

From a very young age, children are socialized according to the appearance of their sexed body. Traditionally, as a child, one will be initiated into a binary gender system comprising the rigid categories of 'man' and 'woman'. In Mexico City, many girls have their earlobes pierced as babies and they are dressed in white dresses and scolded if they get dirty, while boys are permitted to be wild and noisy (Prieur, 1998, p. 119). Most of the women I interviewed were expected to marry and have children. The majority had also been encouraged to work. Women over forty-five years old had been expected to be nurses, secretaries or teachers, while younger women had had more possibilities to study for other careers as well. The traditional ideals on women's sexuality were strongly tied to the reproductive role they were expected to play later in life.

Although social actors such as schools, the media, governmental campaigns on health and population and feminist and LGBT movements have promoted new ideas that at times differ from the Catholic ideals on sexuality (Amuchástegui, 2001), these remained strongly present in the lives of women I interviewed. The Catholic ideals on sexuality categorize women through a binary system where women remain evaluated through the notion of double morality. This notion divides women as 'good' and 'bad', in relation to their sexual behaviour. The system suggests that 'decent' women should be sexually passive, and tie sexuality to procreation and marriage, unlike 'bad' women who actively engage with sexuality regardless of marital status (Rivas Zivy, 1998; Amuchástegui, 2001; Carrillo, 2002; Hirsch, 2003). Today, the religious origin of these ideals is at times left aside (Amuchástegui, 2001). It has been reconstructed as a secular moral system, although it is important to note that in the past decade religious and political discourses have increasingly been intertwined.

Interviewees of all ages voiced that they had received a very distinct sexual education from their brothers. Selene, who was twenty-four years old at the time of the interview, explains:

> Women have always been assigned the passive role. A role where you have to wait to be seduced … someone arrives they flirt and even if you like it, you deny it three times before responding. That is something that we carry, even if you want to get rid of it. A woman that has many male partners … is a prostitute, a *ramera*, etc. Differently, for men it's the symbol of being a good macho …[6]

As Selene suggests, women are socialized to publicly pay little attention to desire. Aligned with the Catholic ideals on sexuality, they are supposed to demonstrate a certain sexual restraint. As Chant (2002, p. 145) point out for the region: 'While virginity is possibly less important as a female credential for marriage than in the past, sexual promiscuity is still less acceptable for women…' than men. Nonetheless, Selene's statement demonstrates that the transgression of traditional ideals does not begin necessarily with sexual relations. Even the act of expressing interest in a man too quickly might place a woman in the 'whore' category, since a woman who approaches a man would be seen as challenging the ideal of female sexual passivity. In her ethnography on marriage in a town of Northern Mexico, Hirsch (2003) describes how young women therefore waited for men to approach them, otherwise facing the risk of being called *aventadas* (too determined).

In contemporary Mexico, various women groups have addressed this binary system, reclaiming their bodies and sexualities. On 6 June 2011, about 10,000 people walked down the streets of Mexico City, in *La Marcha de las Putas* (The March of the Sluts) a global initiative that first took place in Toronto, Canada (Campuzano, 2011). The March of the Sluts had the objective to denounce sexual violence. Anthropologist Martha Lamas (2011), who took part in the march, remarks that the *Marcha de las Putas* is also 'a struggle for the symbolic resignifying, which does not only end with the ideological separation between decent women and *putas*, but it does provoke a very necessary reflection in relation to double morality'. While displaying open interest in men was not always encouraged by families and the community, women often joked among themselves about sex with their peers. In this sense, heterosexuality was also a social ideal in most of the communities interviewees grew up in.

Heterosexuality as a changing social ideal

The General Law of Population that created CONAPO (Consejo Nacional de Población), a governmental institution, was sponsored by the Mexican government in 1974. In the following years, birth-control services were offered to the general population through health institutions across the country. With this law, sex education was also made mandatory beginning in the sixth grade (CONAPO, 1979). Most informants over forty-five years old do not recall any talk about sex education in the classroom. For younger interviewees, sexuality had often been briefly addressed from a biological perspective anchored in a reproductive and heterosexual vision of sexuality. Since 2008, schools in the Federal District address the notion of sexual orientation in a manual on sex education for public schools. However, these changes are very recent. All informants grew up in a context where formal sexual education did not address sexual diversity. This knowledge was not very different from media representations or beliefs circulating in families and communities.

For decades, heterosexuality had been the 'only' possible orientation for women in social imaginaries. Despite the rise of the notion of homosexuality in Mexico since the 1970s, interviewees often remarked that they had lived their formative years in environments where the notion rarely reached them. Many others suggested that it was generally brought up in relation to insults directed at male homosexuals. For example, when I asked 34-year-old Claudia if she remembers what was said on homosexuality in her family, she commented: 'Well, directly nothing but I always remember that my … mother, my father, my brothers made homophobic comments, such as "this *maricón*", "this *joto*",[7] these kinds of derogatory comments.' Selene, who is twenty-four years old, suggested similarly that

> Women as lesbians are completely invisible, so homosexuals are men. At the most, lesbian women are friends who are unable to have a sexual relation. So to be a homosexual is to be a person who dresses up as a woman. For my mother it is a *travesti*, for my father it is a transsexual or a transgender…

In this quote, Selene suggests that homosexuality is commonly associated with male femininity. In the popular imaginary, male same-sex sexuality is represented by *trans* individuals. Some women suggested that the term *tortillera* to signal a very masculine woman was often used in similar derogatory ways. As Claudia and Selene suggest, female same-sex sexuality was far less prevalent in social imaginaries despite the presence of a lesbian movement in Mexico City.

The majority of women I interviewed suggested that they initially encountered difficulties with their families when they announced their preference for women. Mónica, who was almost forty at the time of the interview, remembered how her mother wanted to kick her out of the house in the mid-1990s when she learned Mónica identified as a lesbian:

> She kicked me out but I did not pay attention to her. And I remember that it was a very difficult moment for me because my mother would tell me very hurtful things. She would tell me: 'How is it possible that you are like that?' [She would say] that no one was going to love me, that I would be alone. It hadn't been worth it to pay for my education, if I had turned out to be a *lesbiana*... and stuff like this [...] One day we had a fight and she ran after me with a knife and I told her that I would have her in my life, or live without her or over her, so she could choose. We stopped talking for a month. And then she told me that she loved me very much no matter how I was...

Mónica's story is atypical because only a few stories involved such open insults, violence and the menace of a knife. However, it resembled many other testimonies that suggested an initial misunderstanding followed by relative openness from family members. Mónica's quote ends with her voicing that today her mother is a really good friend of her first girlfriend.

While resistance within the family was often encountered, the context in which young women lived their sexualities has changed in past decades. At a workshop conducted by Musas de Metal, the facilitators asked the two dozen participants: 'Are there spaces where you are not out about your sexual preference?' The question caught my attention since it implied that workshop participants were usually vocal about their preference for women. Many participants had difficulty thinking of a space where this would be the case. If any, women mentioned places related to work and, at times, with some family members.

While women of all ages reported initial conflicts with some of their family members, it is worth noting that younger generations who position themselves as *lesbianas* had access to a distinct vocabulary to challenge their families and communities. The circulation of the term *lesbiana* in public life, and the proliferation of feminist and LGBTTT organizations and places, offered a different set of tools. As mentioned earlier, the lesbian movement had been active in Mexico since the late 1960s, but it is mostly since the 2000s that LGBTTT issues became very visible in public life. After the mid-1990s, discussions around anti-discrimination laws and same-sex marriage brought the notion of homosexuality to the forefront of public life. Particularly in 2010, when I conducted fieldwork, not a day went by without the publication of an article on marriage reform in newspapers of major circulation. The homosexual/heterosexual binary abundantly circulated in public language. In this sense, some of the youngest interviewees grew up in a context where identifying as a *lesbiana* was not always celebrated but truly was a possibility. Yolitzin, who is twenty-two years old, talked about how, when her mother learned that she identified as a lesbian, her uncles and aunts made fun of her mother for being troubled about the news. They suggested that, nowadays, this was rather normal.

Homosexuality was more often related to men and initially not always well received in the family. Nonetheless, due to the efforts of LGBTTT movements and the circulation of new discourses in public life, *lesbiana* identity was now a possibility in contemporary Mexico City. This was particularly evident in legal and cultural changes that rendered these identities more viable than ever before.

Teaching to question gender and sexuality at GLU

Grupo Lésbico Universitario (GLU) deploys different pedagogical tactics to challenge dominant knowledge that circulates on gender and sexuality in Mexico City. Some of these techniques are more formal and include workshops, where participants reflect together on a topic through a pre-planned activity. Other tactics are more informal; for example, participants report learning different ways of understanding gender and sexuality from casual conversations that take place during workshops and the networks of friendship that were later formed in the group. GLU also takes part in public actions that bring visibility to a diversity of sexualities and serve to establish a dialogue in the broader public sphere.

Formal workshops

It is a Saturday afternoon in July 2010 and approximately twenty women are attending GLU's meeting today. I recognize some of the usual faces, but new women I have never seen are here to take part in a workshop on *violencia en la pareja* (violence among couples). One of the main leaders of the group Musas de Metal is facilitating the workshop this afternoon. During the first part of the workshop, participants must offer adjectives or nouns they associate with the categories 'man' and 'woman'. For 'man', participants offer responses such as 'beard, strong, aggressive, dirty…' Araceli, who is sitting at the right far edge of the circle, shouts 'intelligent' for women. Other participants offer expected responses such as 'weak, soft, multi-tasking…' The poster is soon full of responses from the audience. Paulina, the facilitator, now moves to the next part of the workshop. She challenges participants to think if there might be men who have some of the characteristics noted in the 'woman' column. 'Are some men soft?', she asks, questioning the audience's easy assumptions. 'Could some women be described as strong?', she continues. Paulina thus attempts to demonstrate the ways in which common knowledge on gender can be challenged. A young woman wearing a red T-shirt is obviously familiar with cultural constructivism. She comments to *las compañeras* that there is nothing natural in gender; instead, gender is learnt in culture. This simple exercise offers the opportunity to participants to question the characteristics that are associated with 'man' and 'woman' in dominant discourses in Mexico City. While a few remain perplexed in the process, the exercise opens the possibility to question an area of life that might generally be assumed as natural.

Once participants have questioned these categories, the group moves to examine the ways in which gender is implicated in relationships. Traditional gender roles too often prescribe relationships anchored in dependency, inequality, passivity and activity. While participants recognize that there might be other models of relationships, everyone is familiar with the model of the strong male breadwinner figure and the sacrificing mother. The facilitator suggests that violence occurs in all forms of relationships. After all, the workshop is called *violencia en la pareja* (violence among couples). It does not point to a particular gender and suggests that violence happens in relationships regardless of gender identities.

Participants begin sharing their personal stories. Nayeli says that she ended her last relationship because, when she would argue, her partner would slam doors, scream and insult her. After she began noticing a pattern, she got scared and decided to leave this woman. Sofia, who has been with both men and women, tells the group that her relationships with women have been more dramatic than those with men. In her experience, she has lived more verbal and psychological violence with other women. Through these examples, facilitators begin talking about the five types of violence (physical, psychological, economic, verbal and sexual) and the cycle of violence. Participants comment on these ideas and relate it to their own experiences. We run out of time and since the workshop is highly successful, GLU leaders suggest that Musas de Metal come back to conduct the second part of the workshop in two weeks.

Unintended pedagogical moments

While formal workshops lead participants to formally question various cultural assumptions, many interviewees who attended GLU meetings commented that their views were also transformed through informal conversations with their peers. These events constitute unintended pedagogical moments. In spring 2010, I attended a meeting at GLU where the group was trying to evaluate the work that they had been doing. Laura, one of the few participants who was a graduate student, suggested that one of the things she appreciated about the group was the space to learn from others' experiences. Laughing, Laura confessed that she had learned from the group that it might be better not to come out to all of her family at Christmas dinner. A few laughed along with her, saying that they were familiar with this story and how it had been a similar fiasco for one of GLU's members. While experiences were also shared during workshops, informal conversations could be a space to access lived knowledge on 'queer life'. This knowledge was rarely circulated through discourses on sexuality in governmental or religious institutions, in formal education, the media or in women's immediate communities and families.

Many respondents suggested that groups could be a good place to establish social relations with other queer women. Quetzal, who had visited various groups but mostly attended Musas de Metal, said that she began attending groups after her relationship ended with her first girlfriend. When I asked her why, she replied: 'In my family, if there were or not gays or lesbians, those are secrets … I mean my only relation to the gay world was [my ex], Leticia'. In other words, knowledge on queer life did not exist in her immediate family circle. She had to venture out of her usual environment and her usual circle of support that was her immediate family. Unfortunately, Quetzal says that she had difficulties finding her place as a bisexual woman in many of the groups where most participants identified as lesbians.

Other participants suggested that they had formed strong friendships with other GLU members. The formal meetings held at GLU could produce relations that would be developed further in quotidian spaces. As Jafari Allen (2011) argues in his ethnography on the erotics of self-making in Cuba, quotidian spaces and practices of personal agency may be interpreted as political. It is in these informal networks of friendship that knowledge challenging dominant discourses on gender and sexuality may be produced. When I asked 25-year-old Gabs what her friendships were like in the group, in comparison with other groups of friends she had, she commented that she could talk about women with her *compañeras* from GLU. She says:

> I talk about different things with different groups of friends, but the main difference I see is the following one: With my lesbian friends I can talk about sex between women ... there is this possibility. 'She is very cute, have you noticed her prestige, how knowledgeable she is and her education.'[We say] these kinds of things.

As Gabs' remarks demonstrate, there are differences in terms of the kind of topics that can be discussed with different groups of friends. Some of these topics include sex and the ways in which women are attractive. Prior to GLU, Gabs had had a partner but no other lesbian friends. After she began attending GLU sessions, she formed strong friendships with other GLU members. It is in this new network of friendship that Gabs can voice her desires in new ways that assert her attraction to women. While these simple statements might not seem very revolutionary, there is incredible freedom in the possibility of enunciating one's desire, particularly as women. It is in these informal conversations that participants had the opportunity to co-create a common language on gender and sexuality that did not always circulate in other circles. In this sense, as gay and lesbian identities became progressively normalized in Mexico City, groups such as GLU and Musas de Metal decentred heterosexuality through formal workshops as much as through the informal conversations and networks of friendship created during and beyond the group's formal gatherings.

Questioning homonormative trends

In past decades, queer theory has increasingly engaged in discussions about 'the contradictions and complexities of being both "normal" and "dissident"' (Browne, 2007). While Mexico holds the second highest rate of hate crimes related to homophobia in Latin America (Brito and Bastida, 2009), gay and lesbian identities have progressively been normalized in Mexico City largely through the efforts of the LGBTTT movement, leading to legal, political and cultural changes. Nonetheless, as in the rest of the Americas, certain queer identities are deemed more acceptable than others. As Lisa Duggan has suggested, queer politics shifted in past decades. Homonormativity prevails; that is to say, 'a politics that does not contest dominant heteronormative assumptions and institutions, but upholds and sustains them, while promising the possibility of a demobilized gay constituency and a privatized, depoliticized gay culture anchored in domesticity and consumption' (Duggan, 2003, p. 50). While many of GLU's participants also visited spaces such as bars for profit that are generally associated with a depoliticized culture of consumption, GLU meetings took place at a small café that upheld lesbian activist meetings and cultural activities. The group also refused to receive money from funders or institutions that challenge their principles. This refusal is not particular to GLU but rather strongly anchored in larger conversations in the Latin American feminist 'autonomous' and 'institutional' traditions that have largely debated funding from the Global North, governments, corporations, etc. (see for e.g. Alvarez et al., 2003; Bustamante, 2011). In order to make such decisions, the group had to discuss their principles and align themselves with autonomous principles as their webpage suggests.

Other norms circulating in *el ambiente* were addressed in consciousness-raising activities. In some of the workshops that I took part in, GLU or Musas de Metal organized activities that served to question norms that circulated in queer spaces. For instance, middle-class women tended to keep a feminine appearance, while women with masculine appearances were not always well received in these spaces. Aware of these dynamics, Musas de Metal often included in discussions on homophobia, other discussions on other forms of discrimination. The issue of inclusion and exclusion rarely strictly focused on discrimination against oneself; it also focused on the ways in which women participating in queer culture in Mexico City include/exclude others. Such discussions were necessary, as power relations around class, ethnicity and gender identity continue to exercise influence even in queer spaces. Additionally, these discussions were important in an environment where particular queer constituencies were increasingly being accepted in Mexican society.

Conclusion

In this chapter, I have focused on the pedagogical activities of GLU and Musas de Metal in Mexico City. Thus, we saw how formal workshops conducted by these organizations functioned as pedagogical tools to destabilize dominant norms on gender and sexuality while informal conversations and networks of queer friendship also held the pedagogical potential to destabilize hetero and homo normativity. If anything, this demonstrates how educating people about gender occurs in a variety of spaces not restricted only to schools and universities. Lesbian and queer women's organizations educate their specific constituencies as well as the larger general population to challenge heteronormativity in more radical ways than possible in institutionalized spaces and discourses offered by schools, the government, the church and the media.

Acknowledgements

I would like to thank all research participants and in particular the GLU and Musas de Metal. I also want to thank the PUEG at UNAM for welcoming me as a visiting scholar while I conducted fieldwork in 2009–2010.

Notes

1 Informant names correspond to the first name of the person or are a pseudonym. All interviewees decided on the name they wanted me to use in possible publications of this research.
2 In Mexico City, the term queer is rarely used by individuals. The term is however useful to speak of women of various identities that do not position themselves as heterosexuals. In 'How is Queer Thought of in Latin America'? Viteri et al. (2011) suggest that in Latin America and the Caribbean queer theory and politics have been produced and interact with a different set of regional knowledge than in North America, such as sexology and broader health discourses on the normal/abnormal. The articulation of the term in the region has questioned north-south colonial relations, and south-south relations. The term queer has often been mis/translated as *raro*/*rara* (strange) or *teorías torcidas* (literally, "twisted theory" for queer theory).
3 The Café Ellas/Nosotras does not exist anymore.
4 My translation.
5 My translation.
6 All respondent quotes are my translation, unless otherwise indicated.
7 These terms generally circulate in reference to effeminate male homosexuals.

Questions for reflection

a) What do we mean by heteronormativity? What do we mean by queer?
b) What pedagogical strategies do queer organizations use to challenge dominant norms on gender and sexuality that prevail in Mexico City? Discuss the role played by both formal workshops as well as informal networks.

Further Reading

Chant, S. with N. Cracke. (2002), *Gender in Latin America*. New Brunswick: Rutgers University Press.

This book examines continuity and change in gender roles and identities in Latin America, combining detailed case studies with statistical evidence. The book explores a wide range of topics including, but not limited to, feminism, masculinity, sexuality, poverty, population and employment.

Bibliography

Alfarache Lorenzo, A. G. (2003), *Identidades Lésbicas y Cultura Feminista: Una Investigación Antropológica*. México, D.F.: UNAM and Plaza Valdés.

Allen, J. (2011), *¡Venceremos?: The Erotics of Black Self-Making in Cuba*. Durham: Duke University Press.

Alvarez, S. E., Jay Friedman, E., Beckman, E., Blackwell, M., Chinchilla, N., Lebon, N., Navarro, M. and Tobar, M. R. (2003), 'Encountering Latin American and Caribbean feminisms', *Signs: Journal of Women in Culture and Society*, 28, (2), 537–79.

Amuschástegui, A. (2001), *Virginidad e Iniciación Sexual en México: Experiencias y Significados*. México, D.F.: The Population Council and Edamex.

Brito, A. and Bastida, L. (2009), *Informe de Crímenes de Odio por Homofobia*. México.1995–2008. Letra S, Sida, Cultura y Vida Cotidiana A.C. Available at http://www.letraese.org.mx/wp-content/uploads/2010/05/Informe.pdf (accessed 23 May 2012).

Browne, K. (2007), 'Conclusions and future directions or our hopes for geographies of sexualities (and queer geographies)', in K. Browne, J. Lim and G. Brown (eds.) *Geographies of Sexualities: Theory, Practices, and Politics*. Aldershot, Hampshire and Burlington: Ashgate.

Bustamante, X. (2011), 'Del XI EFLAC y otros demonios', *Debate Feminista*, 21, (41), 165–89.

Campuzano, J. (2011), 'Marcha de las Putas'; también en México; convocan en redes sociales', *Milenio*. 13 June 2011.

Carrillo, H. (2002), *The Night Is Young: Sexuality in Mexico in the Times of AIDS*. Chicago: Chicago University Press.

Chant, S. with N. Cracke. (2002), *Gender in Latin America*. New Brunswick: Rutgers University Press.

CONAPO. (1979), *El Programa Nacional de Educación Sexual*. México: CONAPO.

De la Dehesa, R. (2010), *Queering the Public Sphere in Mexico and Brazil: Sexual Rights Movements in Emerging Democracies*. Durham: Duke University Press.

de Metal, Musas. (2013), available at http://musasdemetalgay.blogspot.com/search/label/Historia%20de%20Musas%20de%20Metal (accessed 17 June 2013).

Duggan, L. (2003), *The Twilight of Equality? Neoliberalism, Cultural Politics, and the Attack on Democracy*. Boston: Beacon Press.

Espinosas Islas, S. (2007), *Una Mirada a las Maternidades y Familias Lésbicas en México*. Barcelona: Editoriales Egales.

Friedman, E. J. (2007), 'Lesbians in (Cyber) space: The politics of the internet in Latin America on- and off-line communities', *Media, Culture and Society*, 29, (5), 790–811.

GLU. (2013). '¿Quiénes somos?' *Grupo Lésbico Universitario Blog*. Available at http://glunam.blogspot.com/ (accessed 17 June 2013).

Hirsch, J. (2003), *A Courtship after Marriage: Sexuality and Love in Mexican Transnational Families*. Berkeley: University of California Press.

Lamas, M. (2011), 'La Marcha de las Putas'. *Proceso.com. mx*. 13 June. http://www.proceso.com.mx/?p=272467 (accessed June 2011).

Lumsden, I. (1991), *Homosexuality, Society and the State in Mexico*. Toronto: Canadian Gay Archives; México D.F. Solediciones.

Mogrovejo, N. (2000), *Un Amor que se Atrevió a Decir su Nombre: La Lucha de Las Lesbianas y Sus Relaciones con los Movimientos Homosexuales y Feminista en América Latina*. México, D.F. Centro de Documentación y Archivo Histórico Lésbico (CDAHL).

Prieur, A. (1998), *Mema's House, Mexico City: On Transvestites, Queens and Machos*. Chicago: University of Chicago Press.

Rivas Zivy, M. (1998), 'Valores Creencias y Significaciones de la Sexualidad Femenina: Una reflexión indispensable para la comprehensión de las prácticas sexuales', in I. Szasz and S. Lerner (eds.) *Sexualidades en México: Algunas Aproximaciones desde la Perspectiva de las Ciencias Sociales*. Mexico City: El Colegio de Mexico.

Viteri, M. A., Serrano, J. F. and Vidal-Ortiz, S. (2011), '¿Cómo se piensa lo "queer" en América Latina?', *Iconos: revista de Ciencias Sociales*, 39, 47–60.

Teaching for the Future: Feminist Pedagogy and Humanitarian Education

7

Debotri Dhar

Chapter Outline

The relationship between gender and education is complex, intersecting with the particulars of class, race, age, sexuality, culture, geography, historical context and political milieu to create shifting structures of power and privilege. These structures, in turn, may profoundly shape educational opportunities, interests, expectations and outcomes of individuals and social groups in ways that are not necessarily 'natural', even though they are often perceived as such. An understanding of education as a deeply marked, yet dynamic and potentially transformative, field of endeavour therefore leads many of us to an inevitable question: how can we, as educators, level the playing field, as it were, in order to create genuine equal opportunities for those we teach? This chapter draws upon the links between feminist and other critical theories on one hand and teaching practice on the other to suggest that these pedagogies may hold at least some answers. Indeed, as this chapter will argue, these pedagogies are, at their core, anything but didactic. Instead, being more humanitarian in their context and content, they better serve the purpose of creating gender-just, inclusive learning environments that promote diversity, tolerance and a fuller development of the scholastic abilities of individuals and communities.

The first section of the chapter presents a comprehensive discussion of feminist pedagogy; the second section offers concrete examples of implementing feminist pedagogy in the classroom; and the final section goes on to explore some of the pitfalls as well as the possibilities of these pedagogical strategies geared towards promoting gender equality and ensuring greater learning opportunities and outcomes for students. While the particular examples are based on my experience of teaching a range of Women's and Gender Studies courses at a US public university for the past six years, I contend that many of these strategies may also be adapted to other disciplines, to diverse geographical and cultural contexts as well as to a variety of formal and non-formal educational settings.

Feminist pedagogy: Some notes towards a definition

So what exactly is feminist pedagogy, and what is its relationship with feminist theory? Several scholars (see for instance Rich, 1979; Hooks, 1984; Betteridge and Monk, 1990; De Danaan, 1990; Darder 1991; Mohanty, 1991; Bryson and Castell, 1993; Zimmerman, 1994; Montoya, 1995; Bignell, 1996; Greene, 1996; Reyes, 1997; Srivastava, 1997; essays in Anderson and Hill Collins, 1998; essays in Macdonald and Sanchez-Casal, 2002) have addressed this question from a variety of vantage points. I now attempt to distil some of the salient points of these long-standing discussions.

It may be useful to begin with Terry Eagleton's *The Significance of Theory*, which argues that

> children make the best theorists, since they have not yet been educated into accepting our routine social practices as 'natural', and so insist on posing to those practices the most embarrassingly general and fundamental questions, regarding them with a wondering estrangement which we adults have long forgotten. Since they do not yet grasp our social practices as inevitable, they do not see why we might not do things differently. (qtd Hooks, p. 59)

What Eagleton is getting at is the somewhat artificial binary between the 'natural' and the 'social', with the latter often masquerading as the former. With specific reference to the relationship between gender and education, this would refer to essentialist understandings of how it is 'natural' for girls to be passive and not competitive in the classroom; to be given to emotion rather than reason; to be naturally drawn to subjects such as languages and the humanities instead of Math and Science; to be intrinsically better-suited for certain kinds of 'soft' professions such as nursing and teaching; and to privilege their personal over their academic and professional lives. This naturalizing of what is otherwise a social narrative – which in turn is a result of multiple factors including ideology and gendered socialization rather than (only) biology – has not only polarized 'girls' and 'boys' into two diametrically opposite categories by flattening the important individual and other differences *within* these two categories but also had a pernicious effect on girls' education across cultures.

Thus, several studies down the decades have argued that teachers bring gendered expectations into the classroom, allowing boys to be more rowdy and boisterous while rebuking girls for the same behaviour, or letting boys dominate classroom discussions and holding them up to higher academic standards (See for instance Rich, 1979; Burgess, 1986; Tobin and Gallagher, 1987; Jones and Wheatley, 1990; Liu, 2006; Sanford, 2011). These studies are proof that despite much focus on the issue of gender stereotyping in the classroom and the inevitable progress that must result from such focus, gendered teaching practices have persisted over time, often leading to differences in educational outcomes in ways that make it impossible to delineate cause from effect or the 'natural' from the 'social'. In its simplest formulation, then, feminist pedagogy seeks to identify and articulate these conscious and unconscious gender stereotypes that negatively influence the scholastic expectations, learning experiences and educational outcomes of girls and women and to address these shortcomings through carefully fashioned pedagogical interventions.

However, an emphasis on crafting a more productive relationship between women and education is only one aspect of feminist pedagogy. Just as feminist theory – the academic arm of feminist politics – has adapted to include a variety of perspectives, from first wave feminism's liberal agenda (corresponding to the demand for women's right to vote, to be allowed education and employment etc.) to second wave feminism's somewhat essentialist understandings of femininity and 'sisterhood' even as it probed deeper into the structures of gender domination (through a critique of gendered embodiment, for instance, and a demand for reproductive rights) to third wave feminism's recognition of differences and an expansive engagement with a variety of postcolonial, queer, post-structuralist and other perspectives, the mandate of feminist pedagogy has also expanded. At the core of feminist theory as it stands today – and therefore, of feminist pedagogy – is the understanding that gender cannot be viewed in isolation and must be considered in terms of its complex intersections with other dimensions of identity such as class, race, sexuality, culture, nationality and so forth. As one author writes about feminist pedagogy, 'while the initial aim of these efforts was to create safe classroom environments for women students, these efforts have been extended to include the voices of other groups that have been historically marginalized and silenced' (Sasaki, 2002, pp. 45–6). In other words, even though a traditional understanding of feminist pedagogy may frame it as theoretically distinct from other critical pedagogies (such as those focused on addressing the inequalities of class, race, sexuality and culture), such distinctions, I would argue, are and have always been untenable in practice.

A useful example is Bell Hooks' *Teaching to Transgress* (1984), where she speaks of the limited life choices available to black girls from working-class backgrounds in the apartheid South at the time: 'We could marry. We could work as maids. We could become school teachers' (Hooks, p. 2). Hooks' subsequent experience of formal education, first within segregated black schools and thereafter in desegregated schools, amply demonstrates how the dynamics of gender cannot be easily separated from those of race and class. Feminist scholarship continues to emphasize and critically analyse these race-class intersections (See for instance Darder, 1991; Montoya, 1995; Reyes, 1997; Srivastava, 1997; essays in Anderson and Hill Collins, 1998). Intersections of gender with sexuality, nationality and culture have also been accorded an important role within feminist analysis. Speaking of sexuality, queer theory has displaced and decentred the assumptions of heteronormativity that historically undergirded discussions of gender, thereby fashioning an education that validates the realities of both heterosexual and homosexual students (see for instance Bryson and Castell, 1993; Zimmerman, 1994; Greene, 1996; Khayatt, 1999; Rabinowitz, 2002). Feminist scholarship has also come a long way in terms of its approach to issues of culture and nationality, from the time when Chandra Mohanty wrote about the 'discursive colonization' of 'Third World' women in Western feminist texts and teaching within the metropolitan academy (Mohanty, 1991) to a more contemporary understanding of how cultural essentialism can be as problematic as gender essentialism (Narayan, 2002). We now understand that when easy generalizations about differences between men and women get replaced by equally easy generalizations about 'First World' versus 'Third World' women, or between 'eastern' and 'western' cultures, alternative perspectives are silenced and only hegemonic forms of historical knowledge are allowed to emerge. As a consequence, feminist curriculums have been getting more globalized through curriculum transformation projects from a global perspective (Betteridge and Monk, 1990; De Danaan, 1990; Stetz, 1998).

A third, very important aspect of feminist pedagogy is the role of experiential learning. Way back in 1978, Adrienne Rich (pp. 239–40) had framed some vital questions regarding gender and education. What has been the student's experience of education, Rich asked, in schools that reward female passivity and indoctrinate girls and boys in stereotypic sex roles, and how should we teach women students a canon which has constantly excluded or depreciated female experience? Going on to argue that it is a fallacious assumption that men and women receive an equal education just because they are sitting in the same class, hearing the same lectures and reading the same books, Rich pointed to how the content of the curriculum, the structure of the institution and that of society at large militates against substantive gender equality inside and outside the classroom. Drawing clear links between education and society, Rich provocatively pointed out how

> the capacity to think independently, to take intellectual risks, to assert ourselves mentally, is inseparable from our physical way of being in the world, our feelings of personal integrity. If it is dangerous for me to walk home late evening from the library, *because I am a woman and can be raped*, how self-possessed, how exuberant can I feel as I sit working in that library? (p. 242)

Since then, an array of theorists writing on feminist pedagogy have emphasized the pivotal role of personal experience in feminist pedagogy and the latter's commitment to incorporating the lived experiences of women and other marginalized groups into academic discourse (Hooks, 1984; Collins, 1991; Minnich, 1992; Bignell, 1996; Mayberry and Rees, 1997; MacDonald, 2002). As MacDonald (2002) clarifies,

> feminist inquiry is based on the assertion that the perspectives of women, our experiences and analyses of our existence, have been systematically excluded from mainstream social and intellectual thought. Thus, all varieties of feminist theory and practice are fundamentally concerned with women's experiences. This feature of feminist practice is no different in feminist teaching and learning. Institutionalized and interwoven oppressive forces, including racism, sexism, classism, and homophobia, obstruct women's access to formal education. Once we take our places in schools and universities (in the role of student, teacher or administrator)

> we are forced continually to struggle for the legitimacy of girls' and women's ways of learning. Thus feminist pedagogy is distinguished from other teaching strategies by making women's experiences central in the production of knowledge. (pp. 116–7)

While MacDonald's formulation of 'women's ways of learning' may lend itself to a problematic reading insofar as it suggests that *all* women somehow learn differently from *all* men, she does mention elsewhere that our experiences and identities must be examined in all their complexity, without reducing us to essentialist descriptions of who we are (p. 127). Furthermore, her central thesis holds, echoing the work of feminist theorists down the ages who are all agreed that feminist pedagogy must be grounded in 'a collective struggle for knowledge, stand-point, and the experience of identity', since the experiences that students and faculty bring to the classroom are a valuable source of evidence as well as point of view (MacDonald, p. 113).

Two other related aspects of feminist – indeed, of any critical – pedagogy are democratic, participative learning; and an inherently transformational intent. In 1972, Paulo Freire's groundbreaking *Pedagogy of the Oppressed* had argued against the traditional, hierarchical relationship between the teacher and the taught; against the teacher being seen as the subject of the learning process and the pupil as the object; and against the non-involvement of students in the design and delivery of the curriculum. Critical thinkers such as Freire later became valuable resources for feminist educators like Bell Hooks as they attempted to fashion an engaged, democratic and transformational pedagogy.

Hooks, for instance, says that

> for Black folks teaching – educating – was fundamentally political because it was rooted in antiracist struggle [...] We learned early that our devotion to learning, to a life of the mind, was a counter-hegemonic act, a fundamental way to resist every strategy of white racist colonization. Though they did not define or articulate these practices in theoretical terms, my teachers were enacting a revolutionary pedagogy of resistance [...] Attending school then was sheer joy. I loved being a student. I loved learning [...] Home was the place where I was forced to conform to someone else's image of who and what I should be. School was the place where I could forget that self and, through ideas, reinvent myself. (Hooks, pp. 2–3)

Hooks' narrative of her journey, first as a student and thereafter as an educator, is at once personal and political, her key point being 'the difference between education as the practice of freedom and education that merely strives to reinforce domination' (p. 4). Famously terming theory as liberatory practice, Hooks then tries to imagine ways of teaching that are not centred merely upon inculcating obedience to authority, or upon using 'the classroom to enact rituals of control that were about domination and the unjust exercise of power' (p. 5). This sentiment is echoed in the work of several other feminist educators as they re-envision the classroom as a space of genuine equality and humanitarian justice. As one feminist scholar puts it, 'if the traditional classroom was masculine and depended on teacher's "power over" students, it was felt that the teacher should share that power and give visibility and voice where it had been denied' (Rabinowitz, 2002, p. 181).

To sum up, then, these are the key features of feminist pedagogy. One, to the extent that a dismantling of the binary between the 'natural' and the 'social' has been central to feminism as a set of political and intellectual practices, this also forms the basis of feminist pedagogy. Two, feminist pedagogy is undergirded by an intersectional understanding of social identity; it acknowledges, and seeks to address, the conscious and unconscious influence of gender stereotypes within and outside the educational arena that act in tandem with other markers of social identity such as race, class and sexuality to inhibit students' scholastic achievements. Three, feminist pedagogy affords a critical role to experiential learning. Four, feminist pedagogy advocates the dismantling of traditional hierarchies such as between the teacher and the taught and seeks to establish a democratic and participative learning environment that values the contribution of the student as much as that of the teacher's. And five, feminist pedagogy sees itself as inherently transformational in intent.

From theory to practice: Examples from the classroom

Having thus delineated the theoretical contours of feminist pedagogy, how might educators move from theory to practice? In this section, I present some concrete steps and practical strategies for implementing feminist pedagogy in the classroom, from syllabus design, assignments and curricular innovation to stated and unstated classroom expectations and a variety of other paracurricular choices.

Here is an excerpt from the syllabus of a Women's and Gender Studies introductory course I have taught several times:

> This course is designed to enable an exploration of the themes and concepts that have historically shaped women's – and men's – position in their societies and cultures. We will begin with an introductory overview of Women's and Gender Studies as a dynamic and expansive interdisciplinary field which situates women's voices at the core of analysis. Thereafter, we will go on to examine specific ways in which gender intersects with nation, race, class, ethnicity and sexuality in order to produce systematic structures of power. The course consists of an introduction followed by six sections, with each section focusing on a particular thematic area: 'Masculine' Bodies, 'Feminine' Bodies; Women and Religion; Gender, Labour and Global Capital; Gender and Representation; Gender Violence, Nation and War; and Gender, Human Rights and Social Change. (*Women, Culture and Society*, Spring 2010, Rutgers University)

Similarly, my syllabus for an upper-level Women's and Gender Studies course titled *The Gendered Body* was

> designed to interrogate the ways in which the body is constructed in society and across cultures. We will examine scientific, social, political, economic and literary perspectives on gendering the body, tracing how gender intersects with race, class and other social markers to produce complex bodies-as-effect. Instead of assuming the body to be a natural given, the course therefore looks at how the material body and its discursive regimes are mutually constitutive. (*The Gendered Body*, Winter 2009–2010, Rutgers University)

Feminist Theory: Historical Perspectives, yet another upper-level course I have recently taught, had for its course objectives the following:

> This course explores how feminist theory – as an expansive body of scholarship that situates women's and other marginalized voices at the core of analysis, while accommodating a variety of positions and perspectives – has evolved as a response to (a)historical ways of knowing. Through feminist critiques of historical texts, categories, ideas and epistemologies, we will ask probing questions about the nature of history itself, of historical 'facts', and of the role of power in shaping the shifting global histories of the past and the present.This is a three-part course. The first section uses a feminist lens to interrogate the relationship between history, epistemology and value objectivity. Beginning with juxtaposing a feminist critique of philosophy with a feminist critique of the history of science, we will delve deeper into the gendered histories of knowledge production, from the foundational theories of rationalism and empiricism to anti-foundationalism and critical theory. The second section poses the provocative question: is history 'his

> story' rather than hers? This section examines how women's history is a history of erasure and exclusion rather than of agency; here we will explore how women have figured as silenced subjects of texts, and genres, and as objects of war and paternalistic state polices across the globe. Thereafter, the final section addresses the issue of intersectionality – or, the ways in which gender intersects with race, class, nation, geography and a range of other registers of social and political identity – to produce complex histories of power and privilege that cannot be understood through the simplified prism of gender alone.

As is apparent from the language of the earlier syllabi, courses such as these are uniquely positioned to incorporate the principles of feminist pedagogy. Moving on from course objectives to course materials, 'The Social Construction of Gender' by Judith Lorber and *Ways of Seeing* by John Berger have been required reading in my introductory courses; together, these articles allow the class to understand how gender roles are a consequence of a complex intersection of history, culture, ideology, materiality and society rather than being solely biology-driven. A historical perspective is always useful too; thus, I incorporate texts such as Virginia Woolf's *A Room of One's Own* and Sandra Gilbert and Susan Gubar's *The Madwoman in the Attic: The Woman Writer and the Nineteenth Century Literary Imagination* to establish how gender roles are not static and evolve through time. This understanding then helps students blur the rigid dividing line between the 'natural' and the 'social'.

At the same time, incorporating a variety of female voices rather than only those of the white middle class presents the idea of intersectionality in all its historical richness; for example, material such as Alice Walker's *In Search of Our Mothers' Gardens* has proven effective in my classes. The inherently interdisciplinary nature of my courses also opens up many additional possibilities. A particularly interesting example is when, given my own interest in literary fiction, I decided to teach a social justice course from this perspective, framing the course in the following way:

> Claims to social justice have conventionally been located within the space of the political, and it is in political activism that the struggle to end inequalities pertaining to gender, race, class, sexual orientation, nationality and so forth finds its clearest articulation. However, a move beyond a reductive understanding of politics allows us to appreciate how literature is also inherently political in nature, shaped by the dominant impulses of its times even as it continues to shape them. This course undertakes to interrogate one branch of literature – fiction. More specifically, we will examine how the mainstream literary canon has historically marginalized female experience, and how women's writing has functioned as a creative response to this political marginalization and social inequality.

> Of course, this analytical frame raises all sorts of sticky questions. For instance, what does it take for fiction, whether a novel or a short story, to be considered 'feminist'? Is women's writing synonymous with feminist writing? What is the role of authorial intention? Audience reception? What about genres such as romance? And in privileging gender, what about the other inequalities – of race, class, age and sexual orientation, for instance – that may be overlooked or even enacted by women writers? These concerns lead us into the fractured and ever-expanding terrain of feminist literary theory and criticism, which in turn open up a new set of questions. In order to establish its theoretical position, should feminist literary criticism look to liberalism or realism or romanticism, to Marxism or structuralism or psychoanalysis? What insights do postcolonial feminist theory and Black feminist theory have to offer? Should feminist literary analyses subscribe to a common political position and critical method, or adopt a more playful pluralism? [...]
>
> At the end of the course, students will have gained a broad understanding of the field of feminist literary theory and key debates therein. In addition, they will have learnt to apply the tools of feminist literary criticism in order to read fiction critically, with an eye towards issues of gender equality and social justice. (*Introduction to Social Justice*, Rutgers University)

While the example just stated may be a fairly unique one, at least insofar as students' surprise at expecting social-scientific material and being confronted with fiction is concerned, interdisciplinarity does facilitate a creative mixing of a variety of historical, philosophical, literary, political and other perspectives such that the socially constructed nature of knowledge, the multiplicity of voices and the intersections of gender, class, race, nation, sexuality, etc., can be presented in the classroom in an extremely comprehensive way. For this reason, designing the syllabus has been, for me, one of the most joyful aspects of teaching Women's and Gender Studies courses in the United States, and I routinely also include in my syllabi many of the authors whose works I have outlined in the first section of this chapter such as Adrienne Rich, Bell Hooks, Chandra Mohanty and Uma Narayan.

According to Rabinowitz (2002), 'Curricular transformation work relies on the assumption that our courses can work for social justice – by teaching old material differently; by teaching new material; and by revealing and confronting attitudes and assumptions that we bring to bear as we speak, read, and write' (p. 183). In other words, the principles of feminist pedagogy do not stop with the course objectives and required reading and extend to the rest of the curriculum too; another obvious example is assignments. As an instructor, I have consciously chosen not to administer examinations for my courses, the primary reason being that the critical thinking my courses require of my students cannot, I firmly believe, be tested by means of conventional examinations which privilege rote learning and time management above all else. Instead, I try to design a series of assignments that allow a leisurely yet intellectually engaged exploration of the socially constructed nature of knowledge and the gender, race, class, ideological and material dimensions of power and privilege.

In the first assignment for the social justice course mentioned earlier, for instance, I had the students rewrite sections of prominent short stories, novels, fairy tales and fables. Loosely modelled on the operative idea behind Jean Rhys' postcolonial novel *Wide Sargasso Sea*, in which Rhys gave voice to the mute, mad character of Bertha from Charlotte Bronte's *Jane Eyre*, the purpose of the assignment was to get the class thinking about questions of egalitarianism and social justice in a creative way. The students responded to the assignment with enthusiasm: I got a Cinderella who chose books and education over the Prince, a wife from a Guy de Maupassant short story who stood up to her husband's abuse; an upper-class white woman from an Alice Walker novel who protested against slavery; a Vietnamese immigrant who was able to transform from an angel child to a dragon child to handle the taunts and ridiculing by her racist classmates, and so forth. It has been my experience that creative, even unconventional, first assignments work very well, holding class attention (especially, but not only, for first generation learners) and facilitating a gradual shift towards more scholarly papers that involve textual analyses and other forms of rigorous academic critique.

Given the pivotal role of experiential learning in feminist pedagogy, another first assignment I have designed and used in my introductory courses is the autobiographical essay, which enables the class to explore the connections between gender, race, class, culture and society from the point of view of their own life experiences. As my syllabus says:

> Feminist scholarship teaches us that engaging in a completely 'objective' analysis of social facts in the pursuit of 'knowledge' is impossible, since the knower is deeply implicated in the production of his/her own knowledge [...] Elaborating on our own lived experience and understanding how it shapes our views on society therefore becomes an important intellectual exercise. For example, what do your personal experiences – as women or men, as members of a particular social race or class or nation, of a particular sexual orientation, or of a political or religious group, etc. – tell you about connections between the personal and the political? As you 'move across' nations (especially relevant for those of you who may not be citizens of the United States, have obtained citizenship recently, or have heard of your parents' experiences in obtaining citizenship and assimilating in a new

> culture), what stresses and strains does this impose upon your identity as women or men (i.e. as gendered citizen-subjects) of different cultures? Similarly, those of you who define themselves primarily in terms of 'American culture' (this is to remind you that 'culture' is not an unchanging, monolithic entity but is in fact a dynamic and contested category) may want to reflect on your gendered personal experiences of national events such as war, or of socio-religious issues such as abortion etc., that have been widely debated upon in the public sphere of the United States. These are just indicative guidelines, which you can use to frame your own particular question. In reflecting upon your own experiences, I encourage you to probe deeply, to think critically and to take intellectual risks. (*Women, Culture and Society*, Spring 2010, Rutgers University)

Fashioning a democratic, participatory classroom is another principle of feminist pedagogy I consciously try to follow. Several strategies come in useful here, some of which include designing interactive courses so that students can also contribute to shaping the syllabus; devising innovative seating arrangements (for example, in a course I taught in Fall 2013 titled *Knowledge and Power: Issues in Women's Leadership*, we sat in a circle rather in the rigid rows that usually define classroom experience); making student presentations an integral part of the course so that the politics of space (with the professor standing and lecturing from an elevated podium and students sitting and absorbing) can be further challenged; organizing trips to exhibitions and conferences in order to make the educational experience more meaningful; and incorporating music, art, poetry and film, in order to make the classroom a space of openness, learning and laughter rather than anxiety and ambivalence.

The way ahead: Pitfalls and possibilities

A discussion on feminist pedagogy would be incomplete without adequate attention being paid to some of its potential pitfalls. To this end, feminist scholars have analysed, from a variety of perspectives, the issue of student resistance in the classroom (See for instance Tatum, 1992; Roman, 1993; Srivastava, 1997; Mayberry and Rose, 1999; essays in Macdonald and Sanchez-Casal, 2002).

Blurring the lines between the natural and the social can, for instance, draw sharp, even hostile responses from students whose gendered understandings of identity – a consequence of years of socialization in the family and peer-groups, and further crystallized through religious instruction, media messages and other forms of formal and informal learning – stand severely challenged. As for gender, so for race, class, sexuality, nationality and other dimensions of socio-political identity. In Macdonald and Sanchez-Casal (2002), for instance, Sanchez-Casal writes about the sharp racial lines around which students in her US Latino Studies classroom organized; Hase speaks of the obstacles presented by student nationalism in the classroom to developing a truly global curriculum; and Rabinowitz shares her bittersweet experiences of teaching a queer theory course. Invoking experience as a valid dimension of knowledge also poses its own share of difficulties. As Macdonald (2002) says, these difficulties play out both outside as well as inside the classroom; for instance, her efforts to include student experience in the classroom are scrutinized by senior faculty members, outside the classroom, and 'criticized (as too personal, not philosophical, not intellectual, ideological, prejudicial, and so on)', while in the classroom, she runs into a roadblock when her students fall into a simplistic binary and 'either appeal to an oppressed identity in order to substantiate an argument or just as commonly appeal to their lack of experience of oppression in order to justify their "inability" to analyze an argument' (p. 113).

Similarly, the critical pedagogical notion of democratization within the classroom is a challenging tightrope to walk. Students who have not encountered genuinely democratic teaching often react with confusion when encouraged to develop an equal stake in the process of education and to share their views openly; rather than feeling empowered, they may question whether the teacher has any authority at all. As the boundaries of unstated but implicitly understood traditional ideas about authority collapse, this in turn can have ripple effects in terms of overall classroom discipline. The situation is further complicated by the fact that not all lack of student engagement in the classroom is a result of disempowerment to begin with. As Rabinowitz (2002) explains, some of it may just as well be a sign of arrogance ('I don't have to explain to *you*') since power does not flow in one simple direction from the teacher to the student, and the teacher's race, sexuality and gender may also mitigate against her authority (p. 181).

There are other challenges too. For instance, education systems that are constantly modernizing and that offer relative freedom to individual instructors – who must, in turn, be held accountable to the highest standards of scholarship – to design their courses according to their own intellectual vision, make the implementation of feminist pedagogy much easier. By the same token, these pedagogical principles are most easily adapted to (inter) disciplinary fields such as Women's and Gender Studies, Critical Race and Postcolonial Studies, Sexuality Studies, Transnational Studies, and so forth, at least insofar as these fields have as their stated goal a critical re-envisioning of traditional hierarchies in and out of the classroom. Also, some ideas such as of doing away with examinations may be unviable in the case of many disciplines and methodologies; the STEM fields come directly to mind here, as do many quantitative methodologies within the social sciences. That said, I would argue that the greatest challenge to critical pedagogy is posed not by the structures of the disciplines themselves, or by the examination systems currently in place across the globe, but by the inherited and inhabited frames through which education continues to be viewed by both the teachers and the taught. For, if it were indeed about disciplines, how could we explain that doctoral degrees in Mathematics, Physics and Engineering are also termed 'Doctor of Philosophy'? The point I am trying to make is that, the needs of the job market notwithstanding, the philosophical and expansive exploration of knowledge that undergirds much of liberal studies is not necessarily antithetical to even the STEM fields; indeed, at the heart of the greatest scientific inventions lies a commitment to continuous exploration, improvisation and transformation.

Hence, while not underestimating the pitfalls that line the path of feminist pedagogy, I will argue that its ideas can still be applied to mainstream educational practices, across a variety of contexts, and that the possibilities of such application far outweigh its pitfalls. What is important to keep in mind is that this is not an all-or-nothing argument, since the degree to which such pedagogy is adopted can be carefully calibrated and contextualized. Speaking of curriculum design, for instance, a radical overhauling of the syllabus is not necessary – though such overhauling is not without its merits. Instead, it is quite feasible to incorporate alternative perspectives alongside hegemonic versions such as of history and literature in ways that do not speak of mere tokenism; an example is of courses in the metropolitan academy that may ubiquitously be titled 'World History' or 'World Literature' but continue to be entirely Euro/US-centric. Also, a variety of creative testing methods can be deployed alongside traditional classroom examinations and standardized tests; conventional examinations on their own are rarely an accurate measure of the full spectrum of students' intelligence, and if anything, such a diversification of testing methods would only reflect the rapidly diversifying needs of the global job market. Similarly, making the educational experience more democratic by giving voice to, and validating the personal experiences of, historically under-represented groups has humanitarian benefits for society that far outlast those obtained only in the classroom. These, along with the usual critical pedagogical understandings to be kept in mind while teaching – such as making sure all students participate in class discussions rather than some being allowed to dominate the conversation; being careful not to propagate, consciously or unconsciously, gender, cultural and other stereotypes and assumptions that might have an adverse effect on students' scholastic performance; and being compassionate and flexible in order to accommodate a variety of student needs as they arise – can go a long way towards making education a truly transformative experience.

Of course, equality of opportunity will not always translate into equality of outcome, and to attempt a strict enforcement of the latter is to overlook both individual difference and individual choice. That said, societies that value humanitarian principles owe it to their members to maximize equality of opportunity in a meaningful way; not everyone will pull equally but everyone must pull and must be given the opportunity to do so. Gender-equal, democratic and inclusive teaching creates these opportunities – not by ignoring gender, race, class, sexuality and other markers of social identity but by actively acknowledging their influence and taking remedial measures to ensure a fuller development of individuals' and communities' scholastic abilities.

In other words, while constructing a pedagogy that leads to epistemic wholeness is full of ambiguities and tensions (Macdonald, p. 126), its returns for society are immense, for it can become the first step towards reimagining more egalitarian futures for the students and for the world they will help shape. This positive, transforming power of pedagogy and the humanitarian role it can play for society is succinctly summed up by Rabinowitz (p. 184) who says, 'Is it logical to think there is a causal connection between a course and behavior? Sometimes it works.'

Questions for reflection

a) What are the defining features of feminist pedagogy? What is the relationship between feminist pedagogy and feminist theory?
b) What positive role can experiential learning play in the classroom? What are some of its limitations?
c) What is the link between feminist pedagogy and humanitarian education?

Further Reading

Hooks, Bell. (1984), *Teaching to Transgress*. New York: Routledge.

This book challenges conventional understandings of pedagogy, rethinking teaching and learning practices in an age of multiculturalism. It offers ways to envision education as the practice of freedom from gender, race and class barriers.

Mohanty, Chandra Talpade. (1991), 'Under Western eyes: Feminist scholarship and colonial discourses', in Chandra Talpade Mohanty, Ann Russo and Lourdes Tourres (eds.) *Third World Women and the Politics of Feminism*. Bloomington: Indiana University Press, 51–80.

This seminal article critiques how the Western gaze has historically framed the 'Third world' and its women, and the repercussions of such framing for feminist scholarship and education.

Macdonald, Amie and Susan Sanchez-Casal (eds.). (2002), *Twenty-First-Century Feminist Classrooms: Pedagogies of Identity and Difference*. New York: Palgrave Macmillan.

This is a collection of trenchant essays that explore issues of identity, difference and their relationship with feminist pedagogy. The theoretically nuanced essays address not just the intersections of gender with race, class, sexuality and location but also broader questions concerning epistemic privilege, standpoint and the politics of knowledge.

Bibliography

Anderson, Margaret and Patricia Hill Collins (eds.). (1998), *Race, Class and Gender: An Anthology*. Belmont: Wadsworth.

Berger, John. (1972), *Ways of Seeing*. London: Penguin.

Betteridge, Anne and Monk, Janice. (1990), 'Teaching women's studies from an International perspective', *Women's Studies Quarterly*, 18, (1–2), 78–85.

Bignell, Kelly. (1996), 'Building feminist praxis out of feminist pedagogy: The importance of students' perspectives', *Women's Studies International Forum*, 19, (3), 315–26.

Bryson, Mary and de Castell, Suzanne. (1993), 'Queer pedagogy: Practice makes im/perfect', *Canadian Journal of Education*, 18, (3), 285–305.

Burgess, Robert. (1986), *Sociology, Education and Schools: An Introduction to the Sociology of Education*. London: Batsford.

Collins, Patricia Hill. (1991), *Black Feminist Thought*. New York: Routledge.

Darder, Antonia. (1991), *Culture and Power in the Classroom*. New York: Bervin and Garvey.

De Denaan, Llyn. (1990), 'Center to margin: Dynamics in a global classroom', *Women's Studies Quarterly*, 18, (1–2), 135–44.

Freire, Paulo. (1972), *Pedagogy of the Oppressed*. New York: Herder.

Gilbert, Sandra and Gubar, Susan. (1979), *The Madwoman in the Attic: The Woman Writer and the Nineteenth Century Literary Imagination*. New Haven: Yale University Press.

Greene, Fredrick. (1996), 'Introducing queer theory into the undergraduate classroom', *English Education*, 18, 325–39.

Hase, Michiko. (2002), 'Student resistance and Nationalism in the classroom: Reflections on globalizing the curriculum', in Amie Macdonald and Susan Sanchez-Casal (eds.) *Twenty-First-Century Feminist Classrooms: Pedagogies of Identity and Difference*. New York: Palgrave Macmillan, 87–107.

Hooks, Bell. (1984), *Teaching to Transgress*. New York: Routledge.

Jones, M. G. and Wheatley, J. (1990), 'Gender differences in teacher-student interactions in science classrooms', *Journal of Research in Science Teaching*, 27, 861–74.

Khayatt, Didi. (1999), 'Sex and pedagogies: Performing sexualities in the classroom', *GLQ: A Journal of Lesbian and Gay Studies*, 5, (1), 107–39.

Liu, F. (2006), 'School culture and gender', in C. Skelton, B. Francis and L. Smulyan (eds.) *The SAGE Handbook of Gender and Education*. Thousand Oaks: Sage, 425–38.

Lorber, Judith. (1996), '"Night to His Day": The social construction of gender', in Judith Lorber (ed.) *Paradoxes or Gender*. New Haven: Yale University Press, 13–36.

Macdonald, Amie A. (2002), 'Feminist pedagogy and the appeal to epistemic privilege', in Amie Macdonald and Susan Sanchez-Casal (eds.), *Twenty-First-Century Feminist Classrooms: Pedagogies of Identity and Difference*. New York: Palgrave Macmillan, 111–33.

——— and Sanchez-Casal, Susan (eds.). (2002), *Twenty-First-Century Feminist Classrooms: Pedagogies of Identity and Difference*. New York: Palgrave Macmillan.

Mayberry, Maralee and Rees, Margaret. (1997), 'Feminist pedagogy, interdisciplinary praxis, and science education', *NWSA Journal*, 9, (1), 57–76.

——— and Rose, Ellen Cronan. (1999), *Meeting the Challenge: Innovative Feminist Pedagogies in Action*. New York: Routledge.

Minnich, Elizabeth. (1992), *Transforming Knowledge*. Philadelphia: Temple University Press.

Mohanty, Chandra Talpade. (1991), 'Under Western eyes: Feminist scholarship and colonial discourses', in Chandra Talpade Mohanty, Ann Russo and Lourdes Tourres (eds.) *Third World Women and the Politics of Feminism*. Bloomington: Indiana University Press, 51–80.

Montoya, M. (1995), 'Un/Masking the self while Un/Braiding Latina stories', in R. Delgado (ed.) *Critical Race Theory: The Cutting Edge*. Philadelphia: Temple University Press, 529–39.

Narayan, Uma. (2002), 'Essence of culture and a sense of history', in Barbara Balliet (ed.) *Women, Culture, Society: A Reader*. New Brunswick: Kendall.

Rabinowitz, Nancy. (2002), 'Queer theory and feminist pedagogy', in Amie Macdonald and Susan Sanchez-Casal (eds.), *Twenty-First-Century Feminist Classrooms: Pedagogies of Identity and Difference*. New York: Palgrave Macmillan, 175–200.

Reyes, Maria. (1997), 'Chicanas in academe: An endangered species', in Suzanne de Castell and Mary Bryson (eds.) *Radical Inventions: Identity, Politics and Differences in Educational Praxis*. Albany: State University of New York Press, 15–37.

Rich, Adrienne. (1979), 'Taking women students seriously', in *On Lies, Secrets and Silence: Selected Prose 1966–1978*. New York: Norton, 237–45, Chapter based on a talk delivered on 9 May 1978.

Roman, Leslie. (1993), 'White is a color! White defensiveness, postmodernism and anti-racist pedagogy', in Cameron McCarthy and Warren Crichlow (eds.) *Race, Identity and Representation in Education*. New York: Routledge, 71–88.

Sanchez-Casal, Susan. (2002), 'Unleashing the demons of history: White resistance in the U.S. Latinon studies classroom', in Macdonald, Amie and Susan Sanchez-Casal (eds.) *Twenty-First-Century Feminist Classrooms: Pedagogies of Identity and Difference*. New York: Palgrave Macmillan, 59–85.

Sasaki, Betty. (2002), 'Toward a pedagogy of coalition', in Amie Macdonald and Susan Sanchez-Casal (eds.) *Twenty-First-Century Feminist Classrooms: Pedagogies of Identity and Difference*. New York: Palgrave Macmillan, 31–57.

Shrivastava, Aruna. (1997), 'Anti-racism inside and outside the classroom', in Leslie Roman and Linda Eyre (eds.) *Dangerous Territories: Struggles for Difference and Equality in Education*. New York: Routledge, 113–26.

Stetz, Margaret. (1998), 'Globalizing the curriculum: Rewards and resistance', *Feminist Teacher*, 12, (1), 1–11.

Tatum, Beverly Daniel. (1992), 'Talking about race, learning about racism: The application of racial identity development theory in the classroom', *Harvard Educational Review*, 62, (1), 1–24.

Tobin, K. and Gallagher, J. (1987), 'The role of target students in the science classroom', *Journal of Research in Science Teaching*, 24, (1), 61–75.

Walker, Alice. (1983), *In Search of Our Mothers' Gardens: Womanist Prose*. New York: Harcourt.

Woolf, Virginia. (2012), *A Room of One's Own*. San Diego: Harvest. First published in 1929.

Zimmerman, Bonnie. (1994), 'Lesbian studies in an inclusive curriculum', *Transformations*, 5, 18–27.

Index